ZAGATSURVEY®

2006/07

ATLANTA RESTAURANTS

Local Editor: Shelley Skiles Sawyer

Editor: Yoji Yamaguchi

Published and distributed by
ZAGAT SURVEY, LLC
4 Columbus Circle
New York, New York 10019
Tel: 212 977 6000
E-mail: atlanta@zagat.com
Web site: www.zagat.com

Acknowledgments

We thank the Atlanta Chapter of Les Dames d'Escoffier, The Cook's Warehouse, *flavors – The Forum for Atlanta Food Culture and Dining* magazine, Gena Berry, Gina Christman, Adair, Samuel and Cole Sawyer, Mr. and Mrs. Coleman Sawyer, Steven Shukow and Harrison Von Steiff. We also thank our assistant editor, Josh Rogers, and editorial assistant, Rachel McConlogue, as well as the following members of our staff: Maryanne Bertollo, Reni Chin, Larry Cohn, Andrew Eng, Schuyler Frazier, Jeff Freier, Natalie Lebert, Mike Liao, Dave Makulec, Robert Poole, Becky Reimer, Thomas Sheehan, Joshua Siegel, Sharon Yates and Kyle Zolner.

The reviews published in this guide are based on public opinion surveys, with numerical ratings reflecting the average scores given by all survey participants who voted on each establishment and text based on direct quotes from, or fair paraphrasings of, participants' comments. Phone numbers, addresses and other factual information were correct to the best of our knowledge when published in this guide; any subsequent changes may not be reflected.

© 2006 Zagat Survey, LLC
ISBN 1-57006-795-3
Printed in the United States of America

Contents

About This Survey 5
What's New 6
Ratings & Symbols 7
Most Popular 9
TOP RATINGS
  Food: Cuisines, Features, Locations 10
  Decor: Outdoors, Romance, Rooms, Views .. 14
  Service 15
  Best Buys 16
RESTAURANT DIRECTORY
  Names, Addresses, Phone Numbers,
  Web Sites, Ratings and Reviews
    • Atlanta 17
    • Savannah 126
    • Other Outlying Areas 129
INDEXES
  Cuisines 134
  Locations 142
  Special Features
    Breakfast 150
    Brunch 150
    Buffet Served 150
    Business Dining 151
    BYO 151
    Celebrity Chefs 151
    Child-Friendly 152
    Delivery/Takeout 153
    Dining Alone 155
    Entertainment 156
    Family-Style 156
    Fireplaces 156
    Gracious Hosts 157
    Historic Places 157
    Hotel Dining 157
    Jacket Required 158
    Late Dining 158
    Meet for a Drink 158
    Microbreweries 159
    Natural/Organic 159
    Noteworthy Newcomers 159
    Offbeat 160
    Outdoor Dining 160
    People-Watching 162
    Power Scenes 163
    Private Rooms 163
    Prix Fixe Menus 164
    Quick Bites 164
    Quiet Conversation 165

Raw Bars	166
Reserve Ahead	166
Romantic Places	166
Senior Appeal	167
Singles Scenes	167
Sleepers	168
Special Occasions	168
Teen Appeal	168
Theme Restaurants	169
Transporting Experiences	169
Trendy	169
Views	170
Visitors on Expense Account	170
Wine Bars	170
Winning Wine Lists	171
Worth a Trip	171
Wine Chart	172

About This Survey

Here are the results of our *2006/07 Atlanta Restaurant Survey,* covering 728 establishments as tested, and tasted, by 2,952 local restaurant-goers. To help you find Atlanta's best meals and best buys, we have prepared a number of lists. See Most Popular (page 9), Top Ratings (pages 10–15), Best Buys (page 16) and 47 handy indexes (pages 133–171).

This marks the 27th year that Zagat Survey has reported on the shared experiences of diners like you. What started in 1979 as a hobby involving 200 of our friends rating NYC restaurants has come a long way. Today we have over 250,000 active surveyors and now cover dining, entertaining, golf, hotels, resorts, spas, movies, music, nightlife, shopping, theater and tourist attractions. All of these guides are based on consumer surveys. They are also available by subscription at zagat.com, and for use on PDAs and cell phones.

By regularly surveying large numbers of avid customers, we hope to have achieved a uniquely current and reliable series of guides. More than a quarter-century of experience has verified this. In effect, these guides are the restaurant industry's report card, since each place's ratings and review are really a free market study of its own customers. This year's participants dined out an average of 3.7 times per week, meaning this *Survey* is based on roughly 567,000 meals. Of these 2,000-plus surveyors, 49% are women, 51% men; the breakdown by age is 11% in their 20s; 33%, 30s; 23%, 40s; 19%, 50s; and 14%, 60s or above. Our editors have synopsized our surveyors' opinions, with their comments shown in quotation marks. We sincerely thank each of these people; this book is really "theirs."

We are especially grateful to our longtime editor, Shelley Skiles Sawyer, a freelance food and travel writer and managing food editor for *flavors – The Forum for Atlanta Food Culture and Dining* magazine, based in Atlanta.

Finally, we invite you to join any of our upcoming *Surveys* – to do so, just register at zagat.com. Each participant will receive a free copy of the resulting guide when it is published. Your comments and even criticisms of this guide are also solicited. There is always room for improvement with your help. Just contact us at atlanta@zagat.com.

New York, NY
June 21, 2006

Nina and Tim Zagat

What's New

Encompassing an ever-growing mix of distinct and diverse neighborhoods, Atlanta is cementing its status as the capital of the New South.

Arresting Development: Emblematic of the city's growth is the glitzy mixed-use community Atlantic Station, rising from the grounds of a former steel mill. Dining options abound at the 138-acre site, including Bob Amick's New American Lobby at Twelve in the chic Twelve Hotel; Strip, a steak and sushi venue by Tom Catherall; and an outpost of Rosa Mexicano, NYC's upscale Mexican. The development's central location inside the Perimeter is another plus. With gas prices hovering around $3.00 a gallon, Atlantans are staying closer to home. Roughly two-thirds of our surveyors report that they limit their dining excursions to trips of 30 minutes or less.

Good to Go: Our survey indicates that Atlantans dine out or take out lunch and dinner more than 50% of the time. Those in search of slow food in a fast world can obtain grab-and-go fare from some of the city's top chefs. Todd Mussman (ex South City Kitchen) is realizing his deli dreams at Muss & Turner's in Smyrna, while Bacchanalia's Anne Quatrano has given us Provisions to Go, a gourmet market and deli counter on the Westside that emphasizes local products. Seating is available at both.

Spiritual Companions: Any reader of Southern fiction can tell you that Southerners adore their cocktails. The grub that goes with them, long an afterthought, is gaining ground in these parts. Tiny Krog Bar, at the entrance of Rathbun's in Inman Park, offers antipasti-style bites with its beverages, and Asian-Med small plates are part of the mix at Mix, Haven's spin-off in Brookhaven. An extensive tapas menu is on exhibit at the bar of New American newcomer Table 1280, housed in the High Museum's snazzy new Renzo Piano–designed space.

Eat, Drink, Man, Woman: Sex sells, and some restaurateurs are pushing the envelope to seduce clientele. At B.E.D. in Downtown, diners can lounge on beds and sip libations with names like Pussy Galore, and this summer the LA-based Dolce Group is planning to introduce the erotic-sounding Geisha House to Atlantic Station.

Show Us the Money: While the average cost of a meal in Atlanta has edged up in the past year, to $26.20, it remains nearly $6 below the national average.

Atlanta, GA
June 21, 2006
Shelley Skiles Sawyer

Ratings & Symbols

Name, Address, Phone Number & Web Site

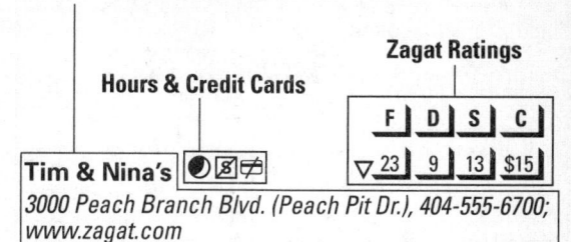

Hours & Credit Cards

Zagat Ratings

F	D	S	C
▽ 23	9	13	$15

Tim & Nina's ◐ ☒ ⊄

3000 Peach Branch Blvd. (Peach Pit Dr.), 404-555-6700; www.zagat.com

"When the little ones howl with hunger", bring 'em to this "behemoth" Buckhead "feedfest", where "from beets to meats to sweets, it's a feat to eat" it all; the Southern spread is popularly known as "the heart of heartburn", the staff is "on permanent cigarette break" and the "plywood-and-staple" interior "wasn't designed by the Johnson Studio", but "who cares" when you "shovel it in" for "practically a plug nickel"?

Review, with surveyors' comments in quotes

Top Spots: Places with the highest overall ratings, popularity and importance are listed in BLOCK CAPITAL LETTERS.

Hours: ◐ serves after 11 PM
☒ closed on Sunday

Credit Cards: ⊄ no credit cards accepted

Ratings are on a scale of **0** to **30**.

F	Food	D	Decor	S	Service	C	Cost
23		9		13		$15	

0–9 poor to fair **20–25** very good to excellent
10–15 fair to good **26–30** extraordinary to perfection
16–19 good to very good ▽ low response/less reliable

Cost (C): Reflects our surveyors' average estimate of the price of a dinner with one drink and tip and is a benchmark only. Lunch is usually 25% less.

For newcomers or survey write-ins listed without ratings, the price range is indicated as follows:

I	$25 and below	**E**	$41 to $65
M	$26 to $40	**VE**	$66 or more

vote at zagat.com

Most Popular

Most Popular

Each surveyor has been asked to name his or her five favorite places. This list reflects their choices.

1. Bacchanalia
2. Rathbun's
3. Bone's
4. Chops/Lobster Bar
5. Aria
6. Canoe
7. Atlanta Fish
8. BluePointe
9. Joël
10. Buckhead Diner
11. Houston's
12. Ritz/Buckhead Din. Rm.
13. Nava
14. Nan Thai
15. Seeger's
16. Kyma
17. Fogo de Chão
18. Pano's & Paul's
19. Floataway Cafe
20. Capital Grille
21. ONE. midtown
22. Maggiano's
23. Sotto Sotto
24. South City Kitchen*
25. Cheesecake Factory
26. TWO. urban licks*
27. Blue Ridge Grill
28. Murphy's
29. Antica Posta
30. La Tavola
31. di Paolo
32. La Grotta
33. Woodfire Grill
34. Pricci
35. Tamarind*
36. MF Sushibar
37. Taqueria del Sol
38. Veni Vidi Vici
39. Horseradish Grill
40. Ruth's Chris

It's obvious that many of the restaurants on the above list are among the Atlanta area's most expensive, but if popularity were calibrated to price, we suspect that a number of other restaurants would join the above ranks. Given the fact that both our surveyors and readers love to discover dining bargains, we have added a list of 80 Best Buys on page 16. These are restaurants that give real quality at extremely reasonable prices.

---

* Indicates a tie with restaurant above

vote at zagat.com

Top Ratings

Excluding places with low voting and those in Savannah and Other Outlying Areas, unless otherwise noted.

Top Food

- **29** Bacchanalia
- **28** Quinones/Bacchanalia
  - Rathbun's
  - Ritz/Buckhead Din. Rm.
- **27** Aria
  - Alon's
  - Bone's
  - Tamarind
  - Park 75
  - di Paolo
  - Seeger's
- **26** Floataway Cafe
  - MF Sushibar
  - McKendrick's Steak
  - Taka
  - Nan Thai
  - Chops/Lobster Bar
  - Joël
  - La Grotta
  - Madras Saravana
  - New York Prime
  - Rest. Eugene
  - Sotto Sotto
  - Paolo's Gelato
  - Nam
  - Pano's & Paul's
  - Sia's
- **25** dick and harry's
  - Canoe
  - Tierra
  - Fogo de Chão
  - Hashiguchi
  - Kyma
  - Muss & Turner's
  - Watershed
  - Capital Grille
  - Eurasia Bistro
- **24** Souper Jenny
  - Greenwoods
  - Nuevo Laredo

By Cuisine

American (New)
- **29** Bacchanalia
- **28** Quinones/Bacchanalia
  - Rathbun's
- **27** Aria
  - Park 75

American (Traditional)
- **24** Greenwoods
  - Sun in My Belly
- **22** Murphy's
  - Wahoo!
- **21** Houston's

Asian/Pan-Asian
- **26** Nam
  - Sia's
- **25** Eurasia Bistro
- **24** Com Dunwoody/Vietnam
  - BluePointe

Barbecue
- **23** Fat Matt's Rib
  - Swallow/Hollow
- **22** Rolling Bones BBQ
  - Harold's BBQ
- **20** Pig-N-Chik

Cajun/Creole
- **24** Hal's on Old Ivy
- **21** Pappadeaux Seafood
- **17** Atkins Park
  - McKinnon's
  - Huey's

Caribbean
- **23** Havana Sandwich
  - Las Palmeras
- **20** Coco Loco
- **19** Fuego Spanish
- **18** Vickery's

Chinese
- **23** Chopstix
  - Canton Cooks
  - Little Szechuan
- **22** Hsu's Gourmet
  - Canton House

Coffee Shops/Diners
- **24** Thumbs Up
  - Sun in My Belly
- **22** Ria's Bluebird
- **21** Crescent Moon
- **20** Original Pancake

10   subscribe to zagat.com

Top Food

Continental/European
- **27** Seeger's
- **26** Pano's & Paul's
- **24** Nikolai's Roof
  Ritz/Buckhead Café
- **23** Babette's Cafe

Delis/Sandwiches
- **27** Alon's
- **25** Muss & Turner's
- **23** New Yorker
  Havana Sandwich
- **22** Fickle Pickle

Dessert
- **27** Alon's
- **26** Paolo's Gelato
- **21** Jake's
- **19** Cafe Intermezzo
- **18** La Madeleine/Bakery

Eclectic
- **25** Muss & Turner's
- **22** SoHo
- **21** Eatzi's
- **19** Eats
- **18** Café Tu Tu Tango

French
- **28** Ritz/Buckhead Din. Rm.
- **26** Floataway Cafe
  Joël
- **24** Atmosphere
- **22** Café Alsace

Greek/Middle Eastern
- **25** Kyma
- **24** Mezza Lebanese
- **21** Avra Greek Tavern
- **20** Nicola's
- **19** Athens Pizza

Indian
- **26** Madras Saravana
- **24** Zyka
- **21** Udipi Cafe
  Bollywood Masala
- **17** Haveli Indian

Italian
- **27** di Paolo
- **26** La Grotta
  Sotto Sotto
- **24** Antica Posta
  Pricci

Japanese
- **26** MF Sushibar
  Taka
- **25** Hashiguchi
- **23** Atlantic Seafood Co.
- **22** Sushi Avenue

Latin American
- **25** Tierra
  Fogo de Chão
- **24** Pura Vida
- **19** Loca Luna
  La Fonda Latina

Mediterranean
- **24** Mosaic
- **23** Café Lily
- **21** Ali-Oli
  Ambra
  Krog Bar

Mexican/Tex-Mex
- **24** Nuevo Laredo
  Taqueria del Sol
- **23** El Taco Veloz
- **21** Pure Taqueria
  Uncle Julio's

Pizza
- **24** Oz Pizza
- **23** Cameli's Pizza
  Savage Pizza
- **22** Baraonda
  Fritti

Seafood
- **26** Chops/Lobster Bar
- **25** dick and harry's
- **24** Prime
- **23** Atlantic Seafood Co.
  Atlanta Fish

Soul Food
- **23** Fat Matt's Rib
- **22** Horseradish Grill
- **20** Fat Matt's Chicken

Southern
- **26** Rest. Eugene
- **25** Watershed
- **24** Greenwoods
  Wisteria
  Ritz/Atlanta Grill

vote at zagat.com

Top Food

Southwestern
- **24** Georgia Grille
- Nava
- Taqueria del Sol
- **23** Agave
- **21** Ambra

Steakhouses
- **27** Bone's
- **26** McKendrick's Steak
- Chops/Lobster Bar
- New York Prime
- **25** Fogo de Chão

Thai
- **27** Tamarind
- **26** Nan Thai
- **23** Little Bangkok
- Mali
- Thai Chili

Vegetarian
- **26** Madras Saravana
- **22** Cafe Sunflower
- **21** Udipi Cafe
- **20** Flying Biscuit
- **19** R. Thomas Deluxe

By Special Feature

Brunch
- **27** Park 75
- **25** Canoe
- Watershed
- **24** Ritz/Atlanta Grill
- Atmosphere

Business Dining
- **27** Aria
- Bone's
- **26** McKendrick's Steak
- Nan Thai
- Chops/Lobster Bar

Hotel Dining
- **28** Ritz/Buckhead Din. Rm.
- Ritz-Carlton Buckhead
- **27** Park 75
- Four Seasons
- **26** La Grotta
- Crowne Plaza Ravinia
- **24** Ritz/Atlanta Grill
- Ritz-Carlton Atlanta
- Nikolai's Roof
- Hilton

Newcomers/Rated
- **28** Quinones/Bacchanalia
- **24** Fleming's/Steak
- Com Dunwoody/Vietnam
- **23** Table 1280
- **21** Pure Taqueria

Newcomers/Unrated
- B.E.D.
- Blue Eyed Daisy
- Ecco
- Lobby at Twelve
- Repast

People-Watching
- **28** Rathbun's
- **27** Aria
- Tamarind
- **26** MF Sushibar
- New York Prime

Prix Fixe/Tasting Menus
- **29** Bacchanalia
- **28** Quinones/Bacchanalia
- Ritz/Buckhead Din. Rm.
- **27** Park 75
- Seeger's

Quick Bites
- **27** Alon's
- **24** Souper Jenny
- Nuevo Laredo
- Taqueria del Sol
- Com Dunwoody/Vietnam

Quiet Dining
- **28** Quinones/Bacchanalia
- Ritz/Buckhead Din. Rm.
- **27** Seeger's
- **26** La Grotta (Buckhead)
- Rest. Eugene

Romantic
- **29** Bacchanalia
- **28** Quinones/Bacchanalia
- Ritz/Buckhead Din. Rm.
- **27** Aria
- Seeger's

Singles Scenes
- **25** Capital Grille
- **24** Fleming's/Steak
- Hal's on Old Ivy
- Pricci
- BluePointe

Top Food

By Location

Alpharetta
- **27** di Paolo
- **23** Pampas Steak
- Atlantic Seafood Co.
- Rainwater
- Ray's Killer Creek

Buckhead
- **28** Ritz/Buckhead Din. Rm.
- **27** Aria
- Bone's
- Seeger's
- **26** Chops/Lobster Bar

Decatur
- **26** Madras Saravana
- **25** Watershed
- Eurasia Bistro
- **24** Mezza Lebanese
- Zyka

Downtown
- **24** Ritz/Atlanta Grill
- Morton's Steak
- Nikolai's Roof
- **23** Ruth's Chris Steak
- **22** Hsu's Gourmet

Duluth
- **26** Sia's
- **24** Stoney River Steak
- **23** El Taco Veloz
- **21** Melting Pot
- **20** Original Pancake

Emory
- **26** Floataway Cafe
- **23** Thai Chili
- **22** Top Spice
- **21** Mellow Mushroom
- Le Giverny

Inman Park/Candler Park
- **28** Rathbun's
- **26** Sotto Sotto
- **24** Wisteria
- Thumbs Up
- **22** Fritti

Marietta
- **25** Hashiguchi
- **22** Aspens/Steak
- **21** Pappadeaux Seafood
- Mellow Mushroom
- **20** Pappasito's Cantina

Midtown
- **27** Tamarind
- Park 75
- **26** MF Sushibar
- Nan Thai
- **25** Tierra

Outlying Areas
- **28** Five & Ten
- **25** Cargo Portside Grill
- **23** East West Bistro
- **20** Williamson Bros. BBQ
- **18** Le Clos

Poncey-Highlands
- **24** Pura Vida
- **23** Babette's Cafe
- **21** Fellini's Pizza
- **20** Java Jive
- **19** La Fonda Latina

Roswell
- **25** dick and harry's
- **24** Greenwoods
- Stoney River Steak
- **23** Swallow/Hollow
- Van Gogh's

Savannah
- **27** Elizabeth on 37th
- **26** Sapphire Grill
- Gottlieb's
- **24** Olde Pink House
- **23** Garibaldi's

South Buckhead
- **26** Rest. Eugene
- **24** Georgia Grille
- **22** Figo Pasta
- Cafe Sunflower
- **21** Taurus

Virginia Highlands
- **27** Alon's
- **26** Paolo's Gelato
- Nam
- **24** Atmosphere
- **23** Mali

Westside
- **29** Bacchanalia
- **28** Quinones/Bacchanalia
- **24** Nuevo Laredo
- Food Studio
- Taqueria del Sol

vote at zagat.com

Top Decor

27 Nan Thai
Ritz/Buckhead Din. Rm.
Quinones/Bacchanalia
26 Joël
BluePointe
Canoe
Nikolai's Roof
25 Bacchanalia
Aria
Rest. Eugene
Seeger's
Park 75
TWO. urban licks
Rathbun's
ONE. midtown
Food Studio
24 Rainwater
Sun Dial
Mix
Capital Grille

Emeril's
Kyma
Globe
Ritz/Buckhead Café
Chops/Lobster Bar
City Grill
Oceanaire
Silk
Nava
Blue Ridge Grill
Taurus
Pampas Steak
Ritz/Atlanta Grill
Krog Bar
Grace 17.20
23 Au Pied de Cochon
Eurasia Bistro
Feast*
Aspens/Steak
MF Sushibar

Outdoors

Anis Bistro
Einstein's
Globe
Haven
Horseradish Grill
Krog Bar
MidCity Cuisine

Mosaic
PieBar
Portofino
Ritz/Atlanta Grill
Six Feet Under
Table 1280
Villa Christina

Romance

Ali-Oli
Antica Posta
Après Diem
Bacchanalia
Dante's Down/Hatch
di Paolo
Eno

Feast
Food Studio
La Grotta
Pano's & Paul's
Quinones/Bacchanalia
Rest. Eugene
Seeger's

Rooms

Aria
Au Pied de Cochon
Bazzaar
BluePointe
Blue Ridge Grill
Ecco
Emeril's

Fleming's/Steak
Grace 17.20
Joël
Nan Thai
Oceanaire
Ritz/Buckhead Din. Rm.
Veni Vidi Vici

Views

Canoe
Capital Grille
Downwind
Horseradish Grill
Nikolai's Roof
ONE. midtown

Ray's on the River
River Room
Sun Dial
Taurus
TWO. urban licks
Vinocity

Top Service

28 Ritz/Buckhead Din. Rm.
Quinones/Bacchanalia
Bacchanalia
Park 75
26 Bone's
Seeger's
25 La Grotta
Fleming's/Steak
di Paolo
Rathbun's
Aria
Ritz/Buckhead Café
Capital Grille
Pano's & Paul's
McKendrick's Steak
Tierra
Nikolai's Roof
Fogo de Chão
24 Nan Thai
Rest. Eugene

Eurasia Bistro
Chops/Lobster Bar
Sia's
New York Prime
Joël
Canoe
Floataway Cafe
Pampas Steak
Krog Bar
23 Pricci
Tamarind
Panahar
Kyma
Grace 17.20
Supper Club
Food Studio
Rainwater*
Blue Ridge Grill
Muss & Turner's
Veni Vidi Vici

vote at zagat.com   15

Best Buys

Top Bangs for the Buck

1. Paolo's Gelato
2. Jake's
3. Souper Jenny
4. Varsity
5. Zesto
6. Rising Roll Sandwich
7. Java Jive
8. Oak Grove
9. Willy's Mexicana
10. Oz Pizza
11. Belly General
12. El Taco Veloz
13. Thumbs Up
14. Chipotle
15. Alon's
16. Fabiano's Deli
17. Ria's Bluebird
18. Bajarito's
19. Fickle Pickle
20. Raging Burrito
21. Havana Sandwich
22. Pangaea
23. Moe's SW Grill
24. Fellini's Pizza
25. New Yorker
26. Sun in My Belly
27. Grant Central Pizza
28. Slope's BBQ
29. Bobby & June's
30. Crescent Moon
31. George's
32. Eats
33. Taqueria del Sol
34. Noodle
35. Tin Drum Asia Café
36. Harold's BBQ
37. Muss & Turner's
38. Jason's Deli
39. Atlanta Bread
40. Brick Store Pub

Other Good Values

Andy's Indian
Barbecue Kitchen
Bread Garden
Busy Bee Cafe
Cameli's Pizza
China Delight
City Garden
Doc Chey's Asian
Dusty's BBQ
88 Tofu House
Figo Pasta
Fortune Cookie
Goldberg's Bagel
Gold Star Cafe
Gumbeaux's
Jalisco
Johnny Rocket's
Joli Kobe Bakery
Little Bangkok
Loaf & Kettle
Matthew's Cafeteria
Old South BBQ
Original Pancake
Panahar
Pho Hoa
Pho 79
P.R.'s BBQ
Rainbow
Rolling Bones BBQ
Savage Pizza
Silver Grill
Silver Skillet
Son's Place
Sprayberry's BBQ
Thomas Mktpl.
Vatica Indian
Vortex B&G
White House
Williamson Bros. BBQ
Zapata

Restaurant Directory

Atlanta

F	D	S	C

Agave   23 | 20 | 20 | $30
242 Boulevard SE (Carroll St.), 404-588-0006;
www.agaverestaurant.com
A "hip Intown crowd" gravitates to this "slice of New Mexico" in Cabbagetown for "top-notch" Southwestern cuisine with some "new twists", which can be "well lubricated" by an "impressive margarita selection"; the "caring owner" and his "awesome" staff aim to please, and the "stylish" space boasts two fireplaces and an "attractive" enclosed patio; though it's "on the pricey side", most consider it a "class act" all around.

Agnes & Muriel's   18 | 18 | 18 | $23
1514 Monroe Dr. NE (Piedmont Ave.), 404-885-1000;
www.mominthekitchen.com
Fans find this "charming" Midtown Southerner a "hoot" as they "carb it up" on "yummy-in-the-tummy" 1950s "housewife cuisine" that matches the "campy" "retro" digs complete with "Barbie dolls", "mismatched dinnerware and tabletops" and "happy aqua walls"; the service is "attentive", with a "sense of humor", but to detractors dismayed by "mediocre" eats and "freakish" decor, what "used to be hip is now past its sell-by date."

Alfredo's   23 | 15 | 22 | $28
1989 Cheshire Bridge Rd. NE (bet. Lavista & Piedmont Rds.),
404-876-1380; www.alfredositalianrestaurant.com
"Like a great old Sinatra song", this Cheshire Bridge "red-sauce" "tradition" is a "classic" offering "healthy portions" of "fantastic" "old-school" Italian eats at "reasonable prices" and "friendly, attentive" service from tuxedo-clad waiters; the "darkly lit" room with "no windows" and "'70s paneling" is "exactly as it has been for decades", which is just fine with the "well-heeled" clientele that keeps it "packed night after night."

Ali-Oli ☒   21 | 21 | 21 | $33
Lenox Mktpl., 3535 Peachtree Rd. (Lenox Rd.), 404-266-0414;
www.aliolirestaurant.com
It's "like taking a quiet vacation in the heart of Buckhead" at this "underappreciated" Med-Italian where "quality eats" and an "outstanding" wine list are served in a "comfortable" space that's "surprisingly posh", given its "strange" parking garage location; it's "one of the hardest places to find" in town, but those who do feel "rewarded"; N.B. there's a Gourmet-to-Go retail shop at the entrance.

Atlanta F | D | S | C

ALON'S   27 | 17 | 19 | $14
1394 N. Highland Ave. (Morningside Dr.), 404-872-6000; www.alons.com
"The oohs and ahs won't stop" at this jam-packed Va-Highlands "bakery fantasy" serving some of the "best bread in America", "sublime" sandwiches, "eye-catching" desserts and "specialty foods galore"; the service is "friendly" and "knowledgeable", but fans wish for "more on-site seating" beyond the outdoor benches and picnic tables, and caution "walk if you can", for "parking can be like hand-to-hand combat."

Ambra ☒   21 | 17 | 18 | $26
1425 Ellsworth Industrial Blvd. (Chattahoochee Ave.), 404-352-2888; www.ambradining.com
Long-distance loyalists find it a "shame" this Westside charmer is "so far away" they need a "compass" to find it and its "creative" Med-Southwestern menu, which has "something for everyone"; "friendly" service and "eclectic" decor in a converted lumber mill help make it "one of the best neighborhood bistros in town."

American Roadhouse   16 | 12 | 17 | $15
842 N. Highland Ave. (bet. Drewry St. & Greenwood Ave.), 404-872-2822; www.american-roadhouse.com
A "laid-back clientele" "brings the family" or their "Saturday morning hangovers" to this "casual" "all-American" diner in Va-Highlands serving an "expansive" menu of comfort food "at its best"; cynics find the fare "mediocre" and the decor in "need of a major fluff-up", but thanks to service "with a smile" and "reasonable prices", there's "usually a wait" on weekends.

Andy's Indian Grill   ▽ 21 | 18 | 20 | $17
3070 Windward Plaza (Windward Pkwy.), Alpharetta, 678-242-0155; www.andysindiangrill.com
Despite its somewhat "unusual name for an Indian" venue, this "joint in the burbs" of Alpharetta is "one of the best north of the perimeter" according to fans, who laud the "excellent" daytime buffet that allows you to "stay within your lunch hour" as well as your budget; a "quaint" setting and "consistent service" make it "worth the effort" to get here.

Anis Bistro   22 | 20 | 19 | $31
2974 Grandview Ave. (Pharr Rd.), 404-233-9889; www.anisbistro.com
This "laid-back" Buckhead boîte "takes ooh-la-la to a new level" with its "authentic" and "reasonably priced" Gallic cuisine, which is brought to table by "delightful" "French-accented" servers; al fresco dining on the "special" year-round patio is a "close-your-eyes-and-you're-in-Provence" experience that's "perfect for a date", but

Atlanta

| F | D | S | C |

detractors fret over an occasionally "absent" staff that seems to be "daydreaming of France."

Annie's Thai Castle | 22 | 16 | 18 | $25 |
3195 Roswell Rd. NE (Peachtree Rd.), 404-264-9546
For "several years running" this "dependable" Buckhead Thai has been serving "straightforward" "favorites to please all palates"; the "dimly lit" interior "leaves a lot to be desired" and frugal foes fume it's "expensive", but "consistent" cooking and "friendly" service keep loyal subjects coming back.

Anthony's ⌧ | 16 | 19 | 18 | $44 |
3109 Piedmont Rd. (bet. E. Paces Ferry & Peachtree Rds.), 404-262-7379; www.anthonysfinedining.com
"Frankly, my dear", the "beautiful surroundings" "remind you of Tara before Sherman" at this New American in the heart of Buckhead; but rebels who aren't "suckered into the faux antebellum experience" report "iffy service", "stale decor" and "tired" food in an "expensive" "institution that's sliding toward relic"; N.B. it now serves only parties of 10 or more and reservations are required.

ANTICA POSTA | 24 | 20 | 21 | $43 |
519 E. Paces Ferry Rd. (Piedmont Rd. NE), 404-262-7112; www.anticaposta.com
"Tuscany, here I come" say fans who feel "transported" to the region by this Buckhead Northern Italian where the "expertly prepared" fare is "simplicity at its finest"; though the space is "a bit cramped", the "cozy" atmosphere makes it a "favorite" for a date and the staff makes you "feel like you're the only one" in the place; to skeptics, though, the service is only "so-so" and the fare "doesn't match the price tag."

Après Diem ● | 17 | 18 | 14 | $21 |
Midtown Promenade, 931 Monroe Dr. NE (bet. Ponce de Leon & Virginia Aves.), 404-872-3333; www.apresdiem.com
"Feel hip lounging in a chaise" "surrounded by deep people" at this "bohemian" Midtown Continental offering "affordable bites", an "amazing dessert case" and an "extensive drink menu" in an "eclectic", "candlelit" space that becomes a "funky twentysomething heaven" when the "very late–night crowd" rolls in; "down-to-earth" servers are "friendly" but "be prepared to wait (and wait and wait) for your check"; N.B. there's live jazz on Wednesdays.

Aqua Blue | 21 | 22 | 20 | $35 |
1564 Holcomb Bridge Rd. (Old Alabama Rd.), Roswell, 770-643-8886; www.atlantaaquablue.com
At this "familiar, upscale" Roswell spot, "unique combinations" of Asian-accented New American fare, "out-of-this-world sushi" and "stellar martinis" are served in a "trendy" space, with a "beautiful bar scene" that may "not

Atlanta   F | D | S | C

be for those with heart conditions"; though some grouse the "sexy" scene is cooled by "mediocre" service and "overpriced" eats, others insist it's "the place to take a date" for a "big city experience in the 'burbs."

ARIA ☒   27 | 25 | 25 | $51
490 E. Paces Ferry Rd. (Maple Dr.), 404-233-7673;
www.aria-atl.com

"Gerry Klaskala continues to be at the top of his game" at this Buckhead "beauty", creating "amazing" New American cuisine "with a soul", while pastry chef Kathryn King's desserts are some of the "best in town"; the "gorgeous" space includes a "cool" bar, "romantic" wine cellar for private dining and "cozy" patio, and though the scene can get "way too loud", "superb" service makes "you feel like a million bucks"; it's "expensive" too, but "you get what you pay for."

Asada   20 | 13 | 18 | $22
1238 Dekalb Ave. NE (Moreland Ave.), 404-522-8666;
www.asada-atl.com

"Tempting tamales" and other Southwestern eats "with an edge", accompanied by "authentic", "refreshing" margaritas, are served at this "underappreciated" "find" in Candler Park that occupies a "funky" converted gas station with a "great" "child-friendly" outdoor patio; skeptics, though, are underwhelmed by "slow" service and "so-so" decor, and insist "you could find better food for the same price."

Aspens Signature Steak   22 | 23 | 21 | $37
Avenues Shopping Ctr., 3625 Dallas Hwy. SW (1 mi. west of Barrett Pkwy.), Marietta, 770-419-1744
Kroger Shopping Ctr., 2942 Shallowford Rd. (Sandy Plains Rd.), Marietta, 678-236-1400
www.knowwheretogogh.com

"Meat-and-taters lovers" in Marietta commend these "fine" midpriced steakhouses offering "high-quality" beef and a "pleasant" experience "without the testosterone" in a "warm", "rustic lodge" setting; the service is "friendly" even when things get "bustling", and while some find it "a bit overpriced" (unless you "go before 6 PM" for the early-bird special Sundays–Fridays), many agree it's "worth the visit."

Athens Pizza House   19 | 12 | 17 | $14
Chamblee Plaza, 5550 Peachtree Industrial Blvd. (Chamblee Dunwoody Rd.), Chamblee, 770-452-8282
Athens Plaza, 1341 Clairmont Rd. (N. Decatur Rd.), Decatur, 404-636-1100
2205 Pleasant Hill Rd. (Satellite Blvd.), Duluth, 770-813-1369
www.athenspizzaatlanta.com

Families and students "on a budget" flock to this trio of independently-owned Greek pizzerias which are "highly

Atlanta

F | D | S | C

recommended" for "fresh" pies ("feta makes it a standout") and "reliable" "authentic" Hellenic eats, served by a "friendly" staff in "comfortable" digs that are "nothing fancy"; naysayers nix the "salty" fare and service that's "hit-or-miss depending on the location", but for others it's a "no-brainer."

Atkins Park ●
17 | 16 | 17 | $20

794 N. Highland Ave. NE (St. Charles Ave.), 404-876-7249
Shops at Village Green, 2840 Atlanta Rd. (Spring St.), Smyrna, 770-435-1887
www.atkinspark.com

"Kick it old-school" at this "classic watering hole", a Va-Highlands "fixture" since 1922, where "wonderful burgers" and other "sturdy" American fare with Cajun accents are served in a "cozy" dining space opposite a "hoppin'" bar; it's "family-friendly until about nine-ish" when the "party crowd" hits and the "good-natured" staff makes it the "closest thing to *Cheers* in Atlanta"; the newer Smyrna location is a "good bet" in that town's "quaint village square."

Atlanta Bread Co.
16 | 12 | 14 | $11

1155 Mt. Vernon Hwy. (Peachtree Rd.), 770-392-1944
Peachtree Ctr., 231 Peachtree St. NE (International Blvd.), 404-688-6393
220 Sandy Springs Circle (Mt. Vernon Hwy. NE), 404-843-0040
Tower Pl., 3365 Piedmont Rd. (Peachtree Rd. NE), 404-814-1302
North Point Mall, 1056 North Point Circle (North Point Ctr. E.), Alpharetta, 770-740-1450
205 E. Ponce de Leon Ave. (Church St.), Decatur, 404-378-6600
Merchant's Walk, 1255 Johnson Ferry Rd. NE (E. Cobb Dr.), Marietta, 770-509-3838
Prado Lane Shopping Ctr., 2555 Prado Ln. (Bells Ferry Rd. NE), Marietta, 770-420-9225
The Forum, 4880 Peachtree Corners Circle (Peachtree Pkwy.), Norcross, 770-662-0900
www.atlantabread.com

A "somewhat healthy alternative to fast food", this "bustling" deli chain dishes out a "broad variety" of "delicious hot soups", "wonderful" sandwiches and "tempting" desserts in a "family-friendly" setting that offsets the generic "cookie-cutter" digs and "lackadaisical" service, while WiFi at most locations is an "added bonus"; foes find the branches "maddeningly inconsistent" and feel the fare "has gone downhill over the years."

ATLANTA FISH MARKET
23 | 19 | 20 | $38

265 Pharr Rd. (bet. Peachtree St. & Piedmont Rd.), 404-262-3165;
www.buckheadrestaurants.com

"If it swims, you can get it" at this "seafood lover's paradise" from the Buckhead Life Group, where an "unrivaled selection" of "schools upon schools" of "fabulous fish"

Atlanta   F D S C

flown in fresh three times daily is prepared "any way imaginable"; you can almost "feel the ocean breezes" in the "welcoming" "nautical" setting, though "even with reservations" it can be a "two-glasses-of-wine wait" when it's packed with as "many tourists" as on a "Carnival Cruise"; regulars recommend this one primarily for "business" or "group" dining.

Atlantic Seafood Company   23 21 20 $34
2345 Mansell Rd. (N. Point Pkwy.), Alpharetta, 770-640-0488;
www.atlanticseafoodco.com
The "best in the 'burbs" is what some finatics call this "upscale" Alpharetta seafooder for its "always fresh" entrees, "excellent" sushi and "efficient" service; it's a "see-and-be-seen" scene (Whitney Houston and Bobby Brown have been sighted here) in this "contemporary fishbowl for adults" with "high ceilings", "elaborate fish tanks" and "booming" acoustics, but some feel it should have "more ambiance for the price point."

Atmosphere   24 21 20 $32
1620 Piedmont Ave. (Monroe Ave.), 678-702-1620;
www.atmospherebistro.com
"Sumptuous" French cuisine, including "excellent specials", and "gracious" service are turning this "hidden gem" in Va-Highlands into a "destination" of those in-the-know for a "special night out", "martinis on the deck" or a "delish" Sunday brunch; the "adorable" family running the show "know their stuff", and you "can hold a conversation" in the "intimate" environs of the "cozy", "nicely renovated Craftsman cottage."

Au Pied de Cochon ●   20 23 21 $48
InterContinental Buckhead, 3315 Peachtree Rd. NE
(Piedmont Rd.), 404-946-9000; www.intercontinental.com
"From Paris with love" comes the "true flavor of France" at this Buckhead brasserie housed in the lobby of the "posh" InterContinental hotel, where an "extensive" menu of "fantastic" French "comfort food" is served in a space graced with Murano glass chandeliers and "romantic" red-velvet-curtain booths; cynics squeal about "slow service", "inconsistent" fare and "second-mortgage" price tags, but night owls declare the "24-hour fine-dining concept is a winner."

Au Rendez Vous ⊠⇗   19 6 16 $21
1328 Windsor Pkwy. (Osborne Rd. NE), 404-303-1968
It may take a "few drive-bys to find it", but those who have tout this Sandy Springs "hole-in-the-wall" as the "only place" for "fabulous" "cheap country French eats", prepared and served by a "gracious" staff; sure, the "nondescript room" is "in desperate need of an interior designer" (picture "eating next to a refrigerator"), but it's still

vote at zagat.com

Atlanta   F | D | S | C

"charming" and one of the "best bargains in town" – just remember to "bring your own wine."

Avra Greek Tavern   21 | 20 | 19 | $31
794 Juniper St. NE (5th St.), 404-892-8890;
www.avragreektavern.com
A chorus shouts "*opa!*" about this family-owned Greek, a "great addition" to Midtown that "fills a niche" with "creatively presented" cuisine (at "tolerable" prices) served by a "courteous", "attentive" staff in an "upbeat environment", with live Hellenic music Wednesdays–Saturdays; well-wishers hope this "first-rate" taverna "will break the curse" of the once "jinxed" renovated two-story house.

Azio Downtown   18 | 16 | 17 | $18
Peachtree Ctr., 229 Peachtree St. NE (International Blvd.), 404-222-0808; www.aziodowntown.com

Little Azio
749 Moreland Ave. SE (Ormewood Ave.), 404-624-0440
903 Peachtree St. NE (8th St.), 404-876-7711
1675 Cumberland Pkwy., Ivywalk Ste. 415 (Atlanta Rd. SE), Smyrna, 678-426-0333
www.littleazio.com
"Eclectic but inexpensive" is how *amici* describe this Downtown Italian and its more casual *bambini*; "fresh" *cucina* and a "beautiful cathedral"-like space make the original location a popular option for the convention and business set, while the smaller, counter-service spin-offs are "pleasant pit stops" for a "hip lunch" with "great people-watching"; skeptics, though, find them "uninspired" and "nothing special."

Babette's Cafe   23 | 20 | 22 | $34
573 N. Highland Ave. (Freedom Pkwy.), 404-523-9121;
www.babettescafe.com
"As reliable as they come", this "neighborhood treasure" in Poncey-Highlands is praised for its "terrific" menu of "robust" European fare and a "fabulous" brunch that "impresses foodies and non-foodies alike; "super service" and a hands-on owner make fans "feel like family" in the "romantic" "charming" house and patio overlooking Freedom Trail – all in all, it's an "unpretentious" experience and a "good value for fine dining."

BACCHANALIA   29 | 25 | 28 | $77
Westside Mktpl., 1198 Howell Mill Rd. (bet. 14th St. & Huff Rd.), 404-365-0410; www.starprovisions.com
"Any conversation about Atlanta's best" must include this "seamless" New American on the Westside, voted the city's Most Popular and No. 1 for Food, with a "big time wow factor" that "could make a rainy Tuesday seem like a special occasion"; "husband-and-wife team" Anne Quatrano and Clifford Harrison's "focused" cuisine guar-

Atlanta F | D | S | C |

antees "gastronomic ecstasy" that's a "true bargain despite the price", and "sublime" service is "choreographed like a ballet" in the "refined" warehouse space with a "laid-back" vibe in spite of its "top-tier status."

Bajarito's 17 | 11 | 15 | $10 |
Cherokee Plaza, 3877 Peachtree Rd. NE (bet. Dresden Dr. & Peachtree Dunwoody Rd.), 404-239-9727
"A nice change from the standard", this "quick-serve" cantina in Brookhaven offers "above-average", "giant" burritos with "novel combinations", "excellent" fish tacos and other "healthy" Mexican fare in a "casual" setting; "extremely fast" service and "reasonable" prices also make it a "reliable" "alternative" to the larger chains.

Bambinelli's 18 | 11 | 18 | $19 |
Sports Authority Vlg., 3202 Northlake Pkwy. NE (Henderson Mill Rd.), Tucker, 770-493-1311;
www.bambinellispizza.com
It's "like having an Italian family invite you for dinner" at this "old-style sauce palace" in Tucker serving "gigantic" portions of "consistent" Southern Italian "favorites" to the strains of "kitschy" piano tunes in a "friendly" atmosphere; *amici* advise just "ignore the decor" and "don't let the strip-mall location deter you."

Bamboo Garden ▽ 20 | 16 | 16 | $16 |
1707 Church St. (Decatur Rd.), Decatur, 404-294-6160
3925 Pleasant Hill Rd. (Peachtree Industrial Blvd.), Duluth, 770-622-1445
www.bamboo-gardens.com
"Flavorful" chile chicken and other "tasty Indian-style" Chinese dishes "will bring out a sweat" from diners at this duo in Decatur and Duluth, but for many the "interesting" fusion "works"; the no-frills decor and "laid-back" service aside, insiders insist you "can't go wrong with anything on the menu."

Bangkok Thai ⌧ ▽ 22 | 11 | 21 | $17 |
Ansley Sq., 1492 Piedmont Rd. (Monroe Ave.), 404-874-2514
For some of the "best Thai takeout in town", Midtowners turn to this "old standby" in Ansley Square that has been serving chicken curry and other "good, plain" eats for nearly three decades; the atmosphere and decor "leave a lot to be desired" but the "food more than makes up for it."

Baraonda 22 | 19 | 19 | $23 |
710 Peachtree St. (3rd St.), 404-879-9962;
www.baraondaatlanta.com
Aficionados who "can't quite afford to get to Italy" head to this "lively" Midtown Italian for "tasty" brick oven–baked pizzas with the "freshest of toppings" and other "simple" fare; "hip" neighbors and pre- or post-theatergoers "crowd" the "cozy" space "to the gills", flowing onto the

Atlanta   F D S C

patio "overlooking shady trees" and providing prime people-watching; though the "hot" waiters have many fans, others complain that the service varies "from pleasant to surly."

Barbecue Kitchen ⊄   ▽ 22 | 7 | 15 | $11
1437 Virginia Ave. (I-85, exit 19B), 404-766-9906
"Solid" Southern "comfort food" at "great prices" makes this "wholesome" meat and three near the airport a "staple" for "airline workers, overnight guests from nearby hotels" and Southsiders; there's "no ambiance" to speak of and the service from "waitresses straight from the *Dukes of Hazard*" can be "hit-or-miss", but they do "keep the people moving."

Basil's   19 | 16 | 19 | $29
2985 Grandview Ave. (Pharr Rd.), 404-233-9755; www.basils.net
"Charming outdoor dining" on the "tree-covered deck" is a "big draw" at this "quaint" Mediterranean in a renovated house in Buckhead, where a "delightful" menu of "reasonably priced" fare also keeps loyalists "coming back"; "no one hurries you for the table" – a "rare treat" in Atlanta – and while some gripe about "uneven" cooking and service, for others it remains a "solid" option.

Bazzaar ⊠   ▽ 16 | 22 | 20 | $25
654 Peachtree St. (Ponce de Leon Ave.), 404-885-7505; www.bazzaaratlanta.com
Next door to the Fox in Midtown, this "cool getaway" with an "awesome" lounge is the "perfect place" for "drinks, nibbles and people-watching" pre- or post-show, where the "beautiful" patrons match the "fabulous" decor; "great DJs" and some of the "best bartenders" around add to the impression that it's "more like a bar than a restaurant"("they serve food?"), but "simple yet creative" small plates of European and American bites add to the scene.

B.E.D.   - | - | - | M
Glenn Hotel, 110 Marietta St. (Spring St.), 404-222-7992; www.bedrestaurants.com
Reserve a bed at this unique venue in Downtown's boutique Glenn Hotel (with siblings in NY and Miami) where daring diners can sack out and sip cocktails with names such as Satin Sheets and Pillow Talk before tucking into Gallic-accented New American dishes perched on lap trays (it also serves breakfast); the Johnson Studio–designed space sports walls of gossamer curtains and a floating spiral staircase, and there are tables for the more conventionally minded; N.B. a rooftop lounge will be available for members only.

Belly General Store   18 | 20 | 16 | $12
772 N. Highland Ave. (St. Charles Pl.), 404-872-1003; www.bellystore.com
"Yuppies" and nostalgic types in Va-Highlands are "glad to have" this renovated drugstore "in the neighborhood" for

Atlanta   F | D | S | C

its basic American eats, including "to-die-for" cupcakes with icing "so good it should be outlawed", a "smiling" staff and a "unique" collection of "interesting" food items, penny candy and household goods; "letdown" locals, though, find it an "overrated" experience "lacking in service and good food", with a "hodgepodge of merchandise" that "begs the question, what exactly is" this place?

Benedetti's   16 | 12 | 16 | $19
2064 N. Decatur Rd. (Clairmont Rd.), Decatur, 404-633-0408
Relive the "red-sauce days of yesteryear" at this strip-mall Decatur "institution" where "generous" portions of "no-frills" Italian cuisine are doled out with "old-school charm" by a "pleasant" staff in a room so "dark" some compare it to Disney's Haunted Mansion"; critics who find the fare "disappointing" and the service "slow" are inclined to "skip it", but many others do not, hence it's "always packed."

Benihana   17 | 17 | 19 | $31
Peachtree Ctr., 229 Peachtree St. NE (International Blvd.), 404-522-9627
2143 Peachtree Rd. (Bennett St.), 404-355-8565
2365 Mansell Rd. (GA 400), Alpharetta, 678-461-8440
www.benihana.com
"What a bunch of cut-ups" are the "high-energy" "knife-twirling" tableside chefs at this Japanese chain putting on an "entertaining" show "perfect" for kids and those "prepared to make friends" with their *teppan* mates; but the "bland", "overpriced" fare is "what you expect" from the "Domino's of hibachi dining" according to foes who feel the "sun has set" on this "passé" posse.

Blackstone   22 | 21 | 22 | $38
Vinings West, 4686 S. Atlanta Rd. (Log Cabin Dr.), Smyrna, 404-794-6100; www.blackstoneatlanta.com
"No need to travel" to "stuffy Buckhead" sniff Smyrna surveyors, thanks to this "neighborly" steakhouse that's "just what this developing area needs", serving "excellent" beef and seafood in a "friendly" setting with a "great bar", working fireplace and live music Tuesdays–Saturdays; critics quibble over "pricey" fare and "spotty" service, but others are "never disappointed."

Blue Eyed Daisy   – | – | – | I
9065 Selborne Ln. (Atlanta-Newnan Rd.), Palmetto, 770-463-8379; www.blueeyeddaisy.com
Cognoscenti report there's "great talent" on display at this Palmetto newcomer in the form of "inspired" sandwiches and "very clever" "home-cooked" Southern fare and baked goods; the service is "personable" and you can "meet and greet the locals" in the "warm", "retro-modern" space that includes reclaimed wood, large windows and a glass case full of sweets.

vote at zagat.com   27

Atlanta | F | D | S | C |

BLUEPOINTE | 24 | 26 | 21 | $47 |
3455 Peachtree Rd. (Lenox Rd.), 404-237-9070;
www.buckheadrestaurants.com
Everything about this New American "marvel" on the "ground floor of a Buckhead high-rise" is "gorgeous", from the "sleek" and "modern" dining room with a lofty "ceiling in the clouds", to the "pure artistry" of the "Asian-inflected", "fish-heavy" cuisine that "hits the right note", to the "electric" lounge scene crackling with "celebrities", "VIPs" and "beautiful women"; despite grumbles about servers with "attitude" and "gold diggers" "hoarding the bar", it's still a "shining star" on the city's "glitterati" dining scene.

Blue Ribbon Grill | 17 | 14 | 19 | $24 |
4006 Lavista Rd. (Briarcliff Rd.), Tucker, 770-491-1570
This "down-home" spot in Tucker gets the ribbon for "attentive" service, "solid" American eats "done the right way" ("homemade chips with blue cheese are worth the trip alone") and "strong and simple cocktails"; while the decor "needs improvement", since it resembles a "truck stop in the middle of suburbia", for "comfort food" it's the "best in the area" in the minds of many.

BLUE RIDGE GRILL | 23 | 24 | 23 | $43 |
1261 W. Paces Ferry Rd. (Northside Pkwy.), 404-233-5030;
www.blueridgegrill.com
Like a "club without the $100K initiation fee", this "relaxing" "mountain-retreat"-inspired Southerner in Buckhead earns "raves" for its "homey" feel and "exceptional bar/lounge" where "lots of regulars", including the "divorcee crowd", mingle; the "high 'suthin'" cuisine, including family-style sides, and "professional" service "up the comfort factor", making it an "impressive" place to entertain out-of-towners and "deal central" for the business set; the tabs can be "dizzying", but most say the "quality and prices are in synch."

Bobby & June's Kountry Kitchen | 17 | 10 | 20 | $12 |
375 14th St. (State St.), 404-876-3872
"Even Yankees like" this "place to grease your chin" in Midtown where "Atlanta's politicians meet up with the good ol' boys" for a passel of "big, cheap" Southern victuals, including "addictive" breakfasts and "tasty" 'cue, that are "as real as it gets", and waitresses "sporting poofy hair and tons of eye shadow" add to the "cultural experience"; just "don't be dawdling at lunch", dahlin', when the "rush is big."

Boi Na Braza | 21 | 18 | 23 | $48 |
3215 Peachtree Rd. NE (Shadowlawn Ave.), 404-814-1086;
www.boinabraza.com
"You don't need a lasso to round up top steer" at this all-you-can-eat Buckhead Brazilian, a "carnivore's paradise"

Atlanta   F D S C

with a "splendid" salad bar and a staff of "attentive" gauchos who are "prompt" with the "protein"; the dining room is "huge" so "there's rarely a wait", making it easy to "loosen the pantyhose or belt" and "let the feeding frenzy begin!"

Bollywood Masala Grill House   21 | 16 | 16 | $17
Center Point Plaza, 2201 Lawrenceville Hwy. (N. Druid Hills Rd.), Decatur, 404-636-6614
"Enjoy a song and a dance" while dining on "spicy" vegetarian and non-vegetarian fare at this Decatur Indian (a sibling of nearby Madras Saravana Bhavan) boasting a "fabulous buffet"; service can be "odd", but there's "lots to look at" thanks to "entertaining" music videos that play on a "super-sized" screen above the "cavernous" space.

Bombay Grill   ▽ 16 | 11 | 17 | $23
2165 Savoy Dr. (bet. Peachtree & Shallowford Rds.), Chamblee, 678-530-9555
The "spicy", "mouthwatering" Indian fare at this no-frills find in Chamblee is the "real deal" according to fans who applaud the "lavish" lunch buffet that "makes up for" any shortcomings in decor or service, which can be either "gracious" or "standoffish"; the "convenient" "by-the-freeway" location is another plus.

BONE'S RESTAURANT   27 | 22 | 26 | $55
3130 Piedmont Rd. (Peachtree Rd.), 404-237-2663; www.bonesrestaurant.com
"Impeccable" right "down to the bone", this "carnivore central" in Buckhead delivers a "wow experience" "time and again" with "classic" steaks "Fred Flintstone would die for", "generous sides", "big, cold drinks" and a "phone book" of a wine list; "polished" servers and "fabulous bartenders" "take excellent care" of the crowd of "old money", "serious business-lunchers", "power players" and others in a "plush red", "old-world" setting that's "drenched in testosterone" as well as "tremendous history and personality"; this "local legend lives on."

Brake Pad, The ◐   19 | 16 | 17 | $15
3403 Main St. (Rugby Ave.), College Park, 404-766-1515
"Woodward kids, Delta lunchers and locals" in College Park flock to this "casual" American "close enough to the airport" for a "layover" meal, serving "great hamburgers and fries" as well as "fresh surprises" such as the "*muy bueno*" tilapia tacos; while it can get "noisy" inside the converted "gas station–cum–neighborhood grill", the seasonal patio is "the place to be on a sunny day", offering "good people- and train-watching" opportunities.

Bread Garden ⊠ ⌿   ▽ 25 | 5 | 14 | $11
549 Amsterdam Ave. (Monroe Dr.), 404-875-1166
"Divine" "made-to-order" sandwiches, "wonderful" breads, "chocolate torte to die for" and other "fabulous

vote at zagat.com   29

Atlanta

finds" make for "damn fine eatin'" at this Midtown bakery that's "on a completely different page" than its larger competitors; despite no decor, the "counter makes a great break" from shopping in the area.

Brickery Grill & Bar | 16 | 10 | 17 | $20 |
Hilderbrand Ct., 6125 Roswell Rd. (Hilderbrand Dr.), 404-843-8002; www.thebrickery.com

This "casual" family-owned American in Sandy Springs has "been around for a long time for good reason" – namely, "consistent" "homestyle meals" and a "friendly" environment that's "popular with the gray-haired set"; all-you-can-eat nights are "great bargains" and help make up for "dreary" decor.

Brick Store Pub ● | 19 | 21 | 20 | $16 |
125 E. Court Sq. (E. Ponce de Leon Ave.), Decatur, 404-687-0990; www.brickstorepub.com

"Everyone knows your name" and the "bartenders remember your beer" at this Decatur public house where "surprisingly solid pub standards" have "a lot of heart", including the "best" fish 'n' chips "this side of the pond", but the "infinite" list of "international" brews is the "real star here"; "gorgeous" exposed brickwork highlights the space set inside a "historic building", and the service is "knowledgeable and friendly"; butt-kickers and others who "hate smoking come here" since it's not allowed, even at the bar.

Bridgetown Grill | 17 | 14 | 16 | $20 |
3316 Piedmont Rd. (Peachtree St.), 404-266-1500
7285 Roswell Rd. (Abernathy Rd.), 770-394-1575
www.bridgetowngrill.com

"Feel like you're in Jamaica, mon" at this "affordable", "low-key" Caribbean duo in Buckhead and Sandy Springs where "delightful" dishes full of "island charm" are served by an "upbeat" staff amid "colorful" surroundings; foes, however, find "no excitement in the menu or atmosphere" and conclude the "luster is gone" from this "corporate chain."

Brio Tuscan Grille | 19 | 19 | 18 | $29 |
700 Ashwood Pkwy. (Ashford Dunwoody Rd.), 678-587-0017
2964 Peachtree Rd. (Pharr Rd.), 404-601-5555
www.brioitalian.com

"Surprisingly good" "for a chain", this "popular" pair is a "safe bet" for a "casual", "reasonably priced" experience featuring an "extensive" menu of "flavorful" Northern Italian fare and "fast" service in a "beautiful" "open" dining room, and "sun dress season" on the patio "can't be beat", especially at the Dunwoody branch overlooking a lake with swans; detractors deplore the "high-decibel dining", "average" food and "uneven" service, but most agree "you could do much worse."

Atlanta

F | D | S | C

Brooklyn Cafe
17 | 14 | 18 | $27

*Springs Landing, 220 Sandy Springs Circle
(bet. Johnson Ferry Rd. & Mt. Vernon Hwy.), 404-843-8377;
www.brooklyncafe.com*

As "comfortable" as an "old shoe", this "unpretentious" strip-mall Northern Italian in Sandy Springs is generally viewed as a "good go-to selection" for "tasty" fare and "friendly" service in an "informal" setting where you can show up "in a suit or sweat suit" with equal aplomb; skeptics feel it's been "losing its zing" of late, but post-*Survey* chef and ownership changes (not reflected in the above scores) may ease those concerns.

Brookwood Grill
19 | 19 | 19 | $26

*880 Holcomb Bridge Rd. (Warsaw Rd.), Roswell, 770-587-0102;
www.brookwoodgrill.com*

"Consistently good" and "hearty" American fare (the "ribs are to die for"), "attentive" service and a "comfortable" brick and hardwood–accented space have enabled this "reliable" Roswell "standby" to "withstand the elements of time"; but hecklers hiss the "predictable" scene "needs an update", because who wants to "party like it's 1988."

Buca di Beppo
16 | 18 | 19 | $24

*2335 Mansell Rd. (GA 400, exit 8), Alpharetta, 770-643-9463;
www.bucadibeppo.com*

Alpharettans "can't help but like" this local link of a national chain known for "lots of rooms crammed" with "over-the-top" decor (e.g. "the Pope's head on a lazy Susan") and "humongous" family-style portions, served by a "witty" staff in a "group-friendly" setting that's a hit with parents "who want to drown out the sound of their own children"; "needa di Pepto!" cry critics put off by "ginormous" helpings, dismissing it as "Olive Garden on steroids."

BUCKHEAD DINER ◐
22 | 21 | 21 | $33

*3073 Piedmont Rd. NE (E. Paces Ferry Rd.), 404-262-3336;
www.buckheadrestaurants.com*

A "sentimental favorite" that's "never out of date", this New American from the Buckhead Life Group "still rocks after 18 years" with "consistently delish" "upscale" "comfort food that makes for a "great late-night bite", as well as the "best brunch in the neighborhood"; "solo diners" "love the counter" in the "incredible art deco" room, where a "pleasant" staff delivers "timely" service, but foes fault the "no-reservations" policy for "long, long waits" (although a priority seating list helps).

Busy Bee Cafe
▽ 26 | 12 | 21 | $11

*810 Martin Luther King Jr. Dr. SW (Joseph E. Lowry Blvd.),
404-525-9212; www.thebusybeecafe.com*

Always "jam-packed", this Downtown stalwart has been serving some of the "best soul food in town" to "a full

vote at zagat.com

Atlanta   F | D | S | C |

house day in and day out" since 1947; the decor "isn't much", but the "wonderful" "down-home cooking", washed down by "tea so good it'll make you slap your mama", "makes up for it."

Byblos   ▽ 20 | 15 | 18 | $24 |
10684 Alpharetta Hwy. (bet. Holcomb Bridge & Mansell Rds.), Roswell, 678-352-0321; www.byblos-atlanta.com

A "great change of pace", this Roswell Lebanese serves up "authentic", "beautifully presented" cuisine, including "bargain" weekday lunch and Thursday night dinner buffets with plenty of options for the "undecided diner"; the staff "exudes warmth and hospitality" and weekend belly dancers add to the "interesting" experience.

Cabernet   23 | 23 | 23 | $45 |
5575 Windward Pkwy. (GA 400), Alpharetta, 770-777-5955; www.cabernetsteakhouse.com

For a "great" steak or "excellent" seafood "in the 'burbs", carnivores tout this "expense-account" meatery in Alpharetta, a "must for power lunches" and even "romantic dinners", with "top-notch" service in an "upscale", "classic steakhouse" setting; while bullish sorts question whether the "bland" scene "warrants the $$$", fans insist it's "on par with the ritzier Downtown and Buckhead joints"; N.B. cigar smoking is allowed at the glassed-in bar area.

Cafe Alsace   22 | 20 | 23 | $25 |
121 E. Ponce de Leon Ave. (Church St.), Decatur, 404-373-5622

"Step back into the old world" at this "delightful" "mom-and-pop" spot in the heart of Decatur, a "one-of-a-kind" place with its "authentic" French cuisine emphasizing the "wonderful flavors of the Alsace region"; lace curtains lend a "homey" feel to the "tiny" space, as do the "charming" owners who make enthusiasts "feel like they really care that you're here."

Cafe Intermezzo ◐   19 | 19 | 13 | $19 |
Park Place Shopping Ctr., 4505 Ashford Dunwoody Rd. (Perimeter Ctr. E.), 770-396-1344
1845 Peachtree Rd. NE (Collier Rd.), 404-355-0411
www.cafeintermezzo.com

Satisfy your "sweet tooth" at this coffee-and-dessert duo in Dunwoody and South Buckhead offering a "never-ending display" of "sinfully delicious" treats and perhaps the "largest drink menu in town", which includes "every type" of java "you can imagine"; "always crowded" with "beautiful" people, they're "perfect" for a "girls' get-together", après-theater or a "late-night I-don't-want-the-date-to-end drink", and even though "laughable" service make many "wish they'd stayed home", most "go back anyway."

subscribe to zagat.com

Atlanta

F | D | S | C

Café Lily 23 | 19 | 22 | $28
The Shops of West Ponce, 308 W. Ponce de Leon Ave. (Ponce de Leon Pl.), Decatur, 404-371-9119; www.cafelily.com

The "sweetest flower in Decatur" is what fans call this "romantic" Mediterranean that "can make any dining experience memorable" with "awesome" cuisine, an "outstanding" wine selection ("terrific list of Zinfandels") and a "delightful" staff making ordering a "breeze"; the "charismatic owner" is "always there" to give you a "big welcome", and "reasonable" prices make it a "repeater" for many; P.S. a recent expansion (not reflected in the above Decor score) may help ease the "lines."

Cafe Prego ⊠ 20 | 15 | 22 | $27
Chastain Sq., 4279 Roswell Rd. (bet. Midvale & Rickenbacker Drs.), 404-252-0032

"Come once and you'll be "welcomed", "come twice and they make you part of the family" at this "quintessential neighborhood" Italian in Buckhead that's "not your average strip-mall eatery"; while the ambiance is "lacking", owner Pietro Fecchio is one of "Atlanta's best hosts" and the fare is "consistently good", so it's usually "stuffed with" a "clubby" bunch of regulars, including an "over-60" contingent, giving the word "'cozy' a whole new definition."

Cafe Sunflower ⊠ 22 | 14 | 20 | $19
Brookwood Square Ctr., 2140 Peachtree Rd. NE (Colonial Homes Dr.), 404-352-8859
Hammond Springs Ctr., 5975 Roswell Rd. (Hammond Dr.), 404-256-1675
www.cafesunflower.com

"Who needs meat?" ponder proponents of these "casual", "inexpensive" vegetarian specialists in South Buckhead and Sandy Springs where the "Birkenstock crowd" and other fans always "feel healthy" dining on "creative", "surprisingly good" meatless offerings (including "unbelievable" vegan desserts) that could "convert even the most die-hard carnivore"; "friendly" service keeps things warm and fuzzy.

Café Tu Tu Tango ● 18 | 21 | 17 | $27
220 Pharr Rd. (Bolling Way), 404-841-6222; www.cafetututango.com

"Get ready to party" at this "funky" Buckhead Eclectic where "fast-paced entertainment" in the form of belly dancers, fire eaters, palm readers, artists and more "spices up" the "interesting" small-plates menu offering "lots of choices"; cynics sneer the "laid-back" service and "food leave a lot to be desired", but because the "high-energy experience" "won't cost an arm and a leg", it's a "favorite" spot for a "group nosh" among "young hipsters" and out-of-towners.

vote at zagat.com

Atlanta

F | D | S | C

Cameli's Gourmet Pizza Joint   23 | 7 | 14 | $12
Ford Factory Sq., 699 Ponce de Leon Ave. (N. Highland Ave.), 404-249-9020; www.camelispizza.com
"*Bene*" say boosters of this Midtown pizzeria that's the "hands-down favorite" of many for its "satisfying" pies with "fresh" "gourmet" toppings, and "enormous" slices that provide "definite bang for your buck"; "looks are deceiving" at this "hole-in-the-wall" where "lots of tats, piercings and purple hair" are on display, but those who brave it always "come back" for more.

CANOE   25 | 26 | 24 | $46
Vinings on the River, 4199 Paces Ferry Rd. (I-75), 770-432-2663; www.canoeatl.com
In a "beautifully landscaped" setting "on the banks of the Chattahoochee River", the "ambiance" of this "fairy-tale" "favorite" in Vinings "goes on for days" while "adventuresome" chef Carvel Grant Gould "successfully navigates" the dining scene with her "stunning" New American cuisine that's heavy on "Southern hunter's fare" ("if you can shoot it in the woods" it's "on the menu"); "impeccable" service adds to the experience so "romantic" that dating doyens declare "if you don't get lucky after going here, then it's time to end the relationship."

Canton Cooks ☻   23 | 9 | 17 | $19
Office Depot Shopping Ctr., 5984 Roswell Rd. NE (Hammond Dr.), 404-250-0515
"You don't have to travel to Buford Highway" for "outstanding" Cantonese say fans of this Sandy Springs Sino spot serving "authentic", "interesting dishes not seen on most Chinese menus"; the strip-mall digs are "not much to look at" and the "service leaves something to be desired", but it's always "crowded" and night owls "love that it's open until 2 AM."

Canton House ☻   22 | 14 | 17 | $17
4825 Buford Hwy. (Chamblee Tucker Rd.), Chamblee, 770-936-9030
At this Chamblee Cantonese, diners are virtually "hanging from the rafters on weekends" for some of the "best dim sum in Atlanta" from a "seemingly endless conga line" of "authentic" "Chinese delights" that are "worth the patience needed" to countenance the "wait" and occasionally "confused" service; the recently renovated space boasts large "airy" rooms with "bright" chandeliers.

CAPITAL GRILLE, THE   25 | 24 | 25 | $53
Capital Bldg., 255 E. Paces Ferry Rd. (Bolling Way), 404-262-1162; www.thecapitalgrille.com
Fans facing capital punishment "would choose" this "classic businessman's" steakhouse in Buckhead for "one last meal" since it delivers the "whole package" – "mouth-

subscribe to zagat.com

Atlanta   F D S C

watering" dry-aged steaks and "exquisite" service in a room with "plenty of mahogany and leather" and "spectacular views of the city"; the clientele is "worth looking at too", and there's a "popular bar scene" for the "afterwork" crowd; though it's part of a chain, it "hides it well."

Caramba Cafe   15 13 14 $17
1409-D N. Highland Ave. (bet. N. Morningside & University Drs. NE), 404-874-1343; www.carambacafe.com
A "huge margarita list" and "decent" "old-school" Tex-Mex fare at "terrific" prices make this family-owned spot in the heart of the action in Va-Highlands "popular" with the locals; it "doesn't look like much" and the service ranges from "surly" to downright "zany", but fans "keep coming back."

Carbo's Cafe ⊠   ▽ 19 18 18 $41
3717 Roswell Rd. NE (Piedmont Rd.), 404-231-4433
While it "flies under the radar" of many, this "wonderful" "old dowager" in Buckhead offers "good" Continental cuisine in an "intimate" dining room with a decidedly "80s feel"; cynics say it's getting "tired", with a menu that "needs updating" and service that's "really gone downhill", but it still has one of the "best piano bars" in town for the "toupee set", and for many it remains a "solid" choice for a "quiet" "special evening."

Carpe Diem   19 23 19 $23
Ice House Lofts, 105 Sycamore Pl. (Commerce Dr.), Decatur, 404-687-9696; www.apresdiem.com
Aesthetes praise the "cool warehouse renovation" of this Decatur Mediterranean in the Ice House Lofts with its "cavernous" dining room, sofa-strewn bar and "inviting" patio overlooking train tracks; some give the kitchen an "A for effort" for the "varied" menu of "tasty" fare, while others find the cooking "spotty" and service "inconsistent", but most agree it's a "great place to relax" and "meet friends."

Carrabba's Italian Grill   20 17 19 $22
2030 Sugarloaf Circle (Satellite Blvd.), Duluth, 770-497-4959
1160 Ernest Barrett Pkwy. (Hwy. 41), Kennesaw, 770-499-0338
1887 Mt. Zion Rd. (Mt. Zion Blvd.), Morrow, 770-968-3233
W. Park Plaza, 500 Commerce Dr. (Hwys. 54 & 74), Peachtree City, 770-631-1057
2999 Cumberland Blvd. (Cobb Pkwy.), Smyrna, 770-437-1444
www.carrabbas.com
On those days "when you just need an Italian fix", these "friendly" links of a Texas-based chain "in the 'burbs" are "hard to beat" for "price and quality", offering "large portions" of "consistently good" red-sauce fare and "cordial" service in a "welcoming" environment; there may be "better" out there, but insiders insist you "get what you expect."

vote at zagat.com

Atlanta

| F | D | S | C |

Cedars 19 | 12 | 17 | $24
Plantation Heights Shopping Ctr., 2770 Lenox Rd. (Peachtree Rd.), 404-261-1826; www.cedarsatlanta.com
"For a taste of Lebanon", "Atlantans of all stripes" crowd around the "terrific" buffet table (at lunch on weekdays, and on Tuesday, Thursday and Sunday evenings) at this Buckhead Mediterranean for "marvelous meze" that are the "real thing" and offer "excellent value"; while "odd", the strip-mall location near Lenox Mall is "approachable" and "gracious" service makes for a "leisurely" experience.

CHEESECAKE FACTORY 18 | 18 | 17 | $25
3024 Peachtree Rd. NE (Pharr Rd.), 404-816-2555
Perimeter Mall, 4400 Ashford Dunwoody Rd. (Abernathy Rd.), 678-320-0201
North Point Mall, 2075 N. Point Circle (N. Point Pkwy.), Alpharetta, 770-751-7011
www.thecheesecakefactory.com
You could dine at these "upscale" American chain links "for six months" and "never eat the same thing twice" thanks to the "encyclopedic" menu of "reliable" fare (including the "unsurpassed" cheesecake) doled out in "gargantuan" helpings; despite "no kids' menu", expect lots of "birthday parties" in a "campy" setting where "chaos rules", and while "unimpressed" critics feel the "wasteful portions" of "feeding trough" fare and "spotty" service don't warrant the "interminable waits", cronies confess "I love this place despite myself."

Chequers Seafood Grill 20 | 17 | 19 | $34
236 Perimeter Center Pkwy. (Hammond Dr.), 770-391-9383; www.chequersseafood.com
An "old reliable that can still charm Neptune", this "solid" seafooder located near Perimeter Mall in Dunwoody reels in afishionados with a "delightful selection" of "fresh" fin fare and a "terrific" Sunday brunch; a "handy location", "attentive" staff and "pleasant" atmosphere help keep it "popular", and while some cynics "don't know why people rave about it", with its "dated" digs and "high" prices, others insist "for business or pleasure", you "can't go wrong" here.

Cherry 15 | 18 | 13 | $30
1051 W. Peachtree St. (11th St.), 404-872-2020; www.aboutcherry.com
"Hipsters sip martinis" and "nibble" on small plates of New American fare and "above-average" sushi at this "swank" Midtown scene for an "attractive" "young" clientele, located in a "large" renovated house with "great views" of the city and a back terrace with a fish pond; but some sniff the "best thing going for it is the bar", and it's "more about the crowd than the food" here.

subscribe to zagat.com

Atlanta

F | D | S | C

Chicago's Steak, Seafood & Pasta 18 | 16 | 18 | $26
5920 Roswell Rd. (I-285), 404-257-8883
990 Whitlock Ave. (Burnt Hickory Rd.), Marietta, 770-590-1500
Shallowford Corners, 4401 Shallowford Rd. (Johnson Ferry Rd.),
Roswell, 770-993-7464
www.chicagosrestaurant.com

This "convenient" suburban steakhouse trio offers "regulars" a "solid lineup" of "proven American favorites", "awesome" martinis and "down-home" service in a "friendly" environment; detractors dub the digs "fern bar central" and demur at the "uninteresting" fare and "erratic" service, but "fair" prices keep it "crowded" with a "faithful" clientele.

China Cooks ● ▽ 23 | 9 | 18 | $19
215 Northwood Dr. (Roswell Rd. NE), 404-252-6611

"Don't let the location scare you", reassure regulars of this "authentic" Chinese on a Sandy Springs side street that's "worth" the jaunt for "some of the best" "traditional" offerings in town, "served piping hot"; night owls appreciate the "nice late eats" (it's open until 2 AM), and those put off by the humble strip-mall digs have it "delivered" or get it "to go."

China Delight ● ▽ 22 | 16 | 20 | $15
2390 Chamblee Tucker Rd. (Cumberland Dr.), Chamblee,
770-986-0898

Enthusiasts extol this Chamblee Chinese serving some of the "most unique and varied" dim sum in town as well as a "large" à la carte menu (in "both Chinese and English") of "excellent" Hong Kong–style Cantonese that's "not fakey", both of which offer "great value"; there's lots of "lively, loud" "celebrating" going on in the adjacent lounge and dance hall.

Chin Chin 18 | 15 | 18 | $18
Cherokee Plaza, 3887 Peachtree Rd. (N. Druid Hills Rd.),
404-816-2229
Ford Factory Sq., 699 Ponce de Leon Ave. (Ponce de Leon Pl.),
404-881-1556
Perimeter Ctr., 1100 Hammond Dr. (Peachtree Dunwoody Rd.),
770-913-0266
3070 Windward Plaza (Windward Pkwy.), Alpharetta,
770-569-7565
6575 Sugarloaf Pkwy. (Satellite Blvd.), Duluth, 770-813-1319
Barrett Parkway Shopping Ctr., 1635 Old 41 Hwy. NW
(Barrett Pkwy.), Kennesaw, 770-218-3993
2100 Hwy 54 E. (Peachtree Pkwy.), Peachtree City, 770-487-9188
2800 Spring Rd. (Cobb Pkwy.), Smyrna, 770-319-8331
Woodstock Ctr., 9820 Hwy. 92 (I-575), Woodstock, 770-928-3896
www.chinchinatl.com

"Reliable" but "not run-of-the-mill", this chain-chain doles out "delicious" Chinese, served by a "witty" staff in "sub-

vote at zagat.com

Atlanta

F | D | S | C

tle" interiors with exhibition kitchens that are "never garish"; while some feel it's "not what it was some years ago" due to excessive "growth", homebodies still "adore" the "quick and easy" takeout and delivery so fast "you need to have the table set before you call."

Chipotle
17 | 14 | 14 | $10

3424 Piedmont Rd. (Lenox Rd.), 404-869-7921
Toco Hills Shopping Ctr., 2963 N. Druid Hills Rd. NE
(bet. Clairmont & Lavista Rds.), 404-929-9907
5250 Windward Pkwy. (Main St.), Alpharetta, 678-867-9459
John's Creek Village, 11720 Medlock Bridge Rd. (McGinnis Ferry Rd.), Duluth, 770-623-1724
2040 Pleasant Hill Rd. (I-85 N., exit 104), Duluth, 678-584-0011
10800 Alpharetta Hwy. (Mansell Rd.), Roswell, 770-642-0710
www.chipotle.com

It may be "McMexican" ("owned by you-know-who") but "it ain't all bad" swear amigos of this "addictive" chain serving "gigantic" burritos and other "fresh" "better-than-fast-food fast food" in "large portions" that "ensure a full belly", all at prices that "can't be beat"; "high-tech", if somewhat "sterile", digs with big patios match the "clean" flavors in a "family-oriented" scene, and the staff delivers counter service with "a smile."

CHOPS/LOBSTER BAR
26 | 24 | 24 | $55

Buckhead Plaza, 70 W. Paces Ferry Rd. (Peachtree Rd.), 404-262-2675; www.buckheadrestaurants.com

A "bit of heaven on earth" for "carnivores and their fish-loving brethren", this "consistently spectacular" Buckhead Life production offers "exemplary" steaks and "unbeatable seafood", paired with a "phenomenal wine list", and "pampering" service that "makes you feel like royalty"; there's a "good bar scene" peopled by the "'in'-crowd" in the "elegant", "man's man" chophouse upstairs, while the "dungeon of deliciousness" downstairs boasts an "awesome" "Grand Central Station"–inspired look.

Chopstix
23 | 19 | 22 | $35

Chastain Sq., 4279 Roswell Rd. (Wieuca Rd.), 404-255-4868; www.chopstixatlanta.net

Popular with the Buckhead "establishment", including a sizable "blue-haired" contingent, this "high-end" purveyor of Middle Kingdom cuisine serves "superb", "imaginative" dishes crafted from "top-quality ingredients" (definitely "not your delivery Chinese"); "courtly" service from "waiters in tuxedos", "elegant" decor ("without those hanging red lanterns") and an "upscale piano bar" all belie the strip-mall location; cognoscenti caution "it'll cost you."

Atlanta   F | D | S | C

Ciao Bella ⓩ   20 | 19 | 20 | $29
309 Pharr Rd. (bet. Grandview Ave. & N. Fulton Dr.), 404-261-6013
To fans, this tiny "laid-back" trattoria is "everything it should be", offering "delicious" "inexpensive" Italian and "top-notch" service in a "quaint" "romantic hideaway" sporting a "cozy" fireplace and a "great patio for warm days", but "without the baggage" that comes with being located in Buckhead; though some critics are "not impressed", cronies insist "you won't be disappointed."

City Garden   – | – | – | I
1829 Peachtree Rd. NE (bet. Palisades Rd. & 28th St. NW), 404-352-5553
Brookwood Hills neighbors in the mood for moo shu "can't lose" when they drop into this "friendly" neighborhood Chinese that offers sushi with the stir fry – it's all "great food for the money" and the staff is "helpful"; if you choose to forgo the brick-walled, window-lined dining room, they deliver with a smile.

City Grill ⓩ   22 | 24 | 23 | $44
50 Hurt Plaza (Edgewood Ave.), 404-524-2489;
www.citygrillatlanta.com
While the dining room is "drop-dead gorgeous" at this "upscale" New American housed in the "elegant" former Federal Reserve Bank in Downtown, fans insist there are "more reasons to visit" – namely, "fine" cuisine and an "amazing wine list", "elegant" service and "quiet" ambiance; foes who feel it's "starting to show its age" contend the "food needs to rise up to the setting", but many in the "suits-and-fur" set continue to bank on it for "über-power lunches", "romantic evenings" and special "events."

Clubhouse   15 | 17 | 16 | $31
Lenox Sq., 3393 Peachtree Rd. NE (Lenox Rd.), 404-442-8891;
www.theclubhouse.com
Fans of this "lively" New American chain link in Buckhead's Lenox Square "never would've guessed it's in a mall" from the "over-the-top" decor featuring "arched ceilings" and a "mahogany" bar; still, it's a "favorite" "after-shopping" stop of many, with an "extensive menu" of "basic clubhouse fare" served in "huge portions" and "desserts bigger than the hips they eventually end up on"; many critics, though, club it for "mediocre" eats and "spotty" service.

Coco Loco   20 | 11 | 17 | $19
Buckhead Crossing, 2625 Piedmont Rd. (Sydney Marcus Blvd.), 404-364-0212; www.cocolocoatlanta.com
"Eat till you burst" at this "little slice of Havana" near the Lindbergh MARTA station in Buckhead serving "wonderful" Cuban and Caribbean grub, including "outstanding" tres leches; the "lack of exterior appeal" is "easily over-

vote at zagat.com   39

Atlanta   F | D | S | C

looked" thanks to "reasonable" prices and a "friendly, anticipatory" staff; it also "works great for takeout."

Colonnade ⊘   20 | 10 | 20 | $18
1879 Cheshire Bridge Rd. (bet. Lavista Rd. & Piedmont Ave.), 404-874-5642

A true "throwback", this "beloved" Cheshire Bridge "charmer" has been around "since snakes had legs" and it's still "busting at the seams" with "trendy gay" men and "every octogenarian within 30 miles" in for a "biscuit fix" and other "lovingly prepared" "Southern comfort food", including its "legendary" fried chicken; "attentive", "beehived waitresses" work the "large" no-frills space that "fills up fast", but "strong drinks" and "entertaining" "people-watching" make the "inevitable waits" "go down easy"; P.S. remember: no "shorts", "flip-flops" or credit cards accepted.

Com Dunwoody   24 | 14 | 19 | $19
5486 Chamblee-Dunwoody Rd. (Mt. Vernon Rd.), 770-512-7410

Com Vietnamese Grill
4005 Buford Hwy. (Clairmont Rd.), 404-320-0405

"Long waits" are the norm at this "awesome" Vietnamese that's a "cut above" the nearby competition "lining Buford Highway", but "worth it" according to insiders who laud its "boldly flavorful" dishes (including "excellent" grilled meats) "not found anywhere else in the city"; "helpful" servers, a "hip vibe" and "dressed-up" "contemporary" decor add to the "festive" experience, and the fact that it's a "real bargain" makes it all the more "delightful."

Corner Cafe   19 | 16 | 16 | $20
3070 Piedmont Rd. NE (E. Paces Ferry Rd.), 404-240-1978;
www.buckheadrestaurants.com

Noshers who "need more than a deli sandwich" head for this "bright, cheery" New American from the Buckhead Life Group, a "known quantity" for its "creative" breakfasts, "tasty" sandwiches and "super brunches" with a "Southern flair", as well as "fantastic" goods from the attached bakery that are "worth the trip alone"; although contrarians feel "for the prices" and pedigree, it "should be more impressive than it is", it's usually "crowded" nonetheless, especially on weekends.

Cowtippers   15 | 13 | 16 | $22
1600 Piedmont Ave. (Monroe Rd.), 404-874-3751;
www.cowtippersatlanta.com

"Fa-a-abulous" gush groupies of this "laid-back" (or Brokeback) Midtown steakhouse where "good-quality" beef and "great margaritas" are doled out by an "efficient and catty" staff in a "tacky" country-themed space reminiscent of a "Cracker Barrel on a tight budget", although the "scenery can't be beat" on the nearly year-round deck

40   subscribe to zagat.com

Atlanta | F | D | S | C |

where "local gays and their admirers" mingle; but "mediocre" fare leads hecklers to hiss the "only thing remotely tasty here is the men."

Crescent Moon | 21 | 17 | 18 | $14 |
174 W. Ponce de Leon Ave. (Commerce Dr.), Decatur, 404-377-5623
Northlake Mall, 4800 Briarcliff Rd. NE (Henderson Rd.), Tucker, 678-937-9020
www.crescentmooneatery.com
"Long lines" are "proof enough" that there's "no finer diner" than these "meccas of breakfasts" in Decatur and Tucker where "mouthwateringly good" "down-home" morning fare is served "all day", as well as "amazing" brunch and "huge" lunch and dinner offerings, in "shiny" "retro" digs; hecklers "hate the uneven service" and "hit-or-miss" food, but others are happy to "wait", "enjoy and waddle home"; the newer Tucker location has a soda fountain.

Daddy D'z | 20 | 9 | 16 | $13 |
264 Memorial Dr. SE (Hill St.), 404-222-0206; www.daddydz.com
"It's a hole-in-the-wall" "like a BBQ joint should be", so 'cuennoisseurs "take the plunge" and ignore the "sketchy neighborhood" around this Southside smoke spot, "a stone's throw" from Turner Field, for "blow-your-mind" ribs, "great smoky" pulled pork, "solid" sides and "ice-cold" beer; sports fans and workers from nearby downtown also groove on "occasional" live blues and "friendly" service – "just be sure to park your car where you can see it."

Dailey's | 20 | 19 | 20 | $35 |
17 International Blvd. (Peachtree St.), 404-681-3303; www.daileysrestaurant.com
A "long-standing" choice of business diners for "basic" American eats, this Downtown sibling of City Grill is "divine" in the eyes of fans mainly for its "incredible" dessert bar, a "feast for the eyes as well as the taste buds", in addition to "consistently wonderful" entrees and "always pleasant" service; the "lovely" upstairs dining room evokes a "New Orleans garden room", while the "swank" downstairs bar mixes "knockout" martinis to the strains of live jazz at night.

Dantanna's ☾ | 17 | 17 | 17 | $30 |
Shops Around Lenox, 3400 Around Lenox Dr. (Peachtree Rd.), 404-760-8873; www.dantannas.com
"Yuppie bar meets sports bar" at this Buckhead surf 'n' turf near Lenox Square, where "SEC darlin's support their 'Dawgs' over "surprising" steaks, "above-average" burgers and "super" seafood (it's "not just wings") in "dark and cozy" digs with "plenty of TVs" and a new cigar room with a "great smoke filtration system"; sensitive sorts report the "friendly" waitresses are "very easy on the eyes."

Atlanta

F | D | S | C

Dante's Down the Hatch ●   17 | 23 | 19 | $37
3380 Peachtree Rd. NE (opp. Lenox Sq.), 404-266-1600; www.dantesdownthehatch.com

For a "little slice of Disney World", fans head to this Buckhead fondue specialist where diners dip into their "cheesy" fare in a "pirate-themed" room dominated by a sailing ship surrounded by live 'gators in a moat; a jazz band plays on deck and "gracious host" Dante and his staff "always go the extra mile", and while some critics find the victuals "mediocre" and the setting "hackneyed", for many others it's a "hoot" that makes for a "memorable evening."

DICK AND HARRY'S ⊠   25 | 19 | 23 | $40
Holcomb Woods Vlg., 1570 Holcomb Bridge Rd. (½ mi. east of GA 400), Roswell, 770-641-8757; www.dickandharrys.com

An "old standby" that "gets better with age", this Roswell New American "consistently" serves "exceptional" seafood-centric cuisine "so fresh" some finatics order "clams for dessert", while "crab-cake snobs" deem its version among the "best in town"; though it's "strangely located" in a "bland" strip mall, "accommodating" service (some find it "snooty") and an "elegant", "upscale" setting help make it a "hot" spot to "celebrate any event."

DI PAOLO   27 | 21 | 25 | $37
Rivermont Sq., 8560 Holcomb Bridge Rd. (Nesbitt Ferry Rd.), Alpharetta, 770-587-1051; www.dipaolorestaurant.com

The "magnificent obsession" of a "loyal army of regulars", Atlanta's No. 1 Italian is "worth the drive to the end of the earth" (i.e. Alpharetta) for "superb" Northern Italian creations from an open kitchen that'll "knock your socks off" and "impeccable" service; there's a "surprise with every detail" in the "quaint", "relaxing" dining room, and though the "old strip-mall location doesn't do it justice", for many it's the "perfect choice for any occasion."

dish   21 | 20 | 20 | $36
870 N. Highland Ave. (Drewry St.), 404-897-3463; www.dish-atlanta.com

"Trendy" fans of "creative" chef Sherri Davis "highly recommend" her "unassuming" New American that's "worth the trip" to Va-Highlands for "sizzling", "creative" dishes and a "fabulous wine selection", served in a "cozy" converted gas station with a "lovely" outdoor patio; it "isn't cheap", and to some the fare "no longer dazzles" and the service is "spotty" at times, but it remains a "big hit for most people."

Doc Chey's Asian Kitchen   17 | 13 | 16 | $13
CityWalk at Sandy Springs, 227 Sandy Springs Pl. NE (bet. Hammond Dr. & Roswell Rd.), 404-943-0113
Highland Walk, 1424 N. Highland Ave. (University Ave.), 404-888-0777

Atlanta | F | D | S | C |

(continued)
Doc Chey's Asian Kitchen
1556 N. Decatur Rd. (Clifton Rd.), 404-378-8188
Ivy Walk at Vinings, 1675 Cumberland Pkwy. (S. Atlanta Rd.), Smyrna, 770-333-9657
www.doccheys.com
The "good karma" of this "ever expanding" noodle chain keeps "carb lovers" "coming back" for "top-notch low-priced meals" that are "creative" and "healthy", though purists find the "pseudo-Asian" eats "overrated"; the "casual" decor "doesn't impress", nor does the "hit-or-miss" service, but the "delightful" patio and "atmosphere" "make up" for many glitches, and did we mention that it's "cheap"?

Dominick's | 20 | 17 | 18 | $22 |
95 S. Peachtree St. NW (Holcomb Bridge Rd.), Norcross, 770-449-1611
This "no-frills" Norcross Italian "favorite" makes "Long Island" natives "homesick" with "large portions" of "classic" red-sauce fare, "addictively good" garlic bread that "will keep vampires away" and "super-cheap house wine"; a crowd of "mostly locals" enjoys the "laid-back vibe" and "friendly" service, and "leave satisfied" with some "cash still in the wallet."

Downwind ⌀ | 14 | 15 | 15 | $15 |
Peachtree-DeKalb Airport, 2000 Airport Rd. (Clairmont Rd.), 770-452-0973; www.downwindrestaurant.com
For flight fans, a "perfect afternoon" is "lunch and a show" at this American venue "along the runway" of PDK airport where you can watch private planes take off and land over "Frisbee-size" burgers and other "casual bar" fare, as well as "good Greek grub"; while the owner is "friendly", the staff appears to be on autopilot at times ("service doesn't exist"), and many feel the "food can't compare" with the "unique setting."

Dreamland Bar-B-Que | 15 | 11 | 14 | $15 |
5250 Peachtree Pkwy. (Peachtree Corner Circle), Norcross, 770-446-6969
10730 Alpharetta Hwy. (Mansell Rd.), Roswell, 678-352-7999
www.dreamlandbbq.com
"You get a lot for your $$$" at these local links of a Tuscaloosa-based BBQ chain known for "generous" portions of "true" 'cue and "exemplary" Brunswick stew that are doled out by an "efficient" crew in "casual" digs; many critics, though, see crimson thinking about the "overrated" eats that are "far from a dream."

Dusty's Barbecue | 18 | 10 | 15 | $12 |
1815 Briarcliff Rd. NE (Clifton Rd.), 404-320-6264; www.dustys.com
Fans of this "fairly priced" "mainstay" near Emory laud its "smoky and delightful" "NC-style" BBQ, served with a

Atlanta   F | D | S | C

"right range" of sauces that you can "buy and take home" ("beware: the hottest will take your head off"), and "properly chunky" Brunswick stew, though a few critics find the fare "mediocre"; the digs are "dingy", but "quick service" and a "convenient drive-thru" window make "getting a 'cue fix extra easy."

East Andrews Cafe & Bar 17 | 18 | 18 | $31
56 E. Andrews Dr. NW (Cains Hill Pl.), 404-869-1132; www.eastandrews.com
Revelers "looking for a drink (or two, three or four)" head to this Buckhead bôite, where the Eclectic eats, served in small plates and as entrées, are "unexpectedly delicious" "for a meat market"; you can "burn it off" on the dance floor upstairs or hang on the "lovely" "European-style" courtyard where the "pretty people" "just out of college" go to "see and be seen"; N.B. the post-*Survey* arrival of chef Diana Watkins may outdate the above Food score.

Eats 19 | 7 | 13 | $10
600 Ponce de Leon Ave. NE (bet. Glen Iris Dr. & Lakeview Ave.), 404-888-9149; www.eatsonponce.net
"Rastas, punks" and "policemen" alike "crowd" into the booths at this Midtown "dive" for "cheap" Eclectic offerings such as "amazing" jerk chicken, "tasty" vegetables and "build-your-own" pasta; though it reminds some of a "soup kitchen" where you basically "wait on yourself", even the "penurious find value" in this "cash-only" "joint" with a mysterious "magnetic pull."

Eatzi's 22 | 16 | 18 | $18
Park Place Shopping Ctr., 4505 Ashford Dunwoody Rd. NE (Perimeter Ctr. E.), 678-634-0000
3221 Peachtree Rd. (Piedmont Rd.), 404-237-2266
www.eatzis.com
"Throw out your pots and pans and become a regular" of these Buckhead and Dunwoody links in a Texas-based chain that's "perfect for the gourmet on the go" and a "godsend" for "working moms", "professionals" and "lazy cooks", purveying an "endless" selection of "tasty" "high-end" Eclectic fare "made fresh daily"; the "food is the decor", but "beautiful" (if "loud") music and lots of "samples" add allure, and while a few feel the food "looks better than it tastes", many others "love everything about it."

Ecco – | – | – | M
40 Seventh St. NE (Cypress St. NE), 404-347-9555; www.fifthgroup.com
The Fifth Group (Food Studio, South City Kitchen, La Tavola) offers a new take on the neighborhood restaurant with this casual Continental housed in a former fencing club in Midtown; chef Micah Willix's simple, seasonal cuisine and small plates are served in a Johnson Studio–designed

Atlanta   F D S C

space that combines modern and old world with a blend of marble, leather and dark walnut, and includes large dining areas, an expansive lounge and an outdoor patio.

Eclipse di Luna   21 | 20 | 17 | $26
764 Miami Circle NE (Piedmont Rd.), 404-846-0449; www.eclipsediluna.com
A "festive alternative" in Buckhead for the "young and beautiful", this Spanish tapastry serves up small plates with "big flavors" and "reasonable prices" that you can wash down with "marvelous mojitos" and "sangria that'll knock your *zapatos* off"; live Latin bands "keep the place groovin'" and the staff delivers "service with a smile", but it almost gets "so loud your ears will bleed", so many opt for the patio, where you "can hear."

Eclipse di Sol   - | - | - | I
640 N. Highland Ave. (North Ave.), 404-724-0711; www.eclipsedisol.com
Eclipse di Luna's groovy yet gracious sibling in Poncey-Highlands serves up a menu of homey New American cuisine, including all-day breakfast fare and a popular Sunday brunch, in a bright bistro setting with solar-themed decor; a covered patio offers refreshing alfresco dining with primo people-watching opportunities.

Edo   18 | 18 | 19 | $27
Toco Hills Shopping Ctr., 2945 N. Druid Hills Rd. (Lavista Rd.), Decatur, 404-728-0228; www.edo-atlanta.com
A "lovely surprise" in a somewhat "ugly" shopping center, this Toco Hills Japanese delivers "worthy" sushi and "huge portions" of "surprisingly good" teppanyaki eats that are sliced, diced and served by "animated", "super-friendly" grill chefs (a "must for kids' birthdays"), although purists find the fare "sadly ordinary"; the space is "big and comfortable", and the "private" tatami rooms have *horigotatsu* tables with "holes in the floor for your legs" to spare you from sitting "Japanese style."

88 Tofu House ◐   ▽ 20 | 7 | 16 | $12
5490 Buford Hwy. (Rte. 285), 770-457-8811
Fans find "more than tofu" at this Buford Highway Korean where "addictive" "heartwarming soups" are served "bubbling hot"; the "incredibly spartan" digs are "less than optimal", but boosters tout it as a "cheap" 24/7 option and an "excellent value", one that "you'll not soon forget."

Einstein's   18 | 21 | 17 | $23
1077 Juniper St. NE (12th St.), 404-876-7925; www.einsteinsatlanta.com
"It doesn't take a genius" to figure out that the "best people-watching patio in town" is the main draw of this Midtown New American, where "beautiful gay men" and a "diverse" crowd dig into "imaginative" eats and "gener-

vote at zagat.com   45

Atlanta

F | D | S | C

ous" drinks; an "impressive renovation" ushers in an "eye-popping" bar and "elegant" "feng shui"–friendly decor, but the space "fills up very quickly", resulting in "painfully slow" service, and, relatively speaking, the fare is "nothing special."

El Azteca
14 | 11 | 15 | $14

1784 Peachtree St. NE (Palisades Rd.), 404-249-1522
939 Ponce de Leon Ave. (Freedom Pkwy.), 404-881-6040
5925 Roswell Rd. (Hammond Dr.), 404-252-7347
9925 Haynes Bridge Rd. (Old Alabama Rd.), Alpharetta, 770-569-5234
13800 Hwy. 9 N. (Bethany Rd.), Alpharetta, 678-867-9950
580 Atlanta Rd. (Hwy. 20), Cumming, 770-886-9927

"Far from gourmet" but "still a top choice" of many for "dependable" "standard" Mexican, this "family-friendly" south-of-the-border chain offers "amazing value", and "people-watching" over "killer" margaritas on its "large" patios remains a popular pastime; many concede, however, that the "social scene" is "better than the food" or "dismal dining rooms."

El Taco Veloz
23 | 4 | 13 | $9

5670 Roswell Rd. NE (I-285), 404-252-5100
Chamblee Commercial Ctr., 3245 Chamblee Dunwoody Rd. (bet. Buford Hwy. & New Peachtree Rd.), Chamblee, 770-458-7779
5084 Buford Hwy. (Chamblee Dunwoody Rd.), Doraville, 770-936-9094 ☾
2700 Buford Hwy. (Old Peachtree Rd.), Duluth, 770-622-0138
2077 Beaver Ruin Rd. (I-85), Norcross, 770-849-0025
925 Windy Hill Rd. (Atlanta Rd.), Smyrna, 770-432-8800

"Go for the food, not the frills" urge amigos of this Mexican chain that resembles "roadside" stands in "South Texas", where the *comida* "rocks" and it's "fun sitting at picnic tables" "with strangers" while digging into "delicious" burritos "as big as your head"; unless *se habla Español* you may have "trouble ordering", but "regardless of language" barriers, it's the "best in town for the peso."

Emeril's Atlanta
18 | 24 | 19 | $50

Alliance Ctr., 3500 Lenox Rd. (Phipps Blvd.), 404-564-5600; www.emerils.com

While the "astonishing" decor of Emeril's Buckhead production "makes an immediate impact" with its "cool" wine tower, "unique" chandeliers and the "woven wood backdrop" of the bar, the "creative" Contemporary Louisiana cuisine, "exceptional" wine list and "attentive" service also impress; still, many who "expected more" were "disappointed" by "overpriced" fare and an "arrogant" staff; P.S. the arrival of displaced NOLA chef Chris Wilson, who has "taken the menu up more than a notch", may not be reflected in the above Food scores.

Atlanta

| F | D | S | C |

Eno ☒   21 | 20 | 20 | $40
800 Peachtree St. (5th St.), 404-685-3191
A "sophisticated spot with big-city ambiance" and "fab outdoor street-watching", this Midtown Mediterranean is a "wonderful option" serving "delicious" Western European–influenced dishes, including "late-night tapas" at the bar, and a "thoughtful" wine list that includes "superb" "wines by the glass"; "well-educated" servers help with "pairings", and the owner's "commitment to detail" shows in the "edgy" dining room and "hip" wine bar.

Enoteca Carbonari ☒   - | - | - | M
710 Peachtree St. NE (3rd St.), 404-810-9110;
www.enotecacarbonari.com
The owners of Baraonda and Bazzaar bring this Tuscan-inspired newcomer to Midtown, where an extensive selection of Italian cheeses, roasted and cured meats and housemade sausages make for tasty small (and large) plates that can be paired with varietals from around the world; heavy wood ceiling beams and the glow from the charcoal rotisserie add warmth to the wine-bottle-lined space, and the secluded outdoor seating has a European feel.

Epicurean, The ☒   - | - | - | E
1361 Clairmont Rd. (N. Decatur Rd.), Decatur, 404-321-0530;
www.theepicureanrestaurant.com
Emory meets the Moulin Rouge at this charming high-end New French in Decatur, where the likes of frogs' legs and pâté are paired with a playful wine list; a professional staff provides white-tablecloth service, while lots of oversized mirrors reflect the original artwork on the walls and create a feeling of depth in the narrow strip-mall space.

ESPN Zone ☽   10 | 18 | 12 | $22
3030 Peachtree Rd. NE (Buckhead Ave.), 404-682-3776;
www.espnzone.com
"If massive portions, chaos and testosterone" are "your dining preferences", this Buckhead American is the "next best place to Turner Field" since the "TVs all over the place" ("even in the bathrooms") ensure "you'll never miss a play", and the game room is "awesome"; the service is "slow" and the "mediocre" "bar" fare gets outscored by the "distractions", but for "kids" and "sports nuts" who "don't go for the food", it's "a blast."

EURASIA BISTRO ☒   25 | 23 | 24 | $30
129 E. Ponce de Leon Ave. (bet. Church St. & Clairmont Ave.),
Decatur, 404-687-8822; www.eurasiabistro.net
Locals "love" this "slice of calm in the middle of Decatur" for "fabulous presentations" of chef Wendy Chang's "refined" Pan-Asian cuisine (including "fish cooked to perfection") from a menu with "no bad options"; it's a "pleasure to be waited on" by the "spectacular" staff in

vote at zagat.com

Atlanta F D S C

the "sophisticated", "romantic" white-tablecloth space with an "upscale" ambiance that "makes you feel like you're Downtown."

Everybody's Pizza 20 | 13 | 16 | $15
1040 N. Highland Ave. (Virginia Ave.), 404-873-4545
Emory Vlg., 1593 N. Decatur Rd. (Oxford Rd.), Decatur, 404-377-7766
www.everybodyspizza.com
"Everybody loves" this "popular" pizza pair in Decatur and Va-Highlands for their "incredibly tasty" pies that "make you feel righteous" ("and your pocketbook says amen") "huge build-your-own salads" that are "only limited by your imagination" and a "vast selection of beers on tap"; the decor is "minimal" but both have "great decks" where a "mixed" crowd of "yuppies", "students, profs and locals" hang, but "make sure you have a lot of time" since service can be "slow."

Fabiano's Italian Deli 20 | 10 | 17 | $11
985 Monroe Dr. NE (10th St.), 404-875-0500
In a "town lacking in the deli department", this Midtown counter-service casual located in a "random" strip mall is a "solid spot" offering a "vast selection" of "quality" deli items, including "huge" sandwiches and "meatballs almost like grandma's", with a "small gourmet market" featuring "hard-to-find Italian favorites"; it's a "perfect stop" for a "Piedmont Park picnic" or a "cozy getaway lunch."

Fadó Irish Pub ● 16 | 22 | 18 | $21
3035 Peachtree Rd. NE (Buckhead Ave.), 404-841-0066;
www.fadoirishpub.com
It's like "stepping into another world" at this Buckhead pub where stones, beams and knickknacks "straight from Ireland" can "transform" your meal or drinks into a "mini-vacation"; for many, the "decent" pub fare ("best fish 'n' chips in town") takes a back seat to the "best pints in town", pulled by "friendly" bartenders; "plan for a crowd" when there are "football (real football) and rugby games" on TV, and a bit of "smoke", which is allowed since children are not.

Fat Matt's Chicken Shack ∉ 20 | 8 | 13 | $14
1821 Piedmont Ave. NE (Rock Springs Rd.), 404-875-2722;
www.fatmattsbbq.com
"Because you can't eat ribs seven days a week", this "affordable" Southern "dive" and sibling to the Rib Shack next door in Va-Highlands is a "recommended" stop for "fried catfish" and "chicken that falls right off the bone"; the "art deco shack" may be in need of "more artistic flair", but it's "true to its name" and "well worth it" – just "remember to bring cash" since they don't take plastic at this "land of fried food."

Atlanta   F | D | S | C

Fat Matt's Rib Shack ●∌   23 | 10 | 14 | $14
1811 Piedmont Ave. NE (Rock Springs Rd.), 404-607-1622;
www.fatmattsbbq.com
"Finger-lickin'" fans flock to the "granddaddy of Atlanta's rib shacks" in Va-Highlands for a "messy and simple" "feast for a king" of "succulent" ribs "to die for (and we probably will)"; add "ice cold beer", "great" live blues and cheap prices and you'll know why there are "lines out the door"; "no frills – no problem", for while "it ain't much to look at", this cash-only "joint" "delivers with a vengeance."

Feast   19 | 23 | 18 | $25
314 E. Howard Ave. (N. Candler St.), Decatur, 404-377-2000;
www.feastatlanta.com
Boosters are "buzzing" over this "marvelous" "addition" to Downtown Decatur, the "new favorite" of many for its "great use of fresh ingredients" in Med-accented New American cuisine offered on "small and large plates great for sharing"; the "eclectic" digs evoke a "gypsy cafe", "warmed" by an open brick oven, with a "cool" "wooden" bar providing a "festive" counterpoint; a few feel it could use more "consistency", but concede that this "inviting" newcomer "has potential."

Feed Store ⌧   21 | 20 | 18 | $30
3841 Main St. (bet. John Wesley & Yale Aves.), College Park,
404-209-7979
"Luckily, forks and knives are provided" instead of "nose-bags" at this "unfortunately named" "surprise find" in College Park, where "trendy and down-home-style" American eats and a "chic" renovation of a former feed store make it a "good choice" for "entertaining clients near the airport"; "poor" service, though, goes against the grain of this otherwise "bright spot" in the neighborhood.

Fellini's Pizza ●   21 | 13 | 16 | $12
1991 Howell Mill Rd. NW (Collier Rd.), 404-352-0799
1634 McLendon Ave. NE (Clifton Rd.), 404-687-9190
2809 Peachtree Rd. NE (Rumson Rd.), 404-266-0082
909 Ponce de Leon Ave. (Linwood Ave.), 404-873-3088
4429 Roswell Rd. NE (Wieuca Rd.), 404-303-8248
333 Commerce Dr. (bet. Hilyer & Sycamore Pls.), Decatur,
404-370-0551
Vista Grove Plaza, 2820 Lavista Rd. (Oak Grove Rd.), Decatur,
404-633-6016
Many "kids of all ages" "would starve without" this "laid-back" Intown pizzeria chain and its "delectable" pizzas available in "gargantuan" slices that are a "meal in themselves"; "quick, no-frills" service and "pocket-change" prices make it a "family-friendly" favorite, while "phenomenal" outdoor patios with "soothing fountains" encourage "warm-weather lingering" – "you can't beat it" for "happy hour" or "an afternoon with friends."

vote at zagat.com

Atlanta   F D S C

Fickle Pickle ⊠   22 | 18 | 18 | $14
1085 Canton St. (Woodstock St.), Roswell, 770-650-9838;
www.ficklepicklecafe.com
At his Roswell New American, chef Andy Badgett's "awesome" fried pickles are "not to be missed" and the rest of the "casual" bill of fare, including "wonderful" "gourmet sandwiches", is "consistently good"; the service is "friendly" and the "desirable" location "close to the town square" makes it a "great place" to "sit outside" "with a friend", especially when it's "crowded in that little house."

Figo Pasta/Osteria del Figo   22 | 16 | 17 | $15
1170B Collier Rd. (Defoors Ferry Rd.), 404-351-9667
1210 Howell Mill Rd. (Huff Rd.), 404-351-3700 ⊠
627 E. College Ave. (Weekes St.), Decatur, 404-377-2121
www.figopasta.com
You may "never make spaghetti at home again" after the "awesome" "homemade pastas" and "exquisitely crafted sauces" that you mix-and-match at this "unpretentious" Italian trio, where "friendly" servers basically "ring up orders" in a "casual" setting; South Buckhead is "tiny", the Westside spot "adds panache" to an "already happening corner" and Decatur has an "old warehouse" feel, but wherever you go, expect "lines snaking out the door."

Fire of Brazil Churrascaria   18 | 17 | 19 | $42
118 Perimeter Ctr. W. (Hammond Dr.), 770-551-4367
5304 Windward Pkwy. (Westside Pkwy.), Alpharetta, 678-366-2411
www.fireofbrazil.com
"Fanatic" carnivores and "business" diners "go for it" at these "manly" Brazilian steakhouse "extravaganzas" in Dunwoody and Alpharetta where "loads of meat on a stick" are paraded by "friendly" waiters; while some are "impressed", critics burned up over "overpriced" fare and "poor" service conclude it's "not as good as others" of its ilk.

Fishmonger   19 | 15 | 18 | $29
4969 Roswell Rd. NE (W. Belle Isle Rd.), 404-459-9003
609 Holcomb Bridge Rd. (Alpharetta Hwy.), Roswell, 770-993-1600
www.fishmongerseafoodgrill.com
This "dependably good" Pisces pair "fills the gap" with "reasonably priced" seafood that's "perfectly cooked" and paired with "good wine values", and served by a "friendly" staff; "neighborhood moms", "friends" and "romantic" couples "relax" in the "quiet" Sandy Springs location with a "lovely patio", while the newer Roswell branch is housed in a former bank that's "nicer than you'd think."

Five Seasons Brewing Co.   23 | 18 | 20 | $25
Prado Shopping Ctr., 5600 Roswell Rd. (I-285), 404-255-5911;
www.5seasonsbrewing.com
A "solid winner" in Sandy Springs, this brewpub "never fails to get the oohs and ahs started" with "fabulous"

Atlanta

microbrews and a "surprisingly" "creative" New American menu on which "fresh, organic ingredients rule"; "helpful", "friendly" service in a "large" space with a "blingy" vibe makes it a "solid choice" for a "pre-Chastain rendezvous", "first date" or "party", and though some find it "far too noisy for good digestion", the "reasonable prices" are easy to swallow.

Fleming's Prime Steakhouse & Wine Bar   24 | 23 | 25 | $54

4501 Olde Perimeter Way (Ashford Dunwoody Rd.), 770-698-8112; www.flemingssteakhouse.com

Local meateries better "watch their back" caution cognoscenti, for this "elegant" link in a steakhouse chain is a "great addition to the scene" in Dunwoody, offering "melt-in-your-mouth" à la carte fare, "awesome" wines by the glass and "top-notch" service; the "clubby" dark-wooded interior that resembles a "den" adds to an experience that leaves groupies gushing "excellence is part of everything they do."

FLOATAWAY CAFE ☒   26 | 22 | 24 | $43

Floataway Bldg., 1123 Zonolite Rd. NE (bet. Briarcliff & Johnson Rds.), 404-892-1414; www.starprovisions.com

Intowners "never tire of" this "foodies' delight", the "more informal" sibling of Bacchanalia and Quinones that wins props for "deceptively simple" and "stunning" French-Italian cuisine emphasizing "local organic produce", an "eclectic" wine list and "gracious" service; nestled in an "oasis of artists' studios" amid an "industrial wasteland" near Emory, the "sleek" space with "ethereal curtains" cultivates an "energetic" vibe – if they could "just get rid of the noise", it "would be the perfect place."

Flying Biscuit   20 | 13 | 17 | $16

1655 McLendon Ave. NE (Clifton Rd.), 404-687-8888
1001 Piedmont Ave. NE (10th St.), 404-874-8887
www.flyingbiscuit.com

"Get up before the roosters crow" to avoid the "never-ending brunch lines" at this "determinedly funky" duo in Candler Park and Midtown, a "breakfast ritual" for Intowners in search of "bountiful" helpings of "healthy" Southern comfort food, including lots of vegetarian options and fried green tomatoes that "make even Yankees swoon"; a "cast of characters" provides service described as "courteous disorganization" in "old-time hippie" settings; P.S. fans also praise the dinner fare as "scrumptious."

FOGO DE CHÃO   25 | 20 | 25 | $52

3101 Piedmont Rd. NE (bet. E. Paces Ferry & Peachtree Rds.), 404-995-9982; www.fogodechao.com

"Get in touch with your Neolithic roots" as you "stuff yourself silly" on the "bountiful bonanza" of "skewer after skewer of succulent meats" at this "best of the breed"

Atlanta

F D S C

Brazilian "beef-a-thon" in Buckhead, where "attentive swarms of servers" "keep it coming till you burst"; "if salad bars were basilicas, this would be St. Peter's" attest the faithful, who "recommend fasting for days beforehand" and "wearing an elastic waistband."

Fontaine's Oyster House ●   17 | 16 | 17 | $20

1026½ N. Highland Ave. NE (Virginia Ave.), 404-872-0869
"Feel like you just walked off Bourbon Street" in this "old-fashioned bar" in Va-Highlands that reels in finatics with "tasty" oysters, the "best lobster bisque in town" and other seafood that "tastes like it came straight off the boat"; an "awesome porch" "any time of year", "fantastic jukebox" and "amazing chandelier" add to the "cool" scene, and while purists consider it "more of a bar than a restaurant", most agree the weekly "food-drink" specials are a "steal."

Food 101   20 | 19 | 19 | $31

4969 Roswell Rd. NE (Belle Isle Rd.), 404-497-9700
1397 N. Highland Ave. NE (E. Rock Springs Rd.), 404-347-9747
www.101concepts.com
"Stick-to-the-ribs" "comfort foods abound" at this Sandy Springs New American that's "setting the bar for neighborhood bistros" with its menu of "Southern favorites" with an "interesting twist" and half-priced wines on Sundays that "can't be beat"; a "great" "pre-Chastain" stop or place to "take the parents", the dining room is "comfortable" (albeit "noisy") and service comes "with a smile", but budget hawks grouse that it's "overpriced"; N.B. the Va-Highlands location opened post-*Survey*.

Food Studio   24 | 25 | 23 | $45

King Plow Art Ctr., 887 W. Marietta St. NW (bet. Ashby St. & Howell Mill Rd.), 404-815-6677; www.thefoodstudio.com
Housed in a Westside "factory-turned–studio performance space", this "dark, moody gem" from the Fifth Group (La Tavola, Sala – Sabor de Mexico, South City Kitchen) is the showcase for chef Mark Alba's "excellent", "clever" New American cuisine, which "never fails to impress" foodies; the "stylish" setting and "hospitable" service make it one of the "most romantic" spots in town, and though it may be "hard to find", fans insist it's "worth getting lost every time."

Fortune Cookie   ▽ 17 | 13 | 16 | $13

Loehmann's Plaza, 2480-7 Briarcliff Rd. NE (N. Druid Hills Rd.), 404-636-8899
Some of the "best Americanized Chinese" fare can be found at this "inexpensive" spot near Emory serving up "satisfying" dishes that "jump with flavor" and a "quality buffet" on Sundays; a "nice" owner and "attentive" staff compensate for the no-frills space at the "back of a strip

Atlanta F D S C

mall", and help make it a "favorite" "everyday" option for many in the neighborhood.

Fratelli di Napoli 20 | 17 | 19 | $28
2101 Tula St. NW (bet. Bennett & Peachtree Sts.), 404-351-1533
928 Canton St. (Atlanta St.), Roswell, 770-642-9917
www.fratelli.net

"*Molto bene*" boast boosters of these midpriced Southern Italian brothers in South Buckhead and Roswell where "family-style" platters full of "rich and tasty" "standard" red-sauce dishes "make you wish you'd been born into that *famiglia*"; while a few find the experience "very up and down", many others feel the "accommodating" service, "convivial" atmosphere that's "kid-friendly without being over-casual" and "big round tables" make them "great for groups" or "girls' night out."

Fritti 22 | 19 | 19 | $23
309 N. Highland Ave. NE (Elizabeth St.), 404-880-9559;
www.frittirestaurant.com

"When your stomach says Sotto Sotto, but your wallet says no go", fans recommend its pizzeria spin-off next door in Inman Park, serving pizzas ranging "from the everyday to the exotic" from its wood-burning oven, as well as "sinfully delicious" Italian dishes such as "truffle oil mushrooms"; a "nice" wine selection and "killer $2 Bloody Marys" at Sunday brunch lubricate the "see-and-be-seen" scene of "yuppies", while a "nice view of Downtown" from the patio makes it a "great first date place."

Fuego Spanish Grill ● 19 | 17 | 17 | $23
(fka Fuego Cafe & Tapas Bar)
1136 Crescent Ave. NE (bet. 13th & 14th Sts.), 404-389-0660;
www.fuegocafe.com

"*Olé*" cry amigos of this small-plate specialist in Midtown that has fans fired up over "amazing" tapas, "authentic" Spanish and Latin entrees and some of the "best sangria in town"; it's "lots of fun for a big group" as well as a "great happy-hour place", with "pleasant" service and live flamenco music on weekends – what's more, it's "not too pricey."

Garrison's Broiler & Tap 19 | 19 | 18 | $34
Perimeter Mall, 4400 Ashford Dunwoody Rd. NE (bet. Hammond Dr. & Perimeter Ctr. W.), 770-350-0134
Vinings Jubilee Shopping Ctr., 4300 Paces Ferry Rd. SE (Spring Hill Pkwy.), 770-436-0102
Medlock Crossing, 9700 Medlock Bridge Rd. (State Bridge Rd.), Duluth, 770-476-1962
www.garrisonsatlanta.com

This "solid" suburban trio earns a "thumbs-up" from fans for a "broad menu" of "consistently" "delicious" American fare,

Atlanta

F | D | S | C

anchored by "fairly priced" steaks and "sublime" desserts; "effusive" service and a "prompt" kitchen make it a "favorite for lunch"; Duluth sports an "attractive" rooftop patio, Vinings boasts "taproom" decor and a patio with a "great view of the village", while fans flock to the Perimeter location "like bees to honey" for the "$6 martinis and free food at happy hour."

Genki
18 | 12 | 13 | $25

3188 Roswell Rd. NW (Sardia Way), 404-869-8319;
www.genki-inc.com

"Creative" sushi and "decent" noodle bowls from this "hip" Buckhead Japanese "hit the mark" for "beautiful" "young locals", especially on the see-and-be-seen patio, and valet parking is a "plus" in this "very busy area"; service varies from "fast" and "helpful" to "horribly rude", and claustrophobes carp it's often "too crowded to enjoy" the experience.

George's
20 | 11 | 19 | $12

1041 N. Highland Ave. NE (Virginia Ave.), 404-892-3648

"Definitely not for fashionistas", this "real deal of a dive" in Va-Highlands has been a "local favorite" for more than four decades thanks to "fantastic" "burgers" and other "standard" American bar fare, a "good beer selection" and a "friendly staff" that "remembers you"; "families", "twenty- and thirtysomethings" and assorted "locals" vie for tables on the "tiny patio" to "people-watch" on the "bustling" corner.

Georgia Grille
24 | 18 | 20 | $33

Peachtree Sq., 2290 Peachtree Rd. NE
(bet. Peachtree Hills Ave. & Peachtree Memorial Dr.),
404-352-3517; www.georgiagrille.com

Namesake "Georgia O'Keeffe would have loved" Karen Hilliard's "comfy" South Buckhead Southwestern where you can "always count on" "delightful" "well thought out" cuisine, including lobster enchiladas "to die for" and "one fantastic brunch"; a "low turnover in staff" "ensures" "amazing service", and the "cozy" space graced with works by the eponymous artist is "good for a date."

Gilbert's Mediterranean Cafe
16 | 14 | 18 | $22

219 10th St. NE (Piedmont Ave.), 404-872-8012;
www.gilbertscafe.com

A "bohemian" "hangout" near Piedmont Park, this "family-owned and -operated" Midtown Mediterranean attracts a "nice crowd in a relaxed mood" with "decent food" and an "excellent weekend brunch", as well as monthly belly dancing and flamenco performances, and an "even better bar scene at night"; while some feel it's a "little pricey for the quality", pros point out you get "a lot of food for the money."

Atlanta F | D | S | C

Globe, The ☒ 21 | 24 | 20 | $29
Technology Sq., 75 Fifth St. NW (Spring St.), 404-541-1487;
www.globeatlanta.com
"Pretty people", the "laptop set" and "metrofolks" in Midtown flock to this "new darling" in Georgia Tech's "buzzing" Technology Square, where a "sleek" space with a "neo-industrial library" look is the backdrop for chef Joshua Perkins' (ex di Paolo) "crisp" New American cuisine, which is paired with an "accessible" wine list; despite some grumbling over "small, expensive" portions and "rocky" service, many are "impressed" by this "up-and-comer."

Goldberg's Bagel Co. & Deli 20 | 10 | 17 | $13
Georgetown Shopping Ctr., 4520 Chamblee Dunwoody Rd. (I-285), 770-455-1119
Roswell Wieuca Shopping Ctr., 4383 Roswell Rd. NE (Wieuca Rd.), 404-256-3751
1272 W. Paces Ferry Rd. NW (I-75), 404-266-0123
Become an "honorary NYer" at this "favorite" deli trio that sets the "gold standard" for local nosh with "excellent" bagels and "hearty" "overstuffed" sandwiches; "everyone knows everyone" at these "power-breakfast headquarters" where the staff "does its best to accommodate the masses", and though the decor could use some "help", the "newly expanded" Buckhead original "includes much more seating."

Goldfish 21 | 20 | 18 | $34
4400 Ashford Dunwoody Rd. NE (Perimeter Ctr.), 770-671-0100;
www.heretoserverestaurants.com
Waves of "suburbanites" come to this "hip" Dunwoody seafooder (sibling of Prime, Twist, Shout and Strip) for "fabulous" sushi and other "fresh" offerings, plus a "decent" wine list; the "slick" space is "always packed to the gills", and the "happening" bar is a "popular" "happy-hour" venue; some critics carp about "awful acoustics", "poor service" and "overpriced" fare, but many others consider it "one of the best choices" around.

Gold Star Cafe & Bakery ▽ 17 | 13 | 17 | $12
(fka Celebrity Cafe & Bakery)
903 Peachtree Rd. NE (8th St.), 404-870-0002
For a "quick lunch" or "tasty breakfast", loyalists of this Midtown American "lick" their "fingers" after downing "homemade-tasting" baked goods and "excellent" sandwiches, all at "reasonable" prices; for those with no time to enjoy the "great outdoor space", box lunches are an option.

Gordon Biersch Brewery ☾ 15 | 17 | 16 | $23
848 Peachtree St. NE (7th St.), 404-870-0805;
www.gordonbiersch.com
A "solid choice" for "casual" "midpriced" American pub fare that's actually "decent" for a national "chain" and

Atlanta

"rotating seasonal" brews that are "always interesting", this "casual" Midtown link is "popular" for a "quick lunch" or as an "after-work" "hangout"; critics are "blah"-sé to the "corporate" eats, and most agree that the "beer's the thing" here.

Grace 17.20 24 | 24 | 23 | $36
The Forum, 5155 Peachtree Pkwy. NW (Jones Bridge Rd.), Norcross, 678-421-1720; www.grace1720.com
For a "sublime dining experience OTP", Norcross neighbors sing hosannas to this "surprisingly sophisticated" "Napa Valley"–inspired New American located in The Forum, where "delicious", "beautifully plated" cuisine is brought to table by "well-informed" servers in an "elegant" space with a "lovely Tuscan" feel; a few find it "stuffy" and "overpriced", but for most it's a "wonderful find."

Grand China 19 | 13 | 20 | $23
2975 Peachtree Rd. NE (Pharr Rd.), 404-231-8690; www.grandchinaatl.com
A Buckhead "mainstay", this Chinese is "thoroughly up to date" when it comes to "reliable" fare of "exceptional" quality at "reasonable prices" and "friendly" service from the "lovely" owner who "personally greets each customer"; the "slightly dowdy" room is "well maintained" nonetheless, but those who "enjoy it more" at home rely on what some claim is the "fastest delivery in the South."

Grant Central Pizza 22 | 12 | 17 | $12
451 Cherokee Ave. SE (Glenwood Ave.), 404-523-8900
1279 Glenwood Ave. SE (Flat Shoals Rd.), 404-627-0007
All you need is a "bit of dough" to score a "wonderful" "authentic Northeast-style" pizza at this "funky" pair in Grant Park and East Atlanta that also dishes out "ginormous calzones", "excellent salads" and "interesting specials"; you feel like you're in "someone's dining room" at these "comfortable" "joints" that transport you to "Hoboken", and "friendly" service helps ensure "they're always busy."

Grape at City Walk 18 | 20 | 20 | $26
CityWalk at Sandy Springs, 227 Sandy Springs Pl. NE (Roswell Rd.), 404-250-9463
Grape at Phipps Plaza
Phipps Plaza, 3500 Peachtree Rd. NE (Oak Valley Rd.), 678-990-9463
Grape at The Forum
5145 Peachtree Pkwy. NW (Medlock Bridge Rd.), Norcross, 770-447-1605
Grape at Vinings
Vinings Jubilee Shopping Ctr., 4300 Paces Ferry Rd. SE (Paces Mill Rd.), 770-803-9463
www.yourgrape.com
This "innovative" bacchic chain is "becoming a favorite" for its "educational" "wine-for-dummies concept" and

Atlanta   F | D | S | C

"broad selection" of "endless options" to "try and buy" that are "paired" with small plates of Mediterranean eats ("lamb chops rock!") and served by a "knowledgeable" staff; "slews of hipsters" settle into "Pinot Noir"–colored velvet banquettes or "flirt and mingle" on expansive patios, and there's "great live music on weekends" at most locations.

GREENWOODS ON GREEN STREET ⌐   24 | 17 | 21 | $23
1087 Green St. (bet. Canton & Woodstock Sts.), Roswell, 770-992-5383

"Be prepared to eat yourself into a food coma" at this "one-of-a-kind" Roswell regional American that "invented the term" "gourmet Southern" with "insanely huge" "family-style" portions of the "best fried chicken on the planet" and "fantastic" "veggies" – but "save room" for the "big and tasty" pies; a "laid-back" vibe and "'hi, honey' service make a meal here "like Sunday dinner at grandma's", except for the "huge crowds", but fans insist it's "worth the wait."

Gumbeaux's, A Cajun Cafe 🅢   ▽ 28 | 20 | 21 | $18
6712 E. Broad St. (Hwy. 92), Douglasville, 770-947-8288; www.gumbeauxs.com

For a "lively" "good time", *amis* tout this Douglasville Cajun place serving "carefully prepared" "bayou"-inspired eats that they call the "best outside New Orleans" and "proof" that étouffée and its ilk "is more than heat"; patient patrons "stand and drink" "while waiting for a table" and an "accommodating" staff "keeps plenty of napkins handy"; P.S. "don't' miss the dollar shots" of their signature six-liquor 'swamp water' whenever "the train rolls by."

Hae Woon Dae Bar B Que ●   ▽ 23 | 13 | 19 | $19
5805 Buford Hwy. (Oakcliff Rd.), Doraville, 770-451-7957

It may be "super hard to find", but "adventurous eaters" and those in search of a "unique" dining experience need "look no further" than this "authentic" "Korean BBQ experience" on Buford Highway where you can "cook it yourself" over a "hardwood fire" at your table or let the "eager" staff "do it for you"; though it's a "hole-in-the-wall", groups can easily "feast" and "have fun" in "semi-private" dining areas, even until 6 AM, when the "regulars" descend.

Hal's on Old Ivy 🅢   24 | 16 | 22 | $44
30 Old Ivy Rd. NE (Wieuca Rd.), 404-261-0025; www.hals.net

While "mountainous" filets of "wonderful" "red meat" and "big drinks" are the main draws of this Cajun-Creole–influenced Buckhead steakhouse, insiders insist owner Hal is a "secret ingredient" for success; "lots of energy" fills the air, especially in the piano bar, where it's "fun to watch" "over-50 good ol' boys and the women who love them" "troll" in the "old Atlanta" setting.

vote at zagat.com   57

Atlanta

F | D | S | C

Happy Valley Seafood ◑   ▽ 21 | 14 | 20 | $17
Plaza Fiesta, 4166 Buford Hwy. NE (bet. Dresden Dr. & Skyland Rd.), 404-633-9383
Sinophiles swear this no-frills Buford Highway Chinese "sets the standard" for Middle Kingdom fare, serving some of the "best dim sum in Atlanta", a "good selection" of "excellent" offerings that keeps on coming; though "you get what you pay for in terms of appearance" and decor, the efficient staff ensures the waits are "not long between carts"; just "get there early" to "avoid the lines."

Harold's Barcecue ☒   22 | 9 | 16 | $12
171 McDonough Blvd. SE (Lakewood Ave.), 404-627-9268; www.haroldsbarbecue.com
265 Hwy. 54 (Rte. 138), Jonesboro, 770-478-5880
The "BBQ couldn't be better" at this decidedly "no-frills" "dive" where "$15 gets you a heap of food", including "hand-sliced" pork "straight from the smoker" and the "best Brunswick stew going", served up by "waitresses who have been there forever"; "you shouldn't even call the decor 'decor'", but, hey, you just "can't beat the convenience to the Federal pen" located next door; N.B. the Jonesboro location is independently owned and operated.

Harry & Sons   22 | 16 | 18 | $22
820 N. Highland Ave. NE (Greenwood Ave.), 404-873-2009; www.harryandsonsrestaurant.com
"When you can't decide" which Asian direction to take, this "unpretentious", "dependable" sibling and neighbor of Surin in Va-Highlands answers the call with "solid" Thai fare and "melt-in-your-mouth" sushi ("Harry Maki roll is da bomb"); it's "damn cheap", and service comes "with a smile", so it's no wonder it's "always packed" with "trendy" locals.

Haru Ichiban   ▽ 29 | 17 | 23 | $31
Mall Corner Shopping Ctr., 36-46 Satellite Blvd. (Pleasant Hill Rd.), Duluth, 770-622-4060
"True sushi lovers seek out" this "reasonably priced" Duluth Japanese, an "unexpected delight" in a "suburban strip center", for "absolutely flawless" and "authentic" offerings, including some seafood that surveyors "didn't even know swam in the ocean", and a regular contingent of "Japanese nationals" is the "best endorsement" to many; "friendly" owners "never forget" your name, and pros promise your "stomach will never forget" the experience.

HASHIGUCHI ◑ ☒   25 | 15 | 19 | $28
Shops Around Lenox, 3400 Woodale Dr. NE (Peachtree St.), 404-841-9229
The Terrace, 3000 Windy Hill Rd. SE (Powers Ferry Rd.), Marietta, 770-955-2337
"Countless regulars" count on these "consistent" Japanese twins in Marietta and Buckhead for "excellent"

Atlanta

eats at "fair prices", including "quality" sushi and a "great variety" of "authentic cooked" offerings, served by a "friendly", "caring" staff; "not many know about" the "hidden" Lenox location, making it a more "intimate" setting, but either venue is a "wonderful" choice for a "quiet business gathering" or a "lively ladies' night."

Havana Sandwich Shop | 23 | 7 | 15 | $11

2905 Buford Hwy. NE (N. Druid Hills Rd.), 404-636-4094

This Buford Highway Cubano "has been around 30 years for a reason" – namely, the "quintessential Cuban sandwich" and other "inexpensive" "kick-ass" fare that "draws big lunch crowds"; "bare-bones" "early bus station lunchroom" decor "doesn't matter" to fans "blinded" by "authentic, flavorful" eats, and the "friendly" staff that's "brief on words" "could beat customers over the head with their sandwiches and people would still come back for more."

Haveli Indian Cuisine | 17 | 9 | 14 | $21

225 Spring St. NW (bet. Andrew Young Blvd. & Harris St.), 404-522-4545
490 Franklin Rd. SE (Rte. 120), Marietta, 770-955-4525

"Come hungry" and "close your eyes" to the spartan digs at these "reliable" Indian twins in Downtown and Marietta where "convenient" "buffets" offer a "good selection" of "standard" offerings; critics who find the "just ok" fare "overpriced" and the service "slack" are "so sad" to see how they've "slipped."

Haven | 23 | 23 | 22 | $37

1441 Dresden Dr. NE (bet. Appalachee Dr. NE & Camille Dr. NE), 404-969-0700; www.havenrestaurant.com

"Sophisticated" New American cuisine "appeals to a wide range" of tastes (albeit at "big price tags"), while "gracious hosts" and a "knowledgeable staff" "get the job done" in a "warm" space with "beautiful art" and a "stylish patio" at this "high-end" venue in Brookhaven; an "eclectic" crowd of "locals", "pretty people" and "nip-and-tuck" types makes for "lively" "people-watching" in spite of the "snob factor"; P.S. "no reservations."

High Cotton | 18 | 14 | 18 | $27

5592 Chamblee Dunwoody Rd. (Mt. Vernon Rd.), 770-395-7004

A "reliable" "comfort-food mainstay", this Dunwoody American is a "safe bet" for "decent" eats and "service with a smile" in "comfortable", "inviting" surroundings, with a bar that's "happenin' on weekends"; cynics may sniff it's "nothing special", but pros point out it's still "easier and cheaper than driving into Buckhead."

Highland Tap | 19 | 16 | 18 | $27

1026 N. Highland Ave. NE (Virginia Ave.), 404-875-3673

"Climb down steep stairs" to this reasonably priced "subterranean steakhouse" in Va-Highlands where carnivores

Atlanta

F | D | S | C

"buckle down (or unbuckle?)" for some "serious beef", including "burgers the way they're supposed to be", while gin-teel types anoint it the "martini champion of Atlanta"; the service is "solid" and the "sexy" "cellar setting" is ripe for "a rendezvous in a dark booth" or a "meeting with friends" in the "smoky" bar.

Hi Life Kitchen & Cocktails ⑤ — 24 | 22 | 23 | $31
3380 Holcomb Bridge Rd. (Jimmy Carter Blvd.), Norcross, 770-409-0101; www.atlantahilife.com
For "upscale dining without the pretentiousness", Norcross residents "can always depend on" this New American sibling of Aqua Blue that's "worth a drive" and the "babysitter bucks" for chef Christopher Pyun's "snappy culinary combinations" and "great wine pairings"; expect "white-tablecloth dining" in a "friendly environment", a "good bar" scene and "swift" "knowledgeable" service – boosters boast "you can't beat it" in the area.

Himalayas Indian ∇ 23 | 14 | 22 | $18
Chamblee Plaza, 5520 Peachtree Industrial Blvd. (Longview Dr.), Chamblee, 770-458-6557
While this "affordable" Chamblee stalwart may be a "dinosaur", devotees still dig in to "consistently good", "well-seasoned" Northern Indian fare that "sometimes wows", and are undaunted by the strip-center location and "no-frills" digs; the "cozy" atmosphere and "professional" service help make it a popular "respite on a busy day."

Hometown Barbecue ⊄ — - | - | - | I
1173 Hwy. 29 S. (Johnson Rd. SW), Lawrenceville, 770-963-5383
It may be "way off the beaten path" in Lawrenceville, but 'cuennoisseurs who've made it to this "traditional BBQ joint" declare the "delicious" "Memphis-style" meats and "solid" Brunswick stew to be "some of the best in the area"; "helpful", "down-home" service is another reason this one's "worth the drive."

Hong Kong Harbour ☾ — 18 | 10 | 16 | $19
2184 Cheshire Bridge Rd. NE (Lavista Rd.), 404-325-7630
"If you get a sudden urge for Chinese in the middle of the night" this "casual" Cheshire Bridge ethnic will "probably be open" (until 1 AM Sundays–Thursdays and 3 AM on weekends) and wokking up "authentic" eats that are "beautifully" served; it's also a "dim sum habit pleaser" since they offer it "every day" in the "tired", "tacky" interior, but there's a "friendly" vibe and hey, it "saves you a drive all the way to Chamblee."

HORSERADISH GRILL 22 | 22 | 22 | $37
4320 Powers Ferry Rd. NW (Wieuca Rd.), 404-255-7277; www.horseradishgrill.com
"Gourmet Southern" is "not an oxymoron" at this "wonderful" Buckhead "charmer" that "lives up to its reputa-

60   subscribe to zagat.com

Atlanta   F | D | S | C

tion" serving up "excellent" "classics" "with a twist", emphasizing the "freshest ingredients"; the "friendly" owners and staff "make you feel welcome" and there's a "real neighborhood feel" to the "beautiful" cottage with "one of the nicest" patios in town; a popular spot for a "sophisticated Sunday brunch" among the "horsey set", it's also a "classy but not pretentious" choice for a "romantic dinner," or a stop "before Chastain concerts."

House of Chan   ▽ 23 | 13 | 20 | $18
Cumberland Square North Shopping Ctr., 2469 Cobb Pkwy. SE (Herodian Way), Smyrna, 770-955-9444
Boosters boast this family-run Smyrna "classic" "kicks" the competition "in the ass" with some of the "best Chinese anywhere", crafted from the "freshest ingredients" and served up in "huge portions"; though the service is "quick", the "small" space, which "hasn't been updated in years", often "gets very crowded", so "come early."

Houston Mill House ⓢ   ▽ 19 | 20 | 19 | $23
849 Houston Mill Rd. NE (Clifton Rd.), 404-727-4033; www.houstonmillhouse.com
"Excellent" for "large gatherings" or as a "quiet" "change of pace" from the "chain and fast food" near the Emory campus, this lunch-only entry is "like a trusted friend" to many, offering a "predictable" menu of American "staples"; it's set in a "historic" field stone home in a "scenic" wooded location "off the beaten path", where you can indulge in some "interesting eavesdropping" dining among "top professors" from the university.

HOUSTON'S   21 | 18 | 21 | $27
4701 Ashford Dunwoody Rd. (Meadow Lane Rd.), 770-512-7066
3321 Lenox Rd. NE (E. Paces Ferry Rd.), 404-237-7534
3539 Northside Pkwy. NW (W. Paces Ferry Rd.), 404-262-7130
2166 Peachtree Rd. NW (Colonial Homes Dr.), 404-351-2442
3050 Windy Hill Rd. SE (Powers Ferry Rd.), 770-563-1180
www.hillstone.com
Many who usually "avoid chains at all costs" "just can't leave" this ubiquitous group that's "taken consistency to an art" with "solid", "comfy" American fare and "attentive" service; the rooms are "cozy" but "dark", so you may need to "bring a flashlight" to "read the menu", as well as a "book" for "excruciatingly long" waits "no matter what time you go."

Hsu's Gourmet   22 | 19 | 20 | $27
192 Peachtree Center Ave. (International Blvd.), 404-659-2788; www.hsus.com
Some of the "best Asian food in the Downtown area" can be found at this "very satisfying" Chinese sibling of Pacific Rim and Silk, a "reliable" purveyor of "tasty, authentic" Szechuan cuisine, including Peking duck that's "worth the

Atlanta   F | D | S | C

trip to the obscure location"; some feel the space is "getting worn", but "not the welcome" from a "friendly" staff, making it a "treasure" for businesspeople and out-of-towners "stuck" in the neighborhood.

Huey's   17 | 14 | 17 | $19
1816 Peachtree Rd. (bet. Collier Rd. & 26th St.), 404-873-2037; www.hueysrestaurant.com

"It's all about the beignets" at this Cajun-Creole spot, a "must" in South Buckhead that "defines Sunday brunch" and does "justice to New Orleans" with its "delightfully prepared" breakfast and lunch fare, "thoughtfully served" with "no pretensions"; the patio is a popular roost on "pretty days."

Il Forno   21 | 13 | 15 | $19
5680 Roswell Rd. NE (I-285), 404-255-8486
13800 Hwy. 9 N. (Bethany Rd.), Alpharetta, 770-664-8877
www.ilfornonypizza.com

"Former NYers" and suburbanites "return again and again" to this "interesting" pizzeria pair in Alpharetta and Sandy Springs for "wonderful" pies that are the "closest thing to real NY pizza in the area", as well as "filling" Italian eats, all at "bargain" prices; "good" service is another reason fans feel it's a "quality place."

Il Localino   19 | 19 | 20 | $36
467 N. Highland Ave. NE (Albion Ave. NE), 404-222-0650; www.localino.info

"If you want to dance with your server", this "festive" Inman Park spot comes highly "recommended" by revelers who've been "swept off their feet" by a "charming" yet "crazy" staff that transforms "good" "family" Italian fare into a "zoo" complete with "campy music", "disco balls" and "party hats"; it's best for "groups", but the "allure is over" for those who kvetch over the "hefty price tag for a lot of kitsch" and food that's "just ok."

Imari   ∇ 23 | 13 | 18 | $29
2221 Peachtree Rd. NE (Biscayne Dr.), 404-603-5282

Those in-the-know declare this tiny Japanese in a South Buckhead strip mall the "real thing" for its "decent selection" of "top-notch" sushi and cooked fare, served in a "soothing" setting that transports you to "Tokyo or the West Coast"; cognoscenti plead "please keep it a secret."

Imperial Fez   18 | 22 | 21 | $54
2285 Peachtree Rd. NE (Peachtree Hills Ave.), 404-351-0870; www.imperialfez.com

"Fill your belly and then dance it off" at this Moroccan "experience" in South Buckhead famous for a "sumptuous" five-course prix fixe of dishes you "eat with your fingers" while lounging shoeless on "floor pillows" in the "elegant" curtain-filled setting; "good service" and "excellent" belly

Atlanta   F | D | S | C

dancers make for a "special night out", and while it's "expensive", fans feel it's "well worth the price."

Ippolito's   19 | 14 | 18 | $19
Abernathy Sq., 6623 Roswell Rd. NE (Abernathy Rd.), 404-256-3546
Abbotts Vlg., 11585 Jones Bridge Rd. (Abbotts Bridge Rd.), Alpharetta, 770-663-0050
12850 Hwy. 9 N. (Windward Pkwy.), Alpharetta, 678-624-1900
Town Center Mall, 425 Barrett Pkwy. NW (I-75), Kennesaw, 770-514-8500
Centennial Shopping Ctr., 2270 Holcomb Bridge Rd. (Eves Rd.), Roswell, 770-992-0781
Dean Taylor Crossing, 2133 Lawrenceville-Suwanee Rd. (Taylor Rd.), Suwanee, 678-985-4377
www.ippolitos.net

"How can a local chain be so good?" ponder paesanos of these "popular" "family-owned" Italians that are the "epitome" of "checkered tablecloth" dining, i.e. "massive portions", "lots of red sauce and cheese", "sinfully good garlic rolls" and "cakes as tall as your forearm"; the digs are "not much to look at", but the prices are "reasonable" and the "personable" staff makes guests "feel like one of the family."

Jake's   21 | 16 | 17 | $8
515 N. McDonough St. (Trinity Pl.), Decatur, 404-377-9300; www.jakesicecream.com

"Ben and Jerry who?" crack cronies of this Decatur dessert specialist where the "fresh", "scrumptious" ice cream is "heaven on earth in a sugar cone", in flavors with "clever names" such as Key Lime Piescream and Good Karma'l; "tasty" sandwiches are also on offer in the "cozy" venue, which shares a roof with a "great kids' bookstore", and though the service can be "questionable", many "can't get enough" of it.

Jalisco ☒   20 | 10 | 21 | $14
Peachtree Battle Shopping Ctr., 2337 Peachtree Rd. NE (bet. Lindbergh Dr. & Peachtree Hills Ave.), 404-233-9244

An "old Atlanta favorite" that's been around since 1978, the Coronado family's South Buckhead "institution" offers "hot and tasty" "old-style" Tex-Mex and Mexican served up "almost too fast"; "Formica-topped tables" highlight the plain room that's "always crowded" with "professionals and housewives" at lunchtime and families at night, but the "Speedy Gonzalez"–like staff "seats you in a snap."

Jason's Deli   17 | 10 | 15 | $11
3330 Piedmont Rd. NE (Peachtree Rd.), 404-231-3333
5975 Roswell Rd. NE (Hammond Dr.), 404-843-8212

(continued)

vote at zagat.com

Atlanta   F | D | S | C

(continued)

Jason's Deli
7300 N. Point Pkwy. (Mansell Rd.), Alpharetta, 770-664-5002
3070 Windward Plaza (Windward Pkwy.), Alpharetta, 770-619-2300
Forum Shopping Ctr., 5131 Peachtree Pkwy. (Medlock Bridge Rd.), Norcross, 770-368-9440
4073 Lavista Rd. (I-285), Tucker, 770-493-4020
www.jasonsdeli.com

These "grab-and-go" delis are "busy" and they "deserve to be", thanks to "obscenely generous" portions of nosh that "rocks", from "fresh fixings" on the salad bar to "mile-high" sandwiches, and free ice cream makes them a "parents' dream"; the "cafeteria-style" service is "efficient" and the "food makes up for any shortcomings" in the "standard" digs with "zero ambiance" that are "noisy enough to bring your loudest kids" without embarrassment.

Java Jive ⌀   20 | 20 | 20 | $12
790 Ponce de Leon Ave. NE (Freedom Pkwy.), 404-876-6161

"Travel back to a simpler time" at this "offbeat" Poncey-Highlands New American praised for the "best pancakes in town" and other "original" breakfast fare (the "gingerbread waffles with lemon curd" are "recommended"), and "delish" coffee "gets you going"; 1950s "kitchen kitsch" and "vintage" "appliances" lend "lots of personality" to the "purple building"; P.S. if you forget "to bring cash" (no credit cards) there's a "fee-gouging" ATM on the premises.

Jitlada   18 | 16 | 20 | $18
Cheshire Square Shopping Ctr., 2329C Cheshire Bridge Rd. (Lavista Rd.), 404-728-9040

"You'd never know how good" this Cheshire Bridge Thai is, "tucked away" in the corner of a "seedy strip mall", but fans say it's "worth seeking out" for the "well-rounded menu" of "delicious" dishes; the "gaudy" decor is oddly "charming" and so are the "excellent" staff and "reasonable prices", and homebodies "wish they delivered."

JOËL ☒   26 | 26 | 24 | $58
The Forum, 3290 Northside Pkwy. NW (W. Paces Ferry Rd.), 404-233-3500; www.joelrestaurant.com

Joël Antunes is a "true artist" creating "brilliant" French cuisine in the "lavishly appointed kitchen" of his Buckhead establishment, while sommelier Philippe Buttin is in "a class of his own" selecting a "formidable" wine list; the "stunning" space boasts "high ceilings" and an "exquisite bar", and while the service strikes a few as "snooty", most find it "superb"; "perfection" may not be "for the faint of pocketbook", but many still keep this "standout" "high on their list for special occasions."

Atlanta

F | D | S | C

Joey D's Oak Room 19 | 18 | 18 | $32
*1015 Crown Pointe Pkwy. (Abernathy Rd.), 770-512-7063;
www.joeydsoakroom.com*

"You get what you expect" at this "popular oasis" in Dunwoody in the form of "plentiful" "above-average" American fare, including "excellent" steaks and a corned beef sandwich that "has no equal", and "consistently good" service in a "classic heavy oak" setting; to many, though, the main draw is the "spectacular" bar "stocked to the ceiling" and manned by "knowledgeable" bartenders.

Johnny Rockets 17 | 15 | 15 | $13
*2970 Cobb Pkwy. (I-285), 770-955-6068
Phipps Plaza, 3500 Peachtree Rd. NE (Lenox Rd.), 404-233-9867
Underground Atlanta, 50 Upper Alabama St. SW (Pryor St.), 404-525-7117
5 W. Paces Ferry Rd. NW (Peachtree St.), 404-231-5555
Arbor Place Mall, 6700 Douglas Blvd. (Bright Star Rd.), Douglasville, 770-577-2636
Gwinett Place Mall, 2100 Pleasant Hill Rd. (bet. I-85 & Satellite Blvd.), Duluth, 770-622-4478
Discover Mills Mall, 5900 Sugarloaf Pkwy. (I-85), Lawrenceville, 678-847-5800
Avenue at East Cobb, 4475 Roswell Rd. (Johnson Ferry Rd.), Marietta, 770-509-0377
www.johnnyrockets.com*

"If you love *American Bandstand*", this "old-fashioned" hamburger chain will have you hopping over "tasty" burgers, "addictive" fries and onion rings and "thick" shakes that are "worth every fat gram" and arrive "Johnny-on-the-spot" "quick"; "personal jukeboxes" at each table play "era-appropriate" tunes, accompanied by a "singing and dancing" staff, so "bring the kids" or anyone "from 3 to 103."

Johnny's New York Style Pizza 19 | 9 | 15 | $13
*1810 Cheshire Bridge Rd. NE (bet. Manchester & Piedmont Rds.), 404-874-8304
280 Elizabeth St. NE (bet. Austin & N. Highland Aves.), 404-523-6339
2850D Holcomb Bridge Rd. (Steeple Chase Rd.), Alpharetta, 770-993-1455
9950 Jones Bridge Rd. (Old Alabama Rd.), Alpharetta, 770-777-9799
11950 Jones Bridge Rd. (Douglas Rd.), Alpharetta, 770-772-4648
869 N. Main St./Hwy. 9 (Windward Pkwy.), Alpharetta, 678-867-6773
911 Market Place Blvd. (Hwy. 20), Cumming, 770-205-9317
340B Church St. (Sycamore St.), Decatur, 404-373-8511
4880 Lower Roswell Rd. (Johnson Ferry Rd.), Marietta, 678-560-2228*

(continued)

Atlanta

F | D | S | C

(continued)
Johnny's New York Style Pizza
Market Square Shopping Ctr., 2970 Canton Rd. (bet. E. Peidmont & Chastain Rds.), Marietta, 678-797-0505
www.jnysp.com
Additional locations throughout the Atlanta area
"No frills, no hassle" and "kid-friendly" to boot, this pizzeria chain is a popular choice for "great" pies, and while "NY it's not", it's "as good as it's going to get this deep into Dixie" and it "keeps your wallet happy"; the "quality varies by location", while the "scruffy" interiors "don't encourage lingering", but "decor and service don't bring in the crowds" – the "pizza does."

Joli Kobe Bakery 23 | 19 | 18 | $16
The Prado Plaza, 5600 Roswell Rd. (I-285), 404-843-3257;
www.jolikobe.com
"Clever salad and sandwich options" and the "best pastries imaginable" ("artistic") make this "better than ever" Sandy Springs bakery and cafe a "hit", where ladies who lunch and locals appreciate "high-quality" Continental fare, "fresh ingredients" and "quick service"; it's a "great escape from Roswell Road" and "worth the wait at lunch", but you can also get it "to go."

Justin's ▽ 13 | 17 | 13 | $39
2200 Peachtree Rd. NW (bet. Collier Rd. & Peachtree Battle Ave.), 404-603-5353
Bring your bling to Sean 'Puffy' Combs' Southern/soul food venue in South Buckhead, where the "large selection of martinis" and "see-and-be-seen" scene are the main attractions, drawing a largely affluent African-American crowd; but while it's "the place to be" for many, cynics snap it's "not the place to eat."

King & I 19 | 8 | 20 | $17
Ansley Sq., 1510F Piedmont Rd. SE (Monroe Dr.), 404-892-7743
"So good and so cheap", this "gay"-friendly Midtown Thai offers "big portions" of "tasty" fare served up by the owner and "lovely staff" who "make you feel right at home" in a "no-frills" space that "looks like it hasn't been redecorated since the '50s"; while many feel "comfortable dining alone", insiders predict you're "bound to see someone you know."

Kobe Steaks ▽ 21 | 17 | 21 | $34
Prado Shopping Ctr., 5600 Roswell Rd. NE (I-285), 404-256-0810
"If you like hibachi", this Sandy Springs Japanese is one of the "best in town" swear "repeat customers" who applaud "amazing aged" beef and other "good" offerings; while the digs may "need a face-lift", the "cook-it-in-front-

Atlanta

F | **D** | **S** | **C**

of-you" show by "entertaining" chefs is an "added bonus" the "whole family can enjoy."

Krog Bar ◐ ☒ — 21 | 24 | 24 | $27
Stove Works, 112 Krog St. NE (bet. Edgewood Ave. NE & Irwin St. NE), 404-524-1618; www.krogbar.com

"Kevin Rathbun has done it again" with this Mediterranean "masterpiece" in Inman Park that "should be on the radar" of everyone in search of "wonderful" "antipasti style" "small plates", a "killer" wine list and a "funky" vibe consistent with this "up-and-coming urban neighborhood"; whether out for a "night on the town" or "just chilling out", aficionados "love, love, love" this "postage stamp of greatness" (ok, it's a "tight fit"), where "they know their vino."

Kurt's ☒ — ▽ 25 | 19 | 20 | $38
4225 River Green Pkwy. (Peachtree Industrial Blvd.), Duluth, 770-623-4128; www.kurtsrestaurant.com

"Exquisite" European cuisine with "refined German" "leanings" makes for seriously "sophisticated dining" "in the 'burbs" at this "big surprise" in a Duluth "industrial park"; whether there for a meal with "the parents", a "business gathering" or on a "romantic" date, "impeccable" service is delivered in the renovated "farmhouse" that exudes a "restful, old-world well-being"; it's a "good value" too, although for fans, "excellent food is value enough."

KYMA ☒ — 25 | 24 | 23 | $47
3085 Piedmont Rd. NE (E. Paces Ferry Rd.), 404-262-0702; www.buckheadrestaurants.com

"I didn't know Atlanta was on the coast" gush groupies about this "brilliant conceptualization" of an "upscale Greek taverna" from the Buckhead Life Restaurant Group where "simple preparations" of the "freshest fish" "allow" the "flavors to shine", and an "amazing wine program" complements "marvelous meze"; a "polished" staff delivers "wonderful" service in the "gorgeous" space, and while the experience may max out your "expense account", for most it's "worth every penny."

La Fonda Latina — 19 | 12 | 16 | $14
1639 McLendon Ave. NE (Page Ave.), 404-378-5200
2813 Peachtree Rd. NE (Rumson Rd.), 404-816-8311
923 Ponce de Leon Ave. (Linwood Ave.), 404-607-0665
4427 Roswell Rd. NE (Wieuca Rd.), 404-303-8201

For "all things Latin", fans flock to these "informal" "kid-friendly" "mainstays", where they tuck into "amazing" fish tacos, "real" salsa and "well-seasoned" paella ("is there any other in Atlanta?"), and wash them down with "extraordinary margaritas"; "no-nonsense" digs include popular outdoor decks and "wildly colored rooms", and while "service can be an issue", the menu still offers "great flavor for the price."

vote at zagat.com

Atlanta

F | **D** | **S** | **C**

LA GROTTA
26 | 22 | 25 | $49

Crowne Plaza Ravinia Hotel, 4355 Ashford Dunwoody Rd. (Hammond Dr.), 770-395-9925
2637 Peachtree Rd. NE (bet. Lindbergh Dr. & Wesley Rd.), 404-231-1368
www.lagrottaatlanta.com

"La Grade A" is what aficionados call this "anniversary-worthy" Northern Italian duo where "fabulous" cuisine that "never disappoints" and "exemplary" service from a "professional" staff represent "fine dining at its very best"; fans of the Buckhead original, including an "older, affluent crowd", are unfazed by the "strange basement location" and enjoy a "sense of calm" and "great acoustics", while the Dunwoody location offers an "elegant", "plush" space that overlooks a garden and waterfalls.

La Madeleine French Bakery
18 | 17 | 14 | $16

Buckhead Mktpl., 35 W. Paces Ferry Rd. NW (Peachtree St.), 404-812-9308
2850 Paces Ferry Rd. (W. Paces Ferry Rd.), 770-434-3900
Perimeter Sq., 1165 Perimeter Ctr. W. (Peachtree Dunwoody Rd.), 770-392-0516
1931 Powers Ferry Rd. (Windy Hill Rd.), 770-952-8426
2255 Pleasant Hill Rd. (Satellite Blvd.), Duluth, 770-814-0355
Providence Sq., 4101 Roswell Rd. (Johnson Ferry Rd.), Marietta, 770-579-3040
www.lamadeleine.com

For a "quick in-and-out meal" "without the fast-food feel", fans tout these "convenient" "self-serve" links in a national chain for their "accessible" French "comfort" fare, including soups "to die for" and "heavenly" baked goods; the "brasserie" settings with "homey" brick fireplaces are "warm and cozy", but "unreliable" cooking and service "ranging from great to awful" lead some to conclude that they're "overpriced."

La Paz
18 | 18 | 17 | $20

Vinings Jubilee Shopping Ctr., 2950 New Paces Ferry Rd. (Paces Ferry Rd.), 770-801-0020; www.lapaz.com

A "no-brainer" for "predictable" but "creatively designed" Tex-Mex fare, this Vinings spot is "worth a drive out of the city" for many, offering "wonderful" margaritas and an "awesome" happy hour in a former church sporting wood furniture from Mexico; "slow" service and "overpriced" eats are excused somewhat by "drink specials that can't be beat"; N.B. the former Woodstock branch is now a private dining and catering venue.

Las Palmeras
23 | 10 | 21 | $17

366 Fifth St. NE (Durant Pl.), 404-872-0846

Like a "sidewalk cafe in Havana", this "*mami* and *papi*" spot "hidden" "behind Piedmont Park" in Midtown attracts *amigos* with "awesome" Cuban cuisine and "wel-

Atlanta

F | D | S | C

coming" service; though the interior of the "little house" could "use remodeling", and it's "tucked away" in an "obscure" neighborhood that "keeps the trendy people away", it's "always busy" nonetheless.

LA TAVOLA   23 | 20 | 22 | $32
992 Virginia Ave. NE (N. Highland Ave.), 404-873-5430;
www.latavolatrattoria.com

"Everything has that homemade touch" at this "stylish" Italian in the "heart of Va-Highlands", where "promising" new chef Craig Richards (ex Falidia in NYC) creates "sophisticated" yet "simple" cuisine that is paired with a "superb" wine list; "attentive" service "makes you feel like a regular" in the "shotgun" space with a "long, gleaming" bar, "romantic" balcony and "intimate" (read "cramped") dining room; P.S. the "fabulous" Sunday brunch is a "well-kept secret."

Lee's Golden Buddha & Mo Mo Ya   18 | 18 | 16 | $24
3861 Roswell Rd. (bet. Le Brun & Piedmont Rds.), 404-261-3777;
www.momoyaga.com

This "beautiful" "three in one" (Chinese, hibachi and sushi) spot in Buckhead "satisfies the whole family" with its "exhaustive" menu of "dependable" Asian eats and "thoughtful" service in a "large yet quiet" dining room overlooking a "calming" koi pond and gardens; "kids love" the "entertaining" teppanyaki chefs and homebodies "couldn't survive" without the "reliable" takeout that's "delivered as soon as you hang up the phone", but critics say it's a "shame" the "food just can't hold a candle" to the "over-the-top" decor.

Le Giverny   21 | 16 | 21 | $29
Emory Inn, 1641 Clifton Rd. (bet. Briarcliff & N. Decatur Rds.), 404-325-7252

When you want to "impress someone" "without breaking the bank", this Emory bistro near the CDC delivers with a "wonderful" selection of "good basic" French cuisine and "fine" service that make it a "favorite" of "doctors", "professors" and "ladies who lunch"; though the decor can be a "total buzz kill" for some, fans still recommend this spot "for a romantic evening" or "end-of-the-week cocktail."

Les Fleurs De Lis Café   ▽ 25 | 20 | 20 | $23
Healey Bldg., 57 Forsyth St. NW (Walton St.), 404-230-9151

"Downtown needs more" places like this tiny French in the historic Healy Building, one of the area's "best-kept secrets" where the "amazing food for the price" is a "pleasant surprise" to those in-the-know; "friendly servers" make the experience even more "relaxing" in quaint digs reminiscent of a "little cafe in Paris", offering further proof that "good things come in small packages."

vote at zagat.com

Atlanta   F | D | S | C

Little Bangkok   23 | 12 | 22 | $16
2225 Cheshire Bridge Rd. NE (Woodland Ave.), 404-315-1530
There's "always a wait" at this Thai even though it's "easy to miss" at its strip-mall address on "gritty" Cheshire Bridge, a "favorite" stop for "locals" and even "chefs from other restaurants" for "awesome" eats, including vegetables "so fresh" they "crunch", and "attentive" servers who "guide you in the right direction" on the menu; aficionados advise "don't let the outside scare you", for inside there's some of the "best food for the price" "in the metro area."

Little Szechuan   23 | 8 | 17 | $16
Northwood Plaza, 5091C Buford Hwy. (Shallowford Rd.), Doraville, 770-451-0192
Surveyors "salivate just thinking about" this "outstanding" Sino spot on Buford Highway offering a "varied" menu "packed" with "tasty choices" of "spectacular" dishes whipped up in a "quick, efficient" manner "by people who know how to cook it"; "inexpensive" "large portions" of what some consider the "best Chinese in town" excuse the "no-frills" decor.

Loaf & Kettle ⊠   ▽ 24 | 15 | 17 | $11
Healey Bldg., 57 Forsyth St. NW (Walton St.), 404-525-8624
Downtowners in search of "something a little different" for lunch head to this "upscale" "hippie-type" Eclectic spot in the Healy Building for "fabulous soups" (try their signature corn, crab and spinach chowder), "inventive sandwiches" and "wonderful" bread pudding; you order at the "self-service" counter and then grab a seat in the "cozy" lobby of the historic edifice (circa 1913).

Lobby at Twelve   – | – | – | M
Twelve Hotel, 361 17th St. NW (Atlantic Dr.), 404-961-7370; www.lobbyattwelve.com
Check into this lively scene, courtesy of Bob Amick and crew (ONE. midtown kitchen, TWO. urban licks and PieBar), in the lobby of Atlantic Station's Twelve Hotel and condominiums where a bustling bar is warmed by a wood oven, and chef Nick Oltarsh (ex Murphy's) presides over the open kitchen that turns out New American cuisine with a Mediterranean accent; the modern space, accented with warm woods and high windows, is appropriate for business meetings, group outings or a romantic tête-à-tête.

Loca Luna ●   19 | 21 | 16 | $24
836 Juniper St. NE (bet. 6th & 7th Sts.), 404-875-4494; www.loca-luna.com
"The music is always a-kickin'" at this "wild" Midtown Pan-Latin where "rowdy crowds" nibble on "surprisingly good tapas" and down "fabulous mojitos" when they're not "dancing" or joining in on the "party" action in the "spacious" dining room or on the "great" outdoor patio;

Atlanta   F | D | S | C

critics feel the "food hasn't quite caught up" to the "lively", "club-like" scene, but while it's maybe "not for a fine night out", it's "certainly a fun one."

Lombardi's   ▽ 18 | 16 | 19 | $23
Underground Atlanta, 94 Upper Pryor St. SW (Martin Luther King Jr. Dr.), 404-522-6568
Its "proximity to the state capitol" makes this Downtown Italian a natural "legislative power-lunch" venue where "lobbyists and politicos" go to "see and be seen"; "hot, fresh" dishes that are "infused with flavor" are served in a Mediterranean-inspired space by a staff that "welcomes you warmly", making it "one of the better options" in the area.

LongHorn Steakhouse   17 | 15 | 17 | $23
Akers Mill Sq., 2973 Cobb Pkwy. SE (Akers Mill Rd. SE), 770-859-0341
2892 N. Druid Hills Rd. (Lavista Rd.), 404-636-3817
2430 Piedmont Rd. (Lindbergh Way), 404-816-6338
6390 Roswell Rd. (Abernathy Rd.), 404-843-1215
10845 Medlock Bridge Rd. (Abbotts Bridge Rd.), Duluth, 770-622-7087
Camp Creek Mktpl., 3840 Camp Creek Pkwy. (I-285), East Point, 404-346-4110
Town Ctr., 2700 Town Center Dr. NW (Busbee Pkwy.), Kennesaw, 770-421-1101
800 Lawrenceville-Suwanee Rd. (Duluth Hwy. NW), Lawrenceville, 770-338-0646
2636 Dallas Hwy. SW (Ridgeway Rd.), Marietta, 770-514-0245
4721 Lower Roswell Rd. (Johnson Ferry Rd.), Marietta, 770-977-3045
www.longhornsteakhouse.com
Additional locations throughout the Atlanta area
"You know what to expect" at this chain of steakhouse "standbys" "located in almost any neighborhood" offering "credible" "tasty" meats "at a reasonable price", served by a "friendly" staff; the "cheesy" decor of "stuffed" "weird creatures" has a "certain corny charm", and while "below-average" dining and "robotic" service drive malcontents to "moo on over" to other pastures, many others report "never having a beef with" this "consistent" performer.

Machu Picchu   ▽ 20 | 11 | 19 | $16
Northeast Plaza Shopping Ctr., 3375 Buford Hwy. (bet. Clairmont & N. Druid Hills Rds.), 404-320-3226
Adventurous diners can "take the chance to really branch out" at this "real deal" Peruvian on Buford Highway and its menu of "traditional", "delicious" eats that also includes "plenty of predictable items" for the more cautious; sure, the "decor could be better", but for a "true experience" that's "cheap" to boot, it's "worth a visit."

Atlanta

F | D | S | C

MADRAS SARAVANA BHAVAN   26 | 10 | 14 | $15
North Dekalb Sq., 2179 Lawrenceville Hwy. (N. Druid Hills Rd.), Decatur, 404-636-4400; www.madrassaravanabhavan.net
Faithful fans wish they had "more arms than Vishnu to shovel in all the wonderful delights" at Atlanta's No. 1 Indian, this "superb vegetarian" in Decatur offering "incredible", "extremely spicy" fare at "affordable prices"; service can be a "crapshoot" and the decor resembles something like "tiki hut meets" the subcontinent, but aficionados just "close their eyes" and "wallow in the smells and tastes" that "take you to India for the price of three coffees from Starbucks."

MAGGIANO'S LITTLE ITALY   20 | 19 | 19 | $28
3368 Peachtree Rd. NE (GA 400), 404-816-9650
Perimeter Mall, 4400 Ashford Dunwoody Rd. (I-285, exit 29), 770-804-3313
www.maggianos.com
"Pack a second stomach" (or a "yard-size Hefty" bag for "leftovers") to dine at these Buckhead and Dunwoody links of a "well-run" chain serving "well-executed Italian-American comfort food" served in "family-style" portions "large enough to feed a small village"; a "solid" staff manages the "long waits" in "comfortable", albeit "noisy", dining rooms, but purists grouse that "everything tastes the same", because "quantity is greater than quality here."

Majestic ●≠   12 | 9 | 12 | $10
Plaza Shopping Ctr., 1031 Ponce de Leon Ave. NE (N. Highland Ave.), 404-875-0276
"If you didn't meet anyone at the bar" you can "convoy with other sloshy strangers" to this 24/7 "old-timey" cash-only diner in Poncey-Highlands where you'll find a "line out the door between 1 and 3 AM" of "weird, colorful characters" jonesin' for a "greasy-spoon" breakfast or late-night burgers; servers are "not overly enthusiastic" but the people-watching "show is free" in the "time-warp" setting.

Malaya   ▽ 20 | 14 | 21 | $18
Howell Mill Vlg., 857 Collier Rd. (Howell Mill Rd.), 404-609-9991; www.malayacuisine.com
"Superb food with a unique flair" is "prepared with care and creativity" at this Asian that's a "real find" for South Buckhead families who appreciate "personal" service that's "friendly in three languages"; the nondescript strip-mall space is "easy to get to", and while some feel the "charm has gone" of late, not "having to go to Buford Highway" keeps others coming back.

Mali   23 | 14 | 21 | $21
961 Amsterdam Ave. NE (N. Highland Ave.), 404-874-1411
"As authentic as you'll get this side of the globe", this "not-so-secret-anymore" Va-Highlands Thai "favorite" "com-

Atlanta F D S C

petently combines" traditional fare with a "boatload" of "beautiful" sushi, and mavens find the menu "magnificent all around"; an "always present" owner and "lovely" staff create a "warm", "charming" ambiance, and one of the "best patios in the neighborhood" make it a "great first date or any date place."

Manuel's Tavern ◐ | 15 | 16 | 17 | $16
602 N. Highland Ave. NE (North Ave.), 404-525-3447; www.manuelstavern.com
A "'W' sticker on a car" in the lot is as "rare as a snowstorm in Miami" at this "well-known" Poncey-Highlands hangout for "Democrats", "Atlanta's progressive community" and "literati" who "gossip over "cold" beers, "wonderful" burgers and other "tasty" tavern fare or take part in the "best trivia [nights] in the lower 48"; those who find the pub grub "incidental" insist the "real draw" is the "cast of characters"; N.B. you must be 18 or older to get in.

Marlow's Tavern ◐ | 18 | 19 | 19 | $21
2355 Cumberland Pkwy. SE (Mt. Wilkinson Pkwy.), 770-432-2526
Camden Vlg., 3719 Old Alabama Rd. (Jones Bridge Rd.), Alpharetta, 770-475-1800
www.marlowstavern.com
These "convivial" tavern twins in Vinings and Alpharetta (siblings of Hi-Life and Aqua Blue) are like "an upscale version of *Cheers*", where a "friendly" staff delivers "full-flavored" American fare that won't "take a chunk out of your wallet"; "each night seems to draw a different age group" so "baby boomers" and the "20s and 30s" crowds alike can "pretend they're 18 again", whether "watching sports", checking out "eye candy" or grooving to live music.

Mary Mac's Tea Room | 18 | 13 | 19 | $16
224 Ponce de Leon Ave. NE (Piedmont Ave.), 404-876-1800; www.marymacs.com
Everyone from "businesspeople" to "blue hairs", "aching" for "down-home" Southern cooking, are drawn to this "sentimental favorite" in Midtown that "mentally whisks you back to grandma's kitchen" with "Atlanta's best veggie plate" and "potent sweet tea"; "spunky waitresses with Southern drawls" "turn on the charm" in the "homespun" setting, and while some feel it's merely "coasting on its reputation", to many others it just "oozes comfort."

Matthew's Cafeteria ⌧ | ▽ 20 | 6 | 13 | $10
2299 Main St. (north of Lawrenceville Hwy.), Tucker, 770-491-9577; www.matthewscafeteria.com
You're apt to "see an Atlanta business mogul eating fried chicken with the guy who cuts his lawn" at this "landmark" "cafeteria-style" Southern in Tucker that's the "definition of a meat and three", where the "real down-home" fare "hasn't changed" in 50 years and the sweet tea will

vote at zagat.com 73

Atlanta

F | D | S | C

"keep you up at night"; while the "dingy" digs are in "need of some TLC" ("my elementary school cafeteria was more welcoming"), the place does have "character."

McCormick & Schmick's 21 | 19 | 19 | $38
600 Ashwood Pkwy. (bet. Ashford Dunwoody Rd. & Meadow Ln.), 770-399-9900
CNN Ctr., 190 Marietta St. NW (Centennial Olympic Park Dr.), 404-521-1236
www.mccormickandschmicks.com
"If you want fresh fish", fans tout these "solid" links in a national chain "that doesn't act like one" for "consistently good" fin fare that's "flown in daily" and an "impressive" selection of "raw oysters"; the Downtown location is "one of the better options" "for a business lunch or dinner", while "outdoor dining by the fountain" makes Dunwoody a local alfresco "favorite", but critics question the "high prices" for an experience that's "nothing to rave about."

MCKENDRICK'S STEAK HOUSE 26 | 21 | 25 | $52
Park Place Shopping Ctr., 4505 Ashford Dunwoody Rd. NE (bet. Hammond Dr. & Perimeter Ctr.), 770-512-8888;
www.mckendricks.com
This "high-end" "power" spot in Dunwoody "competes with the best of Buckhead" with "fabulous" steaks that are "worth the cholesterol", "huge", "tasty sides", an "impressive wine list" and "wonderful" "old-fashioned" service that "makes you feel special"; the atmosphere is "vibrant" (and a "little noisy") in "quintessential" steakhouse surroundings of "dark oak" and "white tablecloths" – just be sure to "bring lots of money" because "everything's à la carte."

McKinnon's Louisiane 17 | 13 | 19 | $36
3209 Maple Dr. NE (Peachtree Rd.), 404-237-1313;
www.mckinnons.com
"Don't judge a book by its cover" insist fans of this "divine strip-mall hole-in-the-wall" in Buckhead that's "been around forever" offering "old-school" Cajun-Creole eats and "cosseting" service in a "comforting" setting with a "hoot" of a piano bar; but "everything seems a bit tired and run-down" to critics, from the "disappointing" fare to the "dated" decor.

Meehan's Public House 16 | 19 | 17 | $18
2810 Paces Ferry Rd. SE (Cumberland Pkwy.), 770-433-1920 ☻
4058 Peachtree Rd. NE (Dresden Dr.), 404-467-9531 ☻
227 Sandy Springs Pl. NE (Roswell Rd.), 404-843-8058 ☻
Grand Pavilion, 11130 State Bridge Rd. (Kimball Bridge Rd.), Alpharetta, 770-475-2468
www.101concepts.com
"For a wee dram", Irish (and other) eyes smile on this quartet of "lively" Celtic taverns with "tons of personality"

subscribe to zagat.com

Atlanta

serving pub "standards", including "excellent" fish 'n' chips, and an "outstanding beer selection"; the similar-looking spaces all boast "lovely patios", and the newest Sandy Springs location, with its "great rooftop deck", "fills a void", and while critics may find "nothing outstanding" on the menu, pros wonder "who goes to a pub for the food, anyway?"

Mellow Mushroom 21 | 12 | 14 | $14

5575 Chamblee Dunwoody Rd. (Dunwoody Village Rd.), 770-396-1393
1679 Lavista Rd. NE (Briarcliff Rd.), 404-325-0330
931 Monroe Dr. (bet. 8th & 10th Sts.), 404-874-2291
2950 New Paces Ferry Rd. SE (Paces Mill Rd.), 770-435-5949
6218 Roswell Rd. (Johnson Ferry Rd.), 404-252-5560
6000 Medlock Bridge Pkwy. (Medlock Bridge Rd.), Alpharetta, 770-813-0818
Commerce Sq., 265 Ponce de Leon Pl. (Commerce Dr.), Decatur, 404-370-0008
736 Johnson Ferry Rd. (Lower Roswell Rd.), Marietta, 770-579-3500
1690 Powder Springs Rd. SW (Macland Rd.), Marietta, 770-425-5511
2421 Shallowford Rd. NE (Trickum Rd.), Marietta, 770-516-1500
www.mellowmushroom.com
Additional locations throughout the Atlanta area

"Wacky toppings lead to happy tummies" at this local "laid-back" pizza chain where "it's all about the dough" that goes into pies "so tasty" "you'll think you're stoned", while the "extensive selection of beers on tap" makes "trivia" nights more interesting and the "screaming kids" more tolerable; decor and service are "highly variable" "depending on location", but most boast a "groovy" vibe and "slacker" servers who are "by no means quick"; homebodies hit with the munchies sigh "if only they delivered."

Melting Pot, The 21 | 17 | 20 | $37

3610 Satellite Blvd. NW (Pleasant Hill Rd.), Duluth, 770-623-1290
2500 Cobb Place Ln. (Cobb Place Blvd.), Kennesaw, 770-425-1411
Shoppes at Mansell, 1055 Mansell Rd. (GA 400), Roswell, 770-518-4100
www.meltingpot.com

"For a classic taste of the '80s", this "cheese"-centric chain offers "all fondue, all the time" (including a "heavenly" dessert version) to those willing to "cook their own dinner"; "attentive" service in a "serene" setting also makes it a winner for a "date", "get-out-of-the-doghouse-with-the-wife" dinner or "special occasion", and while wallet-watchers see theirs get "thinner", it's still a "relaxing" experience for many.

vote at zagat.com

Atlanta   F | D | S | C

Mexico City Gourmet   13 | 11 | 16 | $16
North Decatur Plaza, 2134 N. Decatur Rd. (Clairmont Rd.), Decatur, 404-634-1128
Decaturites looking for a "break from the fast-food burrito scene" head to this "good-time" "hole-in-the-wall" for "all of the trademark Mexican" offerings, "well-seasoned" daily specials and "potent", "giant" margaritas; "happy" servers "make you feel at home" in otherwise "old and worn" quarters that "leave a lot to be desired."

Mezza–A Lebanese Bistro ☒   24 | 16 | 21 | $20
Oak Grove Ctr., 2751 Lavista Rd. (Oak Grove Rd.), Decatur, 404-633-8833; www.mezzabistro.com
A "fantastic choice" for "amazing", "accessible" Lebanese cuisine served up in "small plates of heaven" with lots of "big flavors", this "unpretentious" venue tucked away in a "leafy neighborhood" of Decatur is a "winner"; "helpful", "friendly" service and decor that "reflects the culture" are other reasons local loyalists feel "lucky to have it in our neighborhood."

MF SUSHIBAR   26 | 23 | 21 | $39
265 Ponce de Leon Ave. (Penn St.), 404-815-8844; www.mfsushibar.com
At this Midtown Japanese voted Atlanta's No. 1 for sushi, "lovingly prepared" offerings of "amazingly fresh" fish are "literally art" and the "fresh wasabi" is "not to be missed"; the "cool factor is high" in the "modern" space located in a "wonderfully renovated section" of Ponce that attracts an "eye-appealing" "hip" crowd, so "make reservations" and be prepared to "pay extra" or "forget about eating here."

Mick's   13 | 13 | 15 | $19
557 Peachtree St. NE (North Ave.), 404-875-6425
2110 Peachtree Rd. NE (Bennett St.), 404-351-6425
Underground Atlanta, 75 Upper Alabama St. SW (Peachtree St.), 404-525-2825
116 E. Ponce de Leon Ave. NE (Clairmont Ave.), Decatur, 404-373-7797
www.thepeasantrestaurants.com
"Generous portions at reasonable prices" make these independently owned Americans "standbys" you "can count on" for a "quick dinner" stop or "casual business lunch" served in "comfortable", "open" dining rooms or on "nice" patios; but "mediocrity reigns supreme", from "bland" eats to "slow" service to "poor" decor, say cynics who sniff that it's "only worth a visit for the Oreo cheesecake."

MidCity Cuisine   19 | 21 | 19 | $34
1545 Peachtree St. NE (Spring St.), 404-888-8700; www.midcitycuisine.com
Ownership and multiple chef changes (including one post-*Survey*, which is not reflected in the above Food score)

Atlanta

F | **D** | **S** | **C**

have left surveyors split over this Midtown New American – to fans it's "still fabulous", thanks to the "kid-friendly" Sunday gourmet pizza night, "cool bar" and "awesome" patio; foes feel it's "lost a step", citing "uninspired" service and "unimpressive" fare "for the price"; many others are still "waiting to see" what happens next.

Milan Mediterranean Bistro & Grill
▽ 16 | 19 | 16 | $28

Crowne Plaza Atlanta-Buckhead, 3377 Peachtree Rd. NE (2 blocks south of Lenox Rd.), 678-553-1900; www.milanatlanta.com

"On a sunny day" you "can't beat the patio" at this Buckhead Crowne Plaza Mediterranean with a menu of "fun small plates" that make it a "great option" for lunch or "drinks"; critics, though, find the fare "mediocre"; N.B. a post-*Survey* chef change is not reflected in the above Food score.

Minerva Indian Cuisine
▽ 20 | 11 | 18 | $16

4305 State Bridge Rd. (S. Bridge Pkwy.), Alpharetta, 678-566-7444; www.minervacuisine.com

For a "welcome change in the 'burbs", fans tout this Alpharetta subcontinental specialist offering "true Indian dishes" that are "spicy" but "not too overwhelming" in a spacious, if "sterile", room; as dinner strikes some as rather "boring", insiders recommend the "reasonable" and "assorted" lunch buffet as "your best bet."

Misto
21 | 15 | 20 | $32

1950 Howell Mill Rd. (Collier Rd.), 404-425-0030; www.mistoatl.com

"Those in-the-know" go to this "secret hideaway" "on an ugly street" on the Westside where chef Ryan Aiken (ex Burrito Art) crafts a "well-balanced" menu of Italian and American fare, including "awesome" pumpkin ravioli and other "terrific" "homemade" pastas, paired with a "solid wine list"; the staff is "always friendly" and "accommodating" in the "low-key" converted gas station space.

Mitra ☒
23 | 22 | 20 | $33

818 Juniper St. (bet. 5th & 6th Sts.), 404-875-5515; www.mitrarestaurant.com

"Spicy flavors" and a "funky" atmosphere "meld together" into a "memorable" meal at this "delish" sibling of Sia's in Midtown, where a "well-thought-out" menu of Latin-accented New American fare is "served with flair" to a "stylish, smart and mature crowd"; "attentive" service adds to the "wonderful" ambiance, and the "romantic deck" with "open garage doors" is the place to be in "warm weather."

Mix ☒
19 | 24 | 20 | $31

1441 Dresden Dr. NE (bet. Appalachee Dr. NE & Camille Dr. NE), 404-969-3250; www.mixrestaurant.com

There's a "welcome jolt of Downtown vibe" at this "new kid on the block" in Brookhaven, neighbor Haven's "cool

Atlanta   F | D | S | C

younger" sibling offering an "endless variety" of Asian-Med "small plates" that "complement" "well-poured drinks"; a "good-looking "crowd gravitates to this "see-and-be-seen" "speakeasy", which is set in a "funky space" showcasing rotating local art, "wild" bathroom doors, "hottie bartenders" and "cool DJs."

Moe's & Joe's ●∅   14 | 11 | 14 | $12
1033 N. Highland Ave. (Virginia Ave.), 404-873-6090
This Va-Highlands "institution" "looks exactly like a dive bar should" and "hasn't changed one bit" since 1947, except for the "ever-eclectic crowd" attracted by "cheap" "Pabst Blue Ribbon on draft" and "decent bar food"; if you "don't have high expectations", it's a "great place to relax with friends" "sitting under the trees" "on the sidewalk" or in "red vinyl booths"; N.B. cash only.

Moe's Southwest Grill   15 | 11 | 16 | $10
Ansley Mall, 1544 Piedmont Ave. NE (Monroe Dr.), 404-879-9663
2484 Briarcliff Rd. NE (Woodlake Dr.), 404-248-9399
Colony Sq., 1197 Peachtree St. NE (14th St.), 404-870-8884 ☒
860 Johnson Ferry Rd. NE (Trimble Rd.), 404-303-0081
2915 Peachtree Rd. (Peachtree Ave.), 404-442-8932
3722 Roswell Rd. (Piedmont Rd.), 404-231-1690
8290 Roswell Rd. (Northridge Rd.), 678-585-7573
863 Ponce de Leon Ave. NE (Barnett St.), Decatur, 404-607-7892
125 Ernest W. Barrett Pkwy. (Prado Ln.), Marietta, 678-581-0236
2354 Holcomb Bridge Rd. (Fouts Rd.), Roswell, 770-594-8050
www.moes.com
"You always get a hearty welcome" at this Atlanta-based Southwestern chain serving "quick-serve" eats, including "amusingly named" burritos "bigger than an adult cat" "jam-packed" with "fresh fixings"; while it may be "McMoe's" to detractors, it's a "good value" for "families on a budget", and defenders insist "for what it is, it shines."

Morton's, The Steakhouse   24 | 21 | 23 | $57
(fka Morton's of Chicago)
3379 Peachtree Rd. NE (Lenox Rd.), 404-816-6535
SunTrust Plaza Bldg., 303 Peachtree Center Ave. NE (Baker St.), 404-577-4366
www.mortons.com
"If you're looking for the old-school" "rich ambiance" of a "top-of-the-line" steakhouse, this Buckhead-Downtown duo fits the bill with "mind-blowing, artery-popping" meats "cooked to perfection", "over-the-top lobsters" and "tremendous à la carte sides", paired with an "extraordinary wine list"; it's definitely "not for the tight fisted", and while some are put off by the "gee-whiz presentation", even "infrequent guests" are "made to feel like regulars" in the "classic" "clubby" spaces jazzed up with the strains of "piped-in Sinatra."

Atlanta | F | D | S | C |

Mosaic ⊠ | 24 | 20 | 22 | $42 |
3097 Maple Dr. NE (Peachtree St.), 404-846-5722;
www.mosaicatl.com
A recent change in the kitchen at this "comfortable" Buckhead Mediterranean has made things "very interesting" for neighbors and those in search of a "non-Buckhead" experience, with new chef Darrell Rice creating "inspired" dishes "with a little pizzazz"; the "charming little house" is tucked away on a "quiet" "side street", so outdoor dining "under the stars and trees" is "great for a date night"; "plenty of parking" is another plus.

Mu Lan | 21 | 20 | 20 | $21 |
824 Juniper St. NE (bet. 5th & 6th Sts.), 404-877-5797
This "upscale" Chinese in a "desirable" location in the heart of Midtown "does a solid job" with "unusual" yet "creative" Asian fare, including "great" lunch specials at "incredible prices", and it's the "only" choice for "delivery" for some locals; the owners' "hearts are in the right place" and the staff is "efficient" working the "intimate" renovated Victorian space that's fit for "romantic" "first dates."

MURPHY'S | 22 | 20 | 21 | $26 |
997 Virginia Ave. NE (N. Highland Ave.), 404-872-0904;
www.murphysvh.com
"Sit back, relax and enjoy the people-watching" at this Va-Highlands "standard" that has "withstood the test of time" with "consistent", "satisfying" American cuisine, including a "brunch in a class by itself" and "desserts worth the sin", as well as a "superior" wine list"; "wonderfully fair prices" and "excellent" service in the "relaxed but stylish" "bungalow" setting also make it "worth the hunt for parking."

MUSS & TURNER'S ⊠ | 25 | 19 | 23 | $17 |
1675 Cumberland Pkwy. (Atlanta Rd.), Smyrna, 770-434-1114;
www.mussandturners.com
"These guys know their stuff" gush groupies of this "gourmet" deli in Smyrna that dishes out "amazing" sandwiches that "always hit the spot" and arguably the "coolest takeaway", even if it is "a bit pricey"; "witty" menu descriptions of the "creative" offerings can "make deciding difficult" for some, but the "helpful" "owners and employees love their work" "and it shows"; N.B. beer and wine is served on the premises but no longer sold retail.

Nagoya | ∇ 20 | 13 | 17 | $23 |
48 King St. (S. Atlanta St.), Roswell, 770-998-8899
"Entertaining chefs" man both the teppanyaki and sushi counters at this "neighborhood haunt" in Roswell where the Japanese offerings are "fresh" and "inexpensive", making up for the rather "run-down" digs; purists who find the grilled fare "pedestrian" opt for the "more innovative" raw-fish offerings instead.

vote at zagat.com 79

Atlanta | F | D | S | C |

Nakato
| 19 | 19 | 19 | $32 |

1776 Cheshire Bridge Rd. (Piedmont Rd.), 404-873-6582; www.nakatorestaurant.com

One of Atlanta's "first" Japanese, this Cheshire Bridge "treasure" is the "real deal" say those who appreciate "artistry through sushi" as well as "excellent" teppanyaki prepared by "personable table chefs"; "gracious" service adds to the "serene" mood of the "soothing interior" that's a "quiet place for relaxing" or a "business" meal.

NAM ☒
| 26 | 23 | 22 | $33 |

Midtown Promenade, 931 Monroe Dr. NE (Ponce de Leon Ave.), 404-541-9997; www.namrestaurant.com

"It's not every day you get to gnaw on sugarcane at the table", but this "stellar" Midtown sibling of MF Sushibar has certainly "upped the ante" when it comes to "exotic", "delicious" Vietnamese eats that are a "visual feast" (the "shaking beef is one of the wonders of the world"); the "stylish" and "elegant" environs make you "forget you're in a strip mall in dire need of renovation", while the "impeccable" service and "sexy" vibe add to the "wow factor."

NAN THAI FINE DINING
| 26 | 27 | 24 | $41 |

1350 Spring St. NW (17th St.), 404-870-9933; www.nanfinedining.com

Voted Atlanta's No. 1 for Decor, this "smoothly sexy" "high-end" Midtown Thai (and Tamarind sibling) is "like a trip to Bangkok without the airfare" thanks to a "dazzlingly dramatic" Johnson Studio–designed space that "gushes Asian sophistication and charm" ("even the restroom is gorgeous"); the cuisine is "art on your plate" that's delivered with "impeccable" grace by a "gorgeous" staff, making it "an experience you don't want to miss" and the "best place" to "impress your friends, clients, or in-laws."

NAVA
| 24 | 24 | 22 | $40 |

Buckhead Plaza, 3060 Peachtree Rd. NE (W. Paces Ferry Rd.), 404-240-1984; www.buckheadrestaurants.com

Even those who "don't like Southwestern" may have a "change of mind" at this "upscale" "Santa Fe"–inspired Buckhead Life Group production serving a menu of "spectacular" "fresh flavors" that are a "fiesta for the taste buds" and "flavorful drinks", including "perfect" margaritas that are "worth the trip" alone; a "steady" staff "aims to please" in the "fabulous" "multi-tiered room" or on the "fantastic patio area" by a "cascading fountain", with a new outdoor bar that's a "great addition."

New Yorker Marketplace & Delicatessen ☒
| 23 | 7 | 18 | $12 |

322 Pharr Rd. NE (Peachtree Rd.), 404-240-0260

A "loyal following" is "glad to have" this "killer" deli located in the heart of Buckhead that serves up some of

Atlanta

F | D | S | C

the "best sandwiches in the city", which come "close" to the "ones you find up North"; "get in line" at the no-frills strip-mall spot and grab one of the few tables and "you will not be disappointed"; P.S. the owner is also "one butcher you can count on every time" for "outstanding" cuts of prime beef.

NEW YORK PRIME   26 | 22 | 24 | $57
Monarch Tower, 3424 Peachtree Rd. NE (Lenox Rd.), 404-846-0644; www.centraarchy.com

"Oh yeah, baby" crow carnivores who "rejoice" over this "prime" Buckhead link in a national chain that's "rising in the ranks" with "perfect" steaks that "melt in your mouth", side dishes "to die for" and a "phenomenal" wine list that come together for a "special occasion–" (and "expense account"–)"worthy" experience; the staff of "real pros" is praised for their "attention to detail" in the "masculine" space where there's "always a happening happy hour" ("better not mind cigar smoke").

Nickiemoto's   19 | 19 | 18 | $26
990 Piedmont Ave. NE (10th St.), 404-253-2010

"You can always count on a regular crowd" of "pretty people" to "keep the buzz going" at this "eclectic" "bait-and-booze joint" in Midtown that "pulls it all together" with "excellent" Pan-Asian eats and "creative" sushi; the "patio setting" is "wonderful", "and yes, big Southern boys in dresses" do come out for the "Monday night" "drag show", but "make reservations" because even "on a quiet night, this place is still hopping."

Nicola's   20 | 11 | 20 | $21
1602 Lavista Rd. NE (bet. Briarcliff & Cheshire Bridge Rds.), 404-325-2524; www.nicolas-restaurant.com

"They'll have you on your feet" in no time at this Emory Lebanese that "measures up nicely" with "delicious" "family-style" fare, including "solid" "essentials" (as in "great hummus and pita"), and "caring" service that "adds shine to the old room"; "charming" owner Nicola "does the Macarena" with guests or leads the "belly dancing on weekends."

NIKOLAI'S ROOF ⓢ   24 | 26 | 25 | $79
Hilton Atlanta, 255 Courtland St. NE (bet. Baker & Harris Sts.), 404-221-6362; www.nikolaisroof.com

"Dramatic, wraparound views of the city" from atop the Downtown Hilton figure highly in the "wow factor" of this "pricey" "epicurean experience" that's "still going strong" after 30 years thanks to "excellent" French-Continental cuisine with Russian influences that "takes your taste buds to another level" and "outstanding wine service"; "remarkable" service is another reason it's "still miles above most" others.

vote at zagat.com

Atlanta   F D S C

Nino's   22 | 16 | 22 | $31
*1931 Cheshire Bridge Rd. NE (Piedmont Ave.), 404-874-6505;
www.ninosatlanta.com*
"Step back into a different time" (and maybe "a different place – NJ?") at this "wonderful" "old-style" Italian on Cheshire Bridge that's "like a Billy Joel ballad"; the "hearty" red-sauce fare and "exquisite" wine list would "impress" "your uncle from the old world", while waiters who "know their craft" man the "homey" setting – "*bellissima!*"

Noche   19 | 17 | 17 | $25
*1000 Virginia Ave. NE (N. Highland Ave.), 404-815-9155;
www.heretoserverestaurants.com*
Pros promise an "all-around good time" at this Va-Highlands Southwesterner by Tom Catherall (Twist, Shout, Prime, Strip, Goldfish) serving "fantastic" small plates that represent "excellent value", especially the "Monday all-you-can-eat" option; the servers are "friendly" and the bartenders "are not shy with their pours" when concocting some of the "best margaritas in Atlanta", which make for a "festive" "after-work" scene; when the "small" space gets too crowded, many head for the outdoor patio.

Noodle   20 | 18 | 18 | $14
*903 Peachtree St. NE (8th St.), 404-685-3010
3693 Main St. (Princeton Dr.), College Park, 404-767-5154* ⌧
*205 E. Ponce de Leon Ave. (Church St.), Decatur, 404-378-8622
www.noodlehouse.net*
Though the menu of noodles and rice is "simple", there's "enough variety to suit everyone" at this "affordable" trio serving "tasty" "neo-Asian food with flair" in "large bowls" "chock-full of yummy things"; the "sleek yet inviting" spaces are "kid-friendly" and "casual" and the locations are convenient enough to "calm the savage lunch crowds" of "young urban dwellers"; they're also "solid" "take-out" options.

Norcross Station Cafe ⌧   20 | 20 | 17 | $17
*40 S. Peachtree St. (Holcomb Bridge Rd.), Norcross,
770-409-9889; www.norcrossstation.com*
The "Amtrak Crescent blows by around 8:30 PM these days", passing this "good ol' standby" located in a "quaint" former Norcross train depot that's now "very much a family place" serving "solid", "wholesome" American fare "at a fair price"; the "nice" staff adds to the "charm" and "great decorations" keep the locomotive theme "alive."

Northlake Thai Cuisine ⌧   ▽ 24 | 22 | 24 | $24
*Kroger Shopping Ctr., 3939 Lavista Rd. (Evelyn St.), Tucker,
770-938-2223; www.northlakethai.com*
"Head and shoulders above anything in the neighborhood" and "worth the drive" from anywhere, this "fine-dining" Tucker Thai is lauded for "fantastic" fare "seasoned to

Atlanta

F | D | S | C

perfection" and served with "style"; if "strip-mall chic" exists, it's alive and well in the "elegant" space "hidden" in an "unlikely location" "behind a Kroger"; while almost "nobody knows where it is", those who do confirm it's truly a "real find in a sea of mediocrity."

NUEVO LAREDO CANTINA ⊠   24 | 13 | 17 | $18
1495 Chattahoochee Ave. NW (bet. Collier & Howell Mill Rds.), 404-352-9009; www.nuevolaredocantina.com
"Nothing comes close" to the "authentic" "border cuisine" at Atlanta's No. 1 Mexican, located on an "industrial" stretch of Westside; "go early" or "prepare to camp out" "on the porch" with the rest of the "throngs" who come "from far and wide" for the "tremendous" *comida,* though pitchers of "terrific margaritas" "help" ease the "brutal" waits; "walls lined with snapshots" provide the only decoration in the "down-to-earth" digs.

Oak Grove Market ⊠   21 | 13 | 21 | $11
2757 Lavista Rd. (Oak Grove Rd.), Decatur, 404-315-9831; www.oakgrovemarket.com
"They don't make them like this anymore" say fans about this Decatur deli-cum–butcher shop that "pleases everyone from kids to blue hairs" with "made-to-order" sandwiches, "amazing soups" and "gourmet take-home fare", and fresh meat that's "among the best"; a "pleasant staff" presides over the shiny space with "couches and TVs" and a "nostalgic '50s atmosphere."

Oceanaire, The   23 | 24 | 22 | $49
1100 Peachtree St. (12th St.), 404-475-2277; www.theoceanaire.com
For a "tidal wave of awesome seafood" that's so "fresh" it rivals the "new aquarium", "look no further" than this "elegant" Midtown outpost of a national chain known for "high-end" fin fare served in "luxury liner–size" helpings that make for the "best doggy bags in town", although some wish it would "halve the Paul Bunyan portions" and "lower the prices"; "wonderful" service and a "gorgeous" room make this "expense account" spot a "must" for "entertaining clients or a special night on the town."

OK Cafe   19 | 15 | 19 | $18
West Paces Ferry Shopping Ctr., 1284 W. Paces Ferry Rd. (Northside Pkwy.), 404-233-2888; www.okcafe.com
"Diner-style" "Southern fried bliss" is on the menu at this "Buckhead breakfast haunt" offering "large helpings" of "real country food done right", served up "with a smile" by "perky waitresses in white aprons"; it's a popular spot for "power lunches" or "family" meals, where "you'll see everyone from Ted Turner to the babysitter" "crammed" in the space highlighted by neon and Formica, and those on the go "love" the "take-away" option.

Atlanta

F | **D** | **S** | **C**

Old South Barbecue
▽ 22 | 12 | 20 | $12

601 Burbank Circle (Windy Hill Rd.), Smyrna, 770-435-4215;
www.oldsouthbbq.com

A "great Southern tradition" for those who know about it, this long-standing family-run BBQ in Smyrna has been around for four decades, dishing out "homestyle" slow-cooked 'cue "as it is meant to be" with two different types of sauces in a rustic, cabinlike space; family-style selections and a children's menu are available, and there's also takeout.

111 MLK ⊠
– | – | – | I

111 Martin Luther King Jr. Dr. SW (Peachtree St.), 404-523-0109

Knowledgeable noshers who have discovered this Downtown deli find the spartan space "always packed" with fellow cognoscenti drawn by its "huge" NY-style sandwiches; the brother-and-sister owners "know what they're doing", and their mother makes the daily desserts; N.B. lunch only.

ONE. MIDTOWN KITCHEN ☽
21 | 25 | 20 | $38

559 Dutch Valley Rd. (Monroe Dr.), 404-892-4111;
www.onemidtownkitchen.com

At this "über-trendy" Midtown "favorite" (sibling of TWO. urban licks and PieBar), foodies report new chef Richard Blais "has turned the kitchen around" with New American dishes that "push the boundaries" ("molecular cuisine", anyone?), paired with a "reasonable" wine list (including a "unique" bottomless glass option); an "attentive" staff adds to the "stylish" "see-and-be-seen" "scene" that morphs from "geriatric" to "glitterati" as the evening progresses, and the "beautiful" Johnson Studio–designed space features "languid lighting" and "cool" "New Age" restrooms.

One Star Ranch
20 | 14 | 17 | $15

25 Irby Ave. NW (Roswell Rd.), 404-233-7644
732 N. Main St. (bet. Henderson Village Pkwy. & Vaughn Dr.), Alpharetta, 770-475-6695
www.onestarranch.com

"It ain't elegant dining", but this "little slice of Texas" in Buckhead and Alpharetta serves some of the "best" "Lone Star" state–style BBQ around, including "mouthwatering", "monstrously huge" ribs ("one is a meal") and "excellent" onion rings; you "expect to see Hoss ride up on his horse" to the "casual" "Western-themed" digs where "friendly" folks dole out just "what you're looking for."

Orient at Vinings
19 | 17 | 18 | $22

Vinings on the River, 4199 Paces Ferry Rd. SE (Paces Mill Rd.), 770-438-8866; www.orientatvinings.com

Fans "love the fact" that this Vinings Mandarin is "located in an old train" where passengers can choose "hibachi, sushi or regular" seating and "you can't go wrong" with any of them; detractors who derail it as "beyond bor-

Atlanta

F | D | S | C

ing" find it a mystery that this express is so "popular" among the "locals."

Original Pancake House, The 20 | 8 | 15 | $12
Tara Shopping Ctr., 2321 Cheshire Bridge Rd. (Lavista Rd.), 404-633-5677
3665 Club Dr. (Pleasant Hill Rd.), Duluth, 770-925-0065
Staples Shopping Ctr., 239-243 Marketplace Connector (off Hwy. 54), Peachtree City, 770-486-7634
5099 Memorial Dr. (S. Indian Creek Blvd.), Stone Mountain, 404-292-6914
www.originalpancakehouse.com

"Short order perfection" can be found at this chain of "throwback diners with all the fixin's" offering a "massive menu" of "killer" breakfast fare that'll "please anyone from two to 70", as long as they "forget the carbs and cholesterol"; "waitresses call you 'hon'" in the "no-frills, no-fuss" setting with "few to no screaming children" – the only crying heard are plaints about "atrocious" weekend waits.

Oscar's Villa Capri ▽ 21 | 13 | 20 | $35
Orchard Park Shopping Ctr., 2090 Dunwoody Club Dr. (Jett Ferry Rd.), 770-392-7940; www.oscarsvillacapri.com

Dunwoody denizens "escape" to this "enjoyable" strip-mall spot that "withstands the test of time" with "extraordinary dishes" of "excellent home-cooked" Italian cuisine, brought to table by a "gracious" staff; the ambiance is "warm" and the chef-owner is a "real delight", but a few grouse that it's "overpriced."

Osteria 832 19 | 14 | 17 | $17
832 N. Highland Ave. (3 blocks north of Ponce de Leon Ave.), 404-897-1414; www.osteria832.com

A "neighborhood favorite" that "fits" in "beautifully" with the "personality of Va-Highlands", this "relaxed", "pretty cheap" Italian sibling of Doc Chey's "will transport you to Rome in a mouthful" of its "sophisticated" pastas and "authentic" "thin-crust" pizzas, served by a "kind", "tolerant staff"; "hang with the kids" or enjoy a "first date" on the "big outdoor deck", but "before 8 PM" "be prepared for the Chuck E. Cheese crowd."

Outback Steakhouse 17 | 13 | 16 | $25
Buckhead Court Shopping Ctr., 3850 Roswell Rd. NE (Piedmont Rd.), 404-266-8000
Toco Hills, 2145 Lavista Rd. NE (N. Druid Hills Rd.), 404-636-5110
Kohl's Shopping Ctr., 1715 Market Place Blvd. (Rte. 400, exit 14), Cumming, 678-455-7225
6331 Douglas Blvd. (Chapel Hill Rd.), Douglasville, 770-949-7000
810 Ernest W. Barrettt Pkwy. (I-75, exit 269), Kennesaw, 770-795-0400

(continued)

vote at zagat.com

Atlanta F | D | S | C

(continued)
Outback Steakhouse
Delk Spectrum Shopping Ctr., 2900 Delk Rd. (Powers Ferry Rd.), Marietta, 770-850-9182
Spaulding Woods Vlg., 4015 Holcomb Bridge Rd. (Spaulding Dr.), Norcross, 770-448-6447
995 N. Peachtree Pkwy. (Hwy. 74), Peachtree City, 770-486-9292
655 W. Crossville Rd. (bet. Hackett & Woodstock Rds.), Roswell, 770-998-5630
Park Place Shopping Ctr., 1525 E. Park Place Blvd. (Hwy. 78, exit 30B), Stone Mountain, 770-498-5400
www.outback.com
Additional locations throughout the Atlanta area

For those who want "nothing unexpected", this "dependable" steakhouse chain doles out "hearty", "well-seasoned" steaks at "decent" prices, which help explain the "two hour waits"; service is "friendly" and "quick", and the call-in option, when they "bring your order out to your car", is always popular, but jaded critics jeer at the "bloomin' average" eats and "kitschy" "Aussie" theme.

Oz Pizza   24 | 10 | 16 | $11
309 E. College Ave. (Candler Rd.), Decatur, 404-373-0110
2805 Main St. (White Way), East Point, 404-761-7006
5 W. Broad St. (Campbellton St.), Fairburn, 770-306-0603 ✉

"If they ain't serving these pies in heaven, then I don't wanna go" declare "devotees" who "see the light" when it comes to this cheesy trio voted Atlanta's No. 1 for pizza, thanks to "perfect" crusts and "hearty" sauces that go into its "excellent", "cheap" pizzas; a "funky", "hardworking" staff provides "quick" service in the "dive bar" setting that's "not too much to look at", but whether you decide to "slum it" or opt for "takeout", it's "the best pie you can find" in these parts.

Pacific Rim Bistro   20 | 19 | 20 | $31
SunTrust Plaza Bldg., 303 Peachtree Center Ave. (Baker St.), 404-893-0018; www.pacificrimbistro.com

This Downtown sibling of Hsu's and Silk provides an "excellent variety" of "above-average" Pan-Asian fare (at "above-average prices") including "stellar entrees", "appetizers to write home about" and "fresh" and "varied" sushi; "convenient" for the lunch crowds and "business" set, it's a "comfortable" experience, though perhaps more so "for singles than families."

Pad Thai   21 | 13 | 18 | $21
1021 Virginia Ave. NE (N. Highland Ave.), 404-892-2070

Though it may be the "least flashy" of the "hundreds" of area Thai spots, this Va-Highlands venue (and sibling of nearby Mali) is the "reliable" "favorite" of many because it "knows its strengths and plays to them", offering "first-class" fare "without a lot of attitude"; the mood is

Atlanta

F | D | S | C

"relaxing" in the "small" space, where a "friendly" staff provides "attentive" service."

Palace, The — | — | — | I
6131 Peachtree Pkwy. (Holcomb Bridge Rd.), Norcross, 770-840-7770
"Every option on the menu deserves a try" at this "excellent" Norcross Indian according to those in-the-know, starting with "crisp flatbreads and homemade dips" "and it only gets better from there"; the lunch buffet is "one of the best to be found" in the area, and the "gracious" staff "takes its time (in a good way)."

Palm 23 | 19 | 22 | $54
Westin Buckhead, 3391 Peachtree Rd. NE (bet. GA 400 & Lenox Rd.), 404-814-1955; www.thepalm.com
"Expense-account" dining is the name of the game at this outpost of the national chain in the Buckhead Westin, where "mouthwatering" "huge hunks of beef", "monstrous" lobsters, "excellent" salads and "family-style" sides are served by a "well-mannered" staff; "caricatures" of "local luminaries" adorn the walls of the "clubby", "tough-guy" setting and "your chances of being starstruck are pretty high."

Pampas Steakhouse 23 | 24 | 24 | $40
10970 State Bridge Rd. (Jones Bridge Rd.), Alpharetta, 678-339-0029; www.pampassteakhouse.com
An "unassuming" façade fronts an "upscale yet cozy" interior at this Argentine steakhouse on the outskirts of Alpharetta, where the portions of "tender, juicy" "wood-fire grilled" meats are "enough for a medium-size lion", and the "great selection of different cuts" is complemented by a "very good" wine list; "excellent" service is another reason many deem this carnivores' "paradise" "outstanding."

Panahar 24 | 15 | 23 | $18
Northeast Plaza Shopping Ctr., 3375 Buford Hwy. NE (N. Cliff Valley Way), 404-633-6655; www.panahar.com
The "beautifully made" Bangladeshi cuisine at this Buford Highway specialist is "subtle" and "sophisticated", and the afternoon buffet "delights", as do the "good prices", and BYO with no corkage fee "makes it that much more of a bargain"; the "friendly" owner "charms you into returning again and again" and "gracious", "helpful" (at times "over the top") service makes an "interesting food experience" even more of a "treat."

Pangaea ⌧ 21 | 13 | 17 | $12
1082 Huff Rd. NW (Marietta Blvd.), 404-350-8787; www.globalgrubbin.com
"Hard to find, easy to come back to", this Westside deli is like a "little trip around the world" with "delicious" Vietnamese sandwiches and an array of other "interesting" "ethnic"

vote at zagat.com

Atlanta

PANO'S & PAUL'S 🚫   26 | 23 | 25 | $55
West Paces Ferry Shopping Ctr., 1232 W. Paces Ferry Rd. (Northside Pkwy.), 404-261-3662;
www.buckheadrestaurants.com
At this Buckhead "pinnacle of old-style dining", a "broad and deep wine list" matches the "elegant" Continental menu (including a Dover sole that's "worth the occasional trip to the poorhouse") and "immaculate" dishes arrive "hot and timely" thanks to "crazy perfect" service; the "expense-account crowd" and "comb-over and trophy-wife" types alike celebrate "special occasions" in the "opulent" "early '20s" setting, and while a few feel it's "lost its moorings", defenders insist "Pano's flagship is still sailing" smoothly "after all these years."

Pao de Mel   - | - | - | I
2359 Windy Hill Rd. SE (Cobb Pkwy.), Marietta, 770-690-8007
Pros promise "you won't find a more filling meal for the money" than what's offered at this Brazilian "find" in Marietta where the "low-priced" menu is "nothing short of astounding"; its bakery creates "delectable sweets" that are some of the "best" around and "perfect for entertaining on a budget."

PAOLO'S GELATO ITALIANO ⊄   26 | 15 | 22 | $6
1025 Virginia Ave. NE (N. Highland Ave.), 404-607-0055;
www.paolosgelato.com
"You don't have to be in Italy" to enjoy "honest-to-God gelato" gush fans of the "first-class" confections at this "teensy" Va-Highlands "storefront" (voted Atlanta's No. 1 Bang for the Buck) with "lines out the door" filled with cone-noisseurs who want to "try as many" "interesting flavors" "as they'll allow"; you have to deal with "tireless self-promoter" Paolo and "larger-than-life reproductions" of his "mug" – but then, "would you buy gelato from a guy named Bob?"

Pappadeaux Seafood Kitchen   21 | 18 | 19 | $28
10795 Davis Dr. (Mansell Rd.), Alpharetta, 770-992-5566
2830 Windy Hill Rd. (I-75), Marietta, 770-984-8899
5635 Jimmy Carter Blvd. (I-85), Norcross, 770-849-0600
www.pappas.com
"N'Awlins meets Hotlanta" at this threesome of outposts of an "above average" Texas-based chain that "satisfy" surveyors with the "robust flavors" of "killer" Cajun-Creole seafood that comes "fried, fried or fried" in "huge" portions; "friendly" servers are "right on top of things" in "giant" "family-oriented dining rooms" with a "festive" air, but "unauthentic" "franchise" fare and "inept" service make some critics "want to cry."

Atlanta

| F | D | S | C |

Pappasito's Cantina   20 | 17 | 18 | $23
2788 Windy Hill Rd. (I-75), Marietta, 770-541-6100;
www.pappas.com
"Come hungry, very hungry" to this Marietta link in a Texas-based chain for "plentiful" portions of "dang tasty" Mexican eats and "awesome" margaritas; the service is "reliable" even when it's "busy", and it gets "noisy" in the space that resembles a "south-of-the-border" "Applebee's", where live mariachis on Fridays add to the "festive atmosphere."

PARK 75   27 | 25 | 28 | $60
Four Seasons Atlanta, 75 14th St. (bet. Peachtree &
W. Peachtree Sts.), 404-253-3840; www.fourseasons.com
The "elegant" Four Seasons "lives up to its image" with this "flawless" New American showcasing the "extraordinary flavors" of chef Robert Gerstenecker's "sublime" cuisine, including a "beyond-belief brunch"; the service is "off the charts", mapping "power meals" for "neighborhood lawyers, bankers, headhunters" and other "who's who" guests who gather for "white-tablecloth dining" in the "handsomely appointed" room; P.S. the "divine" chef's table in the kitchen is a "fantastic experience."

Pasta da Pulcinella   23 | 17 | 19 | $23
1123 Peachtree Walk (bet. 12th & 13th Sts.), 404-876-1114
"Pasta heaven" is what devotees dub this Midtown Northern Italian offering a "small but wonderful" menu of "amazing" dishes that "make hearts soar", including the signature apple and sausage ravioli that some pastafarians praise as "the best around"; it's set in a "pretty" "converted house" tucked away in a "puzzle of small streets" "behind mega towers" that makes for a "cozy" "romantic" setting, and it's a "good value" to boot.

Pasta Vino   18 | 9 | 15 | $19
Peachtree Battle Shopping Ctr., 2391 Peachtree Rd.
(Peachtree Battle Ave.), 404-231-4946
11130 State Bridge Rd. (Kimball Bridge Rd.), Alpharetta,
770-777-1213
"You see the same faces week after week" at this "basic red-sauce" pair in Alpharetta and Buckhead that "never changes", serving "fabulous" pizzas and "decent" Italian eats "year after year"; "bustling servers keep the place lively" and "outdoor dining" is a plus, but while the "family-friendly" atmosphere pleases the "PTA crowd", others complain about "kids running amok"; still, most agree it's one of the "best values in town."

Pastis   22 | 17 | 18 | $33
936 Canton St. (Magnolia St.), Roswell, 770-640-3870;
www.roswellpastis.com
"Ah, I'm in France" swoon fans of this "charming" bistro in the center of "old town" Roswell that serves up "excel-

vote at zagat.com

Atlanta   F | D | S | C

lent" French cuisine and an "eclectic" wine list; patrons choose between the "fantastic" upstairs balcony and "nice" downstairs lounge that's "not flooded with immature bar-hoppers"; a "bright and airy Mediterranean feel" fills the "slightly shabby" "white-tablecloth" setting; N.B. mid-*Survey* chef and owner changes are not reflected in the above scores.

Paul's   ▽ 26 | 20 | 23 | $41
10 Kings Circle (Pine Circle), 404-231-4113; www.thechefpaul.com

"Yea, he's back" cheer champions of longtime Atlanta culinary "godfather" Paul Albrecht (ex Pano's & Paul's, Spice) who's "made a good move" with this new South Buckhead American "winner" that "should be right at the top" "in due time"; housed in a popular two-story space in an "out-of-the-way" "Intown" neighborhood, it may still be "working out the kinks", but loyal fans are "keeping an eye on it."

Penang   23 | 15 | 19 | $18
Orient Ctr., 4897 Buford Hwy. NE (Chamblee Tucker Rd.), Chamblee, 770-220-0308

Fans tout this Buford Highway "standout" as a "solid" choice delivering "consistently" "tasty" Malaysian and Thai fare that makes for a "fine foreign feast" to "share" with "friends"; a "helpful" staff guides you through dozens of "exotic specialties", including "exceptional dirt cheap lunch options"; the "wonderfully tacky" "tropical" decor may be "cartoon"-like, but everything else is the "real deal."

Persepolis   ▽ 21 | 13 | 17 | $24
6435 E. Roswell Rd. (Abernathy Rd.), 404-257-9090

"The food will take you to another place and time" at this "delicious" Sandy Springs Persian where "kebabs rule" but there are "lots" of other "amazing" "taste sensations" that will "make you want more", including an "ample" lunch buffet spread; sure, the strip-mall space "could do with a sprucing up", but the "quality" fare and "delightful" service make it "well worth a visit."

Petite Auberge ⓈⒸ   18 | 14 | 20 | $31
Toco Hills Shopping Ctr., 2935 N. Druid Hills Rd. (Lavista Rd.), 404-634-6268; www.petiteauberge.com

This Toco Hills Continental garners a "loyal following of Decatur matrons", "retirees" and others who appreciate the "consistent" "old-world" cuisine devoid of "experimental pretense" and "old-fashioned formal service"; "yeah, the place looks a little dated", but "it still has heart", which "makes up for a lot of things."

P.F. Chang's China Bistro   20 | 20 | 18 | $25
500 Ashwood Pkwy. (Ashford Dunwoody Rd.), 770-352-0500
7925 North Point Pkwy. (Mansell Rd.), Alpharetta, 770-992-3070

Atlanta   F | D | S | C

(continued)
P.F. Chang's China Bistro
*Mall of Georgia, 3333 Buford Dr. NE (Mall of Georgia Dr.),
Buford, 678-546-9005
www.pfchangs.com*

You "know what you're going to get" at this "mainstream" Mandarin trio – namely, a "wide variety" of "addictive", "Americanized" Chinese fare, including "legendary" lettuce wraps that are "worth the waits" and "huge crowds"; the surroundings are "elegant" yet "casual" and service is "friendly", though it sometimes "disappoints", and while some purists dismiss it as "Asian food for amateurs", defenders insist it's "not bad for a chain."

Pho Hoa   ▽ 23 | 5 | 13 | $10
Asian Sq., 5150 Buford Hwy. (I-285), Doraville, 770-455-8729

"One of the oldest in town and still the best" according to phonatics, this Buford Highway Vietnamese "does it right", serving "consistently good", "healthy" pho "without pretension"; while the service and decor barely register with surveyors, the "great value" fare makes it a spot "well worth tracking down."

Pho 79   ▽ 21 | 8 | 18 | $13
*Plaza Fiesta, 4166 Buford Hwy. NE (Clairmont Rd.), Doraville,
404-728-9129*

For "adventurous" "comfort food" "transcending ethnicity" this "excellent" Buford Highway Vietnamese is the "real thing" offering "traditional" fare, including "superb" pho, to the strains of "karaoke" and "Vietnamese music videos"; the "motherly" owner "chats amiably" with fans who deem this one "worth the drive."

Phuket Thai ⊠   20 | 16 | 19 | $17
2839 Buford Hwy. NE (N. Druid Hills Rd.), 404-325-4199

Fans "have fun" just "pronouncing the name" of this "often overlooked" Buford Highway Thai and "rave" about the "divine" cuisine that's both "plentiful" and "inexpensive", washed down with "their own" microbrew beer from Bangkok; "attentive" service makes it a "special dining treat" despite the "crummy strip-mall" space with "dingy Oriental" decor "circa 1950s."

PieBar ☻   13 | 22 | 14 | $26
2160 Monroe Dr. NE (Monroe Pl.), 404-815-1605; www.piebar.com

Aesthetes applaud the "unique" conversion of the former bank in Midtown housing this "über-hip" New American, where a "mix of urban, Buckhead and gay" clientele gathers to "see and be seen" over drinks and "funky" pizzas topped with "everything from rabbit to quail eggs"; but "too much weirdness does not a good pie make" sniff critics who carp over "style over substance", "clueless" service and a room buzzing with "more noise than a 757."

vote at zagat.com

Atlanta   F D S C

Pig-N-Chik   20 7 14 $12
Fountain Oaks Shopping Ctr., 4920 Roswell Rd. NE
(Long Island Dr.), 404-255-6368
5071 Peachtree Industrial Blvd. (Clairmont Rd.), Chamblee,
404-869-0038
www.pignchik.net
The pit masters at this smoky pair in Sandy Springs and Chamblee have "turned BBQ into a science", creating "pure pulled [pork] pleasure" that "lives up to the hype" and Brunswick stew "with a kick"; the "simple" decor isn't an "issue since you're in and out in no time", but if it is, "carryout" is "as good as dine in" – either way, it's "dependable and cheap."

Pittypat's Porch   16 16 15 $32
25 Andrew Young International Blvd. NW (Spring St.),
404-525-8228
"Hoop skirts and magnolia blossoms will have you whistling Dixie" at this Downtown "institution" where "classic" Southern fare and an interior that "evokes images of *Gone With the Wind*" make it a "must see" for "newbies to Atlanta"; skeptics dismiss it as a "tourist trap with all the trimmings" that "might have been good in Margaret Mitchell's day", but now "the bloom is off the mint julep."

Pleasant Peasant   20 17 20 $30
555 Peachtree St. NE (Linden Ave.), 404-874-3223;
www.thepeasantrestaurants.com
While it may "not [be] edgy", for "consistency and value" this veteran Midtown American is "still a winner", and the "perfect choice" for "business" lunches and pre- and après- "Fox" or "symphony"; the "intimate" setting is "upscale" but "relaxed", and while a few feel it's getting "tired", for many others it remains a "nostalgic favorite."

Portofino   21 19 21 $36
3199 Paces Ferry Pl. (bet. E. Andrews Dr. & W. Paces Ferry Rd.),
404-231-1136; www.portofinobistro.com
A "well-rounded menu" of "dynamite" Italian fare, and "extensive wines by the glass" and flights from the "excellent" "but inexpensive" list are the "real attraction" of this "charming" Buckhead venue, although "'tis a dream to dine in the spring" on the "lovely" "brick" patio "under the trees" as well; the "splendid" staff "tries hard" to please, and prices that "won't break the bank" make it "a place to come back to again and again."

PRICCI   24 21 23 $42
500 Pharr Rd. (Maple Dr.), 404-237-2941;
www.buckheadrestaurants.com
"Everything old is new again" at this Buckhead Life Group Italian that "has morphed back onto the scene in a big way" thanks to "remarkable" chef Piero Premoli's "out-

Atlanta

standing" "old-country" fare and "exceptional" service that "makes you feel like royalty"; the city's "glitterati" goes for the "lively" scene amid "retro '80s glam" surroundings, where "comfortable booths" and an open kitchen add to the "cosmopolitan" setting, and while a few find it "overpriced", for the rest it remains a "keeper."

Prime | 24 | 21 | 21 | $44

Lenox Square Mall, 3393 Peachtree Rd. (Lenox Rd.), 404-812-0555; www.heretoserverestaurants.com

"Escape the crowds" of Lenox Square Mall for a "primo" experience at this "upscale" surf 'n' turf sibling of Goldfish, Twist, Shout and Strip, featuring "terrific" steaks, "fresh sushi to die for" and early-bird specials that are among the "best deals in town"; the servers are "attentive" yet "unobtrusive" (sometimes to the point of "disappearing") in the "spacious" room with "tall ceilings", where it's "always a scene" filled with a "sophisticated" "attractive" crowd.

Provisions to Go | ▽ 25 | 18 | 20 | $18

Westside Mktpl., 1198 Howell Mill Rd. (Huff Rd.), 404-365-0410; www.starprovisions.com

"Expect to be delighted" by the "gourmet carryout" at this Westside market by the owners of Bacchanalia, who have done a "real service to the community" by offering "great deli" items, "off-the-chart pastries" and other "assorted delights" – if you can't wait, you can pull up a stool or a table outside; the rest of the space offers an "eclectic selection" of "gifts for that unique someone on your list", making it easy to "come for cheese and leave with a blender."

P.R.'s Barbeque | ▽ 17 | 12 | 16 | $11

867 Buford Rd. (Atlanta Hwy.), Cumming, 770-844-9446

While "locals" "still miss the old dive", this "new location" of the Cumming smoke shack is "better designed" and "clean", but it still serves "the same solid BBQ", slathered with "tasty" sauces, and "homemade sides" that keep 'cuennoisseurs coming "back again and again"; it may not be fancy but it's "filling and fast" and full of "local flavor."

Pung Mie | ▽ 21 | 18 | 20 | $20

5145 Buford Hwy. NE (Shallowford Rd.), Doraville, 770-455-0435

"Glam meets China" at one of Buford Highway's "longer running establishments", where the most "amazing" "dumplings in town", "buns to die for" and other "excellent" Chinese eats are delivered "fast" by waiters "who remember what you order"; add to that "clean" surroundings and you've got the makings of a "favorite" destination.

Pura Vida | 24 | 19 | 19 | $26

656 N. Highland Ave. NE (bet. North Ave. & Ponce de Leon Blvd.), 404-870-9797; www.puravidatapas.com

Amigos take their "hats off" to the "cutting-edge", "flat-out great" small-plate "inspirations" that come out of Hector

Atlanta

F | **D** | **S** | **C**

Santiago's kitchen at this Poncey-Highlands Pan-Latin venue, where "drinking consultants" concoct sangrias that "will rock your world" and the "best mojitos hands down"; snappy live music and lots of "salsa" dancing is common in the colorful dining room that's a "great place to celebrate anything", and an "enthusiastic" staff adds to the "vibe."

Pure Taqueria
21 | 18 | 16 | $18

103 Roswell St. (Old Milton Pkwy.), Alpharetta, 678-240-0023
Arguably "the hippest new restaurant" on the north side, this "upscale" Alpharetta taqueria from the owners of Van Gogh's, Aspen's and Vinny's on Windward is dishing out "unique" Mexican cuisine full of "new and inventive flavors" in a "renovated" warehouse structure named after the old gas station next door; while some feel it "needs to work on staff training", pros promise a "magical" experience.

QUINONES ROOM AT BACCHANALIA ⊠
28 | 27 | 28 | $122

Courtyard of Bacchanalia, 1198 Howell Mill Rd. NW (bet. 14th & Huff Sts.), 404-365-0410; www.starprovisions.com
Bacchanalia may have "one-upped" itself with this "truly remarkable" New American prix fixe–only "experience" in the same Westside complex, where "every bite" offers an "unforgettably superb taste" and "fantastic wine pairings" "won't disappoint"; "impeccable", "synchronized" service and a "gorgeous", "intimate" room with "wonderful linens" add to the "$$$'s no object special-occasion" experience that's "worth every penny" according to fans, who feel it should be on everyone's "once-before-I-die list."

Raging Burrito
19 | 14 | 16 | $12

141 Sycamore St. (Church St.), Decatur, 404-377-3311; www.ragingburrito.com
"If you like burritos without the big corporate spin", this Decatur Cal-Mex "may be the border for you to cross", serving "overflowing" "custom-made" eponymous eats, "tasty" margaritas and a "great selection of microbrews" and draught beers; the "hip" staff is a little "slow" but "tourists", "business" types and "college students on a budget" manage to "chill" anyway in the "grubby-pubby" digs or outside on one of the "best" patios "on the square."

Rainbow Restaurant ⊠
▽ 18 | 5 | 16 | $10

(fka Rainbow Natural Foods)
North Decatur Plaza, 2118 N. Decatur Rd. (Clairmont Rd.), Decatur, 404-633-3538; www.rainbowgrocery.com
"Delicious", "healthy" vegetarian fare at a "reasonable" price can be found at this venue housed in a Decatur natural foods store; little more than a "prefab paneled corner" with salad and hot bars and a few tables, it's "not the best atmosphere" around, but the "takeout is a timesaver" for residents in the area.

Atlanta

F | **D** | **S** | **C**

Rainwater ⓈⒻ   23 | 24 | 23 | $40
11655 Haynes Bridge Rd. (Rainwater Dr.), Alpharetta, 770-777-0033; www.rainwaterrestaurant.com

"It'll never rain on your parade" at this "beautiful" Alpharetta New American with a "Southern touch" showcasing chef Jay Swift's "exquisitely prepared" cuisine in a "gorgeous" "villa"-esque setting; it may "look imposing" from the outside, but "lovely small dining areas" and "incredible" service with a "personal touch" make it a "quiet" "treat" whether for a "romantic dinner for two or a business dinner for 20."

Raja Indian   ▽ 21 | 10 | 19 | $25
2955 Peachtree Rd. NE (bet. Peachtree Ave. & Pharr Rd.), 404-237-2661

"Amazing" tikka masala and other "old-fashioned" dishes served by a "no-nonsense" staff make dining "truly enjoyable" at this Buckhead Indian, where the kitchen can accommodate even the most "wimpy" of palates; it's "nothing too fancy", just a "relaxed" and "reliable" "neighborhood" option that's "always a pleasure."

RATHBUN'S Ⓢ   28 | 25 | 25 | $45
Stove Works, 112 Krog St. NE (bet. Edgewood Ave. NE & Irwin St. NE), 404-524-8280; www.rathbunsrestaurant.com

Aficionados aver "the raves are true" about this "trendy but not pretentious" New American in a "refurbished industrial area" of Inman Park that "leaves the hip pretenders in the dust" thanks to Kevin Rathbun's "spectacular", "visually appealing" "creations" from daily "hand-scrawled" menus that offer "something for everyone" and "every budget", topped off with "small and perfect" desserts; "homey" "greetings from the man himself" are part of the "charming" service, and the "beautiful" "rehabbed stove plant" resonates with a "lively" vibe (but "bad acoustics") that "makes life seem glam and fun."

Ray's in the City   22 | 18 | 19 | $32
240 Peachtree St. NE (bet. Andrew Young Int'l Blvd. & Harris St.), 404-524-9224; www.raysrestaurants.com

This urban version of "uptown brother" Ray's on the River is "much needed" on the Downtown scene, "pleasantly surprising" nine-to-fivers with a "variety" of "super-fresh" and "beautifully prepared" seafood and sushi; "reasonable prices" and "courteous" "quick" service make it "great for a business lunch" or "quiet dinner", but foes find the "inconsistent" fare a bit fishy.

Ray's Killer Creek   23 | 23 | 22 | $39
(fka Killer Creek Chophouse)
1700 Mansell Rd. (GA 400), Alpharetta, 770-649-0064; www.raysrestaurants.com

"Do suburbanites deserve such luxuries?" ponder OTPers about this "excellent" steakhouse in Alpharetta (sibling of

vote at zagat.com   95

Atlanta

F | D | S | C

Ray's on the River and in the City) that reduces the "need to drive down 400" for "damn good" "prime" steaks at "decent prices"; the "beautiful" "rustic" setting is one of the "best looking rooms in the 'burbs" and a "favorite refuge" of many, and the staff is "knowledgeable", though some feel it could use "more personality."

Ray's New York Pizza
16 | 6 | 12 | $12

3021 Peachtree Rd. (Pharr Rd.), 404-364-0960
Sandy Spring Plaza, 6309 Roswell Rd. (Mt. Vernon Rd.), 404-252-9888
5230 Windward Pkwy. W. (GA 400), Alpharetta, 770-521-0222

"If you can't make it to NY for pizza", this "no-frills" trio is the "next best thing" according to pie-sanos who swear by its "delicious" "thin-crust" creations with "quality toppings"; "delivery" is "best" for those put off by "divey" digs and "very slow" service, but while it's a "decent pie for the South" that "works just fine" for many, purists sniff "I'm from NY, and it's not."

Ray's on the River
21 | 22 | 20 | $35

6700 Powers Ferry Rd. (I-285), 770-955-1187;
www.raysrestaurants.com

"Class on the Chattahoochee" is how fans describe this "old-school" Cobb County seafooder serving "fresh", "handsomely presented" fin fare in a "beautiful" setting with "great views of the river"; even though it can get "crowded" (it's a "favorite" "prom" and "graduation" spot), a "cheery" staff delivers "top-notch" service, but some still find the whole affair "overpriced"; P.S. the "amazing" Sunday brunch is "one of the best in town."

Real Chow Baby, The
18 | 16 | 16 | $18

1016 Howell Mill Rd. NW (10th St.), 404-815-4900;
www.therealchowbaby.com

"Let out your inner chef" and "make it the way you like it" at this American "twist on Mongolian BBQ" where Westsiders line up, "bowl" in hand, at the stir-fry bar loaded with "plenty of veggies", "fresh" "protein" and a "great selection of sauces and spices" that get cooked up on a large grill; the industrial, "fast-foody" space accommodates "huge crowds" and "patient" servers explain the drill, and "if you don't like the food, it's your own fault."

Real Food
17 | 17 | 16 | $24

3070 Windward Plaza (Windward Concourse), Alpharetta, 770-442-3123; www.realfoodeatery.com

"Families", "locals" and the OTP "business" set "luv" this "little sister to Horseradish Grill" in Alpharetta for its "homey" Southern fare that's "belly-filling good" and blueplate specials that are an "excellent value", served in a "tasteful" space with a "great fireplace"; but "unprofessional" service and "bland" cooking rile razzers.

Atlanta

F | D | S | C

Red and Green Pan Asian ▽ 20 | 24 | 19 | $33
4160 Old Milton Pkwy. (State Bridge Rd.), Alpharetta, 770-667-7711; www.redandgreenpanasian.com
"Each mouthful is a treat" at this new Alpharetta Pan-Asian that creates "delights for the palate and the eyes" that are "arrayed like photo shoots on designer plates"; the "serene" "white-tablecloth" room with a "Zen-like class" and the "coolest decor" in the area and the "accommodating" staff also make it stand out in a "row of chain" restaurants.

Redfish, a Creole Bistro – | – | – | M
687 Memorial Dr. SE (Cameron St. SE), 404-475-1200; www.redfishcreole.com
Jack Sobel (of Agave) and Gregg Herndon (ex Tiburon Grille) team up to bring this Cajun-Creole newcomer to Grant Park, where the seafood-heavy menu features classics such as étouffée, jambalaya and gumbo, which can be washed down with Louisiana-bred libations such as Abita Turbodog beer and hurricanes; the warm yellow space is adorned with aquariums and a rotating collection of well-chosen local art, and an outdoor patio and easy parking are added bonuses.

Red Snapper 22 | 11 | 20 | $25
2100 Cheshire Bridge Rd. (Lavista Rd.), 404-634-8947; www.redsnapperatlanta.com
Fans exhort "channel your inner geezer" and dive into this Cheshire Bridge seafooder that "hasn't changed in umpteen years" and is still "flooring" fans with "delicious" fin fare ("how many ways can they prepare red snapper?") that "really appeals to the older set" but which "trendy reviewers" just "don't get"; the service is "efficient and attentive", and the space "doesn't look like much from the outside", while inside is a "step back in time" to the "early '80s."

Repast ⊠ – | – | – | M
620 Glen Iris Dr. NE (North Ave.), 404-870-8707; www.repastrestaurant.com
Spouses Joe Truex and Mihoko Obunai are honoring their vows – as trained chefs – at this establishment in the Ponce Springs Lofts in Midtown where they create edgy New American cuisine featuring globally sourced ingredients; the casual yet cutting-edge two-story industrial space features exposed concrete, wooden beams and a gleaming open kitchen punctuated by a huge column, and there's also an outdoor lounge.

RESTAURANT EUGENE 26 | 25 | 24 | $56
The Aramore, 2277 Peachtree Rd. (Peachtree Memorial Dr.), 404-355-0321; www.restauranteugene.com
"Tradition and innovation pat each other on the back" in the kitchen of this "first-class" New American in South Buckhead where the "husband-and-wife duo has got it

vote at zagat.com

Atlanta F | D | S | C

going on" with a "constantly changing menu" of "fresh", Southern accented fare emphasizing "local" ingredients and an "impressive boutique wine list"; "impeccable" service "makes everyone feel special and welcome" in the "beautiful" "quiet" room, and satisfied surveyors go so far as to say it's "a pleasure to pay the bill."

Ria's Bluebird   22 | 14 | 17 | $12
421 Memorial Dr. SE (Cherokee Ave.), 404-521-3737; www.riasbluebird.com
"Meat eaters and vegheads" alike feel "at home" at this "popular" "bohemian" diner in Cabbagetown that offers "fantastic" all-day breakfast fare and "scrumptious" "vegetarian options", served by a "sassy, no-nonsense" staff that's "brusque" – "in a good way"; the "cozy-hippie" spot near "historic" Oakland Cemetery sports a cheery "expanse of floor-to-ceiling windows" that cast light on "great people-watching" and "piercings" and "tattoo" spotting, but "be prepared" to "wait on weekends."

Rib Ranch   ▽ 19 | 14 | 18 | $15
2063 Canton Rd. (Sandy Plains Rd.), Marietta, 770-422-5755; www.theribranch.com
It may be "in the middle of nowhere", but this "friendly" Marietta BBQ is the center of the universe for longtime fans who make the "tender" "saucy" beef and "Texas-style" ribs a "part of all family functions"; a "new expansion" brings a "plasma TV" that "kills the old roadhouse feel" to some degree, but there's still "tons of junk to look at on the walls", such as snakes and license plates.

Rice Thai Cuisine ⊠   22 | 17 | 22 | $25
1104 Canton St. (Woodstock St.), Roswell, 770-640-0788; www.goforthai.com
"Sit on the porch" and "watch Roswell go by" at this "fantastic" Thai that comes "highly recommended" by "regulars" who relish the "wonderfully subtle" "gourmet" fare and "pleasant greetings" from the "polite" staff; "original art" on the walls adds an "interesting" touch to the "charming bungalow" that sits "in the heart" of this "historic" town.

Righteous Room ☻   16 | 10 | 13 | $16
1051 Ponce de Leon Ave. NE (N. Highland Ave.), 404-874-0939
It may be "funky to the max", but this Poncey-Highlands strip-mall watering hole is a "must visit" for many, serving "cheap drinks" and some of the "best bar food in Atlanta", including "healthy" options such as the "incredible" veggie burgers; "slackers" and "theater"-goers put up with "hit-or-miss" service in the "dark", "smoky" space.

Rio Grande Cantina   13 | 12 | 14 | $17
3227 Roswell Rd. (Peachtree Rd.), 404-237-3243
"While nothing fancy", this Roswell Road cantina is popular for its "large front deck" overlooking Buckhead's bus-

Atlanta   F | D | S | C

tle, where families with "kids" and the "happy-hour" gang dig into basic "Mex with a little Tex" – but "get there early" on hopping nights since it gets "jam-packed"; critics who pan the fare as "poor" prefer to "pass on dinner and go straight to the margaritas."

Rising Roll Sandwich Co. ⊠   21 | 13 | 20 | $11
Atlantic Center Plaza Bldg., 1180 W. Peachtree St. (14th St.), 404-815-6787
11417 Haynes Bridge Rd. (GA 400), Alpharetta, 770-752-8082
832 Virginia Ave. (Doug Davis Dr.), Hapeville, 404-669-1170
1812 N. Brown Rd. (Sugarloaf Pkwy. NW), Lawrenceville, 678-847-6088
www.risingroll.com
The lunch bunch "can't get enough of" this deli foursome that "hits all the right notes" with a "mind-boggling" selection of "exceptional" "huge" sandwiches made with "best in class" bread baked "daily on-site", as well as other "fantastic lunch options", doled out by a "friendly" crew; they're "always busy for a reason", and while wallet-watchers claim "prices have crept into the realm of gasp", satisfied sorts insist "you get what you pay for."

Ritz-Carlton Atlanta Grill   24 | 24 | 23 | $53
Ritz-Carlton Atlanta, 181 Peachtree St. NE (Ellis St.), 404-659-0400; www.ritzcarlton.com
Be it for a "business lunch", "high tea", "after-hour cocktails" or a "romantic" dinner behind "red curtains" in their "private" "cheater booth", this "exquisite" Downtown hotel dining room delivers with "delicious" Southern fare and "white-glove" (albeit sometimes "slow") service; even "eating alone becomes a pleasure" in the "lovely room", and "excellent veranda views" make for "great people-watching" on the streets below.

Ritz-Carlton Buckhead Café   24 | 24 | 25 | $48
Ritz-Carlton Buckhead, 3434 Peachtree Rd. NE (Lenox Rd.), 404-237-2700; www.ritzcarlton.com
Waiters who say "my pleasure" add to the "perfection" of this "elegant" all-day cafe that's fitting for "business" or "social" meals of "consistently excellent" Continental cuisine, and the "extensive" "killer brunch" is the "best in Atlanta, hands down" according to fans; the "quiet" "luxurious" setting is appropriate for the "razzle-dazzle" clientele, though some find it a bit "stuffy", and "pleased" patrons concede it's "worth the fortune charged."

RITZ-CARLTON BUCKHEAD   28 | 27 | 28 | $82
DINING ROOM ⊠
Ritz-Carlton Buckhead, 3434 Peachtree Rd. NE (Lenox Rd.), 404-237-2700; www.ritzcarlton.com
Near "perfect from beginning to end", this "elegant", upscale "grande dame" was voted Atlanta's No. 1 for Service

Atlanta

F | D | S | C

thanks to a "kind" and "impeccable" staff that "makes all diners feel special", a "knowledgeable" sommelier who is "helpful" with her "wine novella" and "the best maitre d' in town"; chef Arnaud Berthelier's New French–Med cuisine "holds a universe of remarkable flavors" that are "simply unforgettable" and the green damask setting with "cozy" booths is another "treat for the senses" that "makes you feel like a Rockefeller"; N.B. jackets required.

River Room
21 | 21 | 20 | $36

Riverside by Post, 4403 Northside Pkwy. NW (bet. Chattahoochee River & Mt. Paran Rd.), 404-233-5455; www.riverroom.com

The signature "crab cakes alone are reason to find" this "tremendous" Vinings New American where the "revamped menu" is "more interesting" than ever, making it a "solid" choice for "business lunches" and "first dates", in a location "convenient" for folks "in the 'burbs to meet friends from the city"; while the service can be "inconsistent", the "delightful town square" setting near the Chattahoochee is "awesome."

Roasted Garlic
20 | 15 | 18 | $24

Alpharetta Square Shopping Ctr., 281 S. Main St. (Old Milton Pkwy.), Alpharetta, 770-777-9855

"Don't eat all day, you'll need the room" for the "huge portions" of "delicious" Italian-Mediterranean cuisine crafted from "original recipes" served up at this Alpharetta "gem" (but you'd better "like garlic"); though it's "crammed into the corner" of a shopping center, many agree it's a "great escape from the chains" as well as an "excellent value."

Roasters
19 | 11 | 19 | $14

2770 Lenox Rd. NE (Buford Hwy.), 404-237-1122
6225B Roswell Rd. NE (Johnson Ferry Rd.), 678-701-1100
Abbotts Vlg., 11585 Jones Bridge Rd. (Abbotts Bridge Rd.), Alpharetta, 770-753-0055
2997 Cumberland Blvd. (Cumberland Mall), Smyrna, 770-333-6222
www.roastersfresh.com

"Pig out and still feel self righteous" at this American quartet praised for its "healthy" "rotisserie-style" fare, including "succulent" "chicken any which way", "excellent homestyle veggies" and "mighty tasty" complimentary corn muffins; "fast", "friendly" and "easy on the pocketbook", they're "dependable" options for a "family" meal or a snack after the "gym", so decor that deserves a "negative" score doesn't deter fans.

Rolling Bones Premium Pit BBQ
22 | 15 | 15 | $14

377 Edgewood Ave. SE (Jackson St.), 404-222-2324; www.rollingbonesbbq.com

"Craveable" Texas-style BBQ with a "Caribbean" accent is on offer at this Downtown pit stop, including "fantastic

Atlanta

| F | D | S | C |

fall-off-the-bone" ribs and "heaping plates" of "smoky" pork "hand chopped" by a "friendly" "server so adept with his knife" that "you're glad he's smiling"; the converted gas station sports "lots of glass and chrome", making it "the shiniest building" in this "up-and-coming" neighborhood, and there's also drive-thru, though "slow" service makes it "more like a park-thru" at times.

Roman Lily Cafe | 18 | 12 | 17 | $19 |
668 Highland Ave. (Sampson St.), 404-653-1155
The food "shines" at this "funky" Inman Park Eclectic, an "old reliable" in the neighborhood for "simple" and "tasty" "comfort food" "with a home-cooked feel to it", which also comes in "half-portions"; the "quirky bathrooms" are "worth checking out", but otherwise the decor is "easy going" to the point of "shabby", and while the staff may be "pierced and tattooed", it is "friendly."

Rosa Mexicano | – | – | – | E |
245 18th St. (17th St.), 404-347-4090
The NYC–based Mexican makes its first foray into the deep South with this Atlantic Station outpost that serves high-end south-of-the-border cuisine, including guacamole made tableside in impressive *molcajetes* (lava-rock mortars), signature pomegranate margaritas and unique specialties such as a layered tortilla pie with shredded chicken, Chihuahua cheese and chile poblano sauce; warm hues, glowing lights and an 18-foot waterfall wall sculpture add to the drama.

Roy's | 23 | 22 | 22 | $45 |
3475 Piedmont Rd. NE (Lenox Rd.), 404-231-3232;
www.roysrestaurant.com
"Fantastic Asian fusion" cuisine does the Hawaiian "hula" at this "delightful" Buckhead link in a "first-class chain" that's "less time consuming than a trip to the islands", and while you won't get the "amazing sunsets" you will find "beautifully crafted" dishes of "fresh" fish and "memorable sushi" delivered with "aloha" service; "linger in the bar" or "comfortable" outdoor patio for "elegant skyline drinks" and expect a "lovely" "tropical environment" despite the "strange" "office park" location.

R. Thomas Deluxe Grill ◐ | 19 | 18 | 17 | $17 |
1812 Peachtree Rd. NW (bet. Collier Rd. & 26th St.),
404-881-0246; www.rthomasdeluxegrill.com
It's "like stepping through the looking glass" at this "funky" 24/7 South Buckhead "destination for homeopaths and granolaheads" that "caters to anyone's taste" with "tasty" New American and vegetarian fare; "eclectic" waiters blend in with a "bohemian" outdoor scene that also includes "gorgeous" live birds, "psychics" and "lawn ornaments" – "what more could you want late at night?"

Atlanta   F | D | S | C

Ru San's   18 | 12 | 16 | $20
Ansley Sq., 1529 Piedmont Rd. NE (Monroe Dr.), 404-875-7042
Tower Pl., 3365 Piedmont Rd. NE (Peachtree Rd. NE), 404-239-9557
2313 Windy Hill Rd. SE (Cobb Pkwy.), Marietta, 770-933-8315
This "American-friendly" Japanese trio is "immensely popular" for its "enormous menu" of "sushi with training wheels" (read: "cooked fish"), "unusual" "cross-cultural rolls" and "super" lunch buffet, served in a "rowdy" setting with "techno music", a "spirited" staff and the "highest decibels in town"; purists pan the "yard-sale quality" eats, but if you "don't take it too seriously", it's "a riot" – and a "cheap" one at that.

Rustic Gourmet Ⓢ   ▽ 25 | 21 | 25 | $32
FloatAway Bldg., 1145 Zonolite Rd. NE (Briarcliff Rd.),
404-881-1288; www.rusticgourmet.com
A "lovely find" in an industrial section near Emory, this "delightfully different" New American offers "limited" but "satisfying" prix fixe menus "determined daily" by "what's fresh", and a "well-selected" and "affordable" wine list; the "low-key" setting is "conducive to conversation" and provides a "nice escape from the normal Atlanta din"; N.B. there's a specialty wine shop on-site.

RUTH'S CHRIS STEAK HOUSE   23 | 19 | 22 | $53
Atlanta Plaza, 950 E. Paces Ferry Rd. (Lenox Rd.), 404-365-0660
Embassy Suites Hotel, 267 Marietta St. (International Blvd.), 404-223-6500
5788 Roswell Rd. (I-285, exit 25), 404-255-0035
www.ruthschris.com
Carnivores crow "you just can't go wrong" with these "solid" links of the steakhouse chain offering "mouthwatering" steaks in "sizzling butter" and "excellent sides", served by a "professional" staff in a "dark" "businessman setting" that's "not as stuffy" as you might expect; foes, however, feel the "marginal" fare and "obsequious" service "don't measure up" to the "big prices."

Sage on Sycamore   21 | 21 | 20 | $25
121 Sycamore St. (Church St.), Decatur, 404-373-5574;
www.thebistros.com
For a bit of "laid-back luxury", Decaturites descend on this New American in the historic town square for "delicious" eats at "excellent prices" "balanced by" a "great wine list", served by a "friendly" staff in a "warm", "easy environment"; while some sniff that it "never quite excites", most agree the "whole experience" is "always a good one."

Sala – Sabor de Mexico   19 | 20 | 19 | $28
1186 N. Highland Ave. NE (Amsterdam Ave.), 404-872-7203;
www.sala-atlanta.com
At this Fifth Group production in Va-Highlands, an "authentic Mexican experience, from margaritas to mole", can be

Atlanta F | D | S | C

had in a "very cool" space" "right out of South Beach", featuring "delicious", "upscale" fare, "killer" margaritas "shaken at the table", an "amazing selection" of tequilas, a "big wine list" and "polished" service; "live music" Thursday nights is a "big plus" and the outdoor patio is a "perfect way to spend a sunny afternoon."

Sal Grosso ▽ 19 | 18 | 23 | $39
1927 Powers Ferry Rd. SE (Windy Hill Rd.), 770-850-1540; www.salgrosso.com

"When you have a hankering for every type of meat possible", fans recommend this Cobb County outpost of a Sao Paolo–based churrascaria chain offering an "overwhelming" array of "amazing" cuts and "delicious" salad bar; "you feel welcome the moment you walk in" thanks to the "unassuming attitude" of the "good-looking" gauchos; "go at lunchtime for the best deal" counsel cognoscenti.

Salsa ⓢ ▽ 15 | 17 | 14 | $15
Howell Mill Vlg., 2020 Howell Mill Rd. NW (Collier Rd.), 404-352-3101
749 Moreland Ave. SE (Ormewood Ave.), 404-624-3105

The "Caribbean"-accented Cuban cuisine is "just outside the mainstream" at this family-owned South Buckhead venue and its East Atlanta younger sibling, which deliver "consistent" eats that make folks "want to come back for more"; colorful paintings add some warmth to the setting, but the cool staff "could be more friendly."

Salvatore Trattoria ⓢ ▽ 20 | 10 | 16 | $28
292 S. Atlanta St. (½ mi. south of Marietta Hwy.), Roswell, 770-645-9983

Regulars of this "down-home" Roswell red-sauce spot that's "always packed" praise the "authentic" eats that'll "save you a plane ride to Naples", at prices "you can't beat"; the "cramped quarters" "look like a dive", and while insiders appreciate the "personal service by the owner", newcomers find the staff "uncaring" "unless they know you."

Santoor Indian Cuisine ▽ 21 | 14 | 22 | $19
3050 Mansell Rd. (Old Alabama Connector), Alpharetta, 770-650-8802

"If it's Indian you're looking for", "call for directions" to this Alpharetta spot that's "difficult to track down", but worth the effort for "amazing", "fresh" fare and "personal" "service with a smile"; it's "not much to look at on the outside" but inside it's "full of expats" and "people who know" their tikka masala.

Savage Pizza 23 | 13 | 15 | $14
484 Moreland Ave. NE (bet. Euclid & Mansfield Aves.), 404-523-0500; www.savagepizza.com

With "more personality than your average pizza place", this "friendly neighborhood" "joint" full of "Little Five

vote at zagat.com

Atlanta

F D S C

Points charm" is "an experience that shouldn't be missed", featuring "fantastic" pizzas with "amazing toppings" and "perfect crusts"; a "tattooed and pierced" staff mans the "Generation X" digs where "comic book characters adorn the walls" and "old action figures" and "plastic toys" "keep the younger ones occupied."

Savu
▽ 17 | 19 | 17 | $38

W Hotel, 111 Perimeter Ctr. W. (Ashford Dunwoody Rd.), 770-280-0700; www.whotels.com

The only dining option in Dunwoody's "cool" W Hotel, this "very hip place" offers "imaginative" "Asian flavors" from a "thoughtful" (albeit "pricey") menu; the "minimalist" space features a "nice patio" with a fireplace, and while the "lobby ambiance" "doesn't work" for some, it "leaves nothing to be desired" for the rest.

Sawadee - A Taste of Thailand
▽ 20 | 14 | 18 | $18

Fountain Oaks Shopping Ctr., 4920 Roswell Rd. (Long Island Dr.), 404-303-1668

"The kitchen speaks for itself" at this Sandy Springs Thai serving "solid", "upscale" cuisine, including some "innovative" dishes; "personalized" attention from "the owner" is a plus, but service can be "slow" and the "standard storefront" decor fails to impress, which may be why some recommend it for "takeout."

Seasons de Provence ☒
▽ 27 | 22 | 25 | $36

4416 Senator Russell Sq. (Main St.), Acworth, 678-574-7188; www.seasonsdeprovence.com

"Culinarily deprived foodies of Cobb and Cherokee" counties count this "delightful" Provençal bistro in Acworth a "blessing", thanks to "excellent" cuisine, "exquisite" cheese and wine selections from "specific regions" of France, the "charming" owner who "enthusiastically welcomes" all and his "attentive" staff; despite its "strange location" in the "back of a building", it's an "overall great experience", so now many "Intown" folks no longer "mind driving OTP for dinner."

SEEGER'S ☒
27 | 25 | 26 | $101

111 W. Paces Ferry Rd. (E. Andrews Dr.), 404-846-9779; www.seegers.com

"Like being in Europe without having to clear customs", this Buckhead contemporary European is a "foodies' paradise" thanks to "genius" chef-owner Guenter Seeger, whose "love affair with food" shows up in "every luminous dish"; a "professional" staff delivers just the "right balance of attention and privacy" and the "stunning new decor" of the cozy house "envelops you" "like a dream"; a few wags rename it "Meagers" for the "small", "expensive" portions, but most laud it as an "elegant" "gift" that "could stand up anywhere in the world"; N.B. jackets required.

Atlanta

F | **D** | **S** | **C**

Shipfeifer on Peachtree
▽ 18 | 6 | 15 | $13
1814 Peachtree St. (Collier Rd.), 404-875-1106
Named after a tribe of gypsies, this South Buckhead Mediterranean has "passed the test of time" with "solid" and "inexpensive" eats, including "great gyros", that excuse the "quirky" service; despite being a "little tattered around the edges", it's a sunny spot on "busy" Peachtree that's "great" for "lunch"; N.B. it no longer serves alcohol.

Shorty's
▽ 22 | 16 | 20 | $18
2884 N. Druid Hills Rd. (Clairmont Rd.), Decatur, 404-315-6262
A "non-chain" newcomer with a "true neighborhood joint feel", this pizzeria near Toco Hills in Decatur makes fans "happy" with "excellent", "clever" pies from a wood-fired oven, the "freshest, most creative" salads "ever seen within 100 yards of a pizza" and "chunky, fresh" guacamole considered the "best in town"; expect a "surprisingly nice" "blue jeans setting", "friendly" servers and an owner who "actually cares if you had a great meal."

Shout
15 | 22 | 15 | $31
Colony Sq., 1197 Peachtree St. NE (14th St.), 404-846-2000; www.heretoserverestaurants.com
"It's all about the party" at Tom Catherall's Midtown Eclectic where a "cool" vibe resonates throughout the "chic", "eye-pleasing" Johnson Studio space that includes a "comfortable" dining room, "swanky" sushi lounge and rooftop bar with cabanas that evokes "Miami Beach"; small plates showcase a "hodgepodge" of cuisines from Europe and Asia, but it's "less about the food" – or the "mediocre service" – and "more about who's who" among the "young and beautiful" that people the "vibrant", "loud" scene – "there's a reason they call it 'Shout.'"

SIA'S
26 | 22 | 24 | $45
10305 Medlock Bridge Rd. (Wilson Rd.), Duluth, 770-497-9727; www.siasrestaurant.com
For "cutting-edge" cuisine "without the drive to Buckhead", aficionados recommend Sia Moshk's (also owner of Mitra) "wonderfully inventive" Asian-Southwestern in Duluth, an oasis of "flair and finesse" "in the midst of the big box chains" that delivers a "little spice" to the 'burbs; a "friendly" staff provides "consistent" service in an "attractive" "art deco"–inspired room – they "do it all well."

Silk
21 | 24 | 18 | $40
919 Peachtree St. NE (8th St.), 678-705-8888; www.silkrestaurant.com
"Hipsters and foodies can coexist" at this "funky" Pan-Asian (sibling of Hsu's and Pacific Rim) "in the heart of the thriving Midtown food scene", where "fusion and flair abound" in an abundance of "tasty" small plates, "fabulous sushi" and a "surprisingly innovative wine list"; the

vote at zagat.com   105

Atlanta

F | D | S | C

"gorgeous" space is "quiet" and "romantic", but an "overpriced" menu and "inconsistent" service mar an otherwise "awesome dining experience."

Silver Grill
▽ 21 | 12 | 21 | $13

900 Monroe Dr. NE (8th St.), 404-876-8145

"Everyone knows your name – and remembers it" at this cash-only Midtown "meat-and-three institution" that's been family-owned for three generations, where many of the "extraordinarily friendly waitresses" have also "been there for years"; "reasonably priced", "good old-fashioned" Southern victuals attract a "diverse crowd" of "families with kids", "drag queens", "blue- and white-collar" types and assorted "miscreants" who occupy the "old-time luncheonette" space.

Silver Skillet
16 | 9 | 16 | $12

200 14th St. NW (I-75), 404-874-1388; www.thesilverskillet.com

"Everyone should go at least once" – and "go hungry" – to this "legendary" Midtown diner where "business" diners, "academic types" and others "in-the-know" tuck their napkins in for "wonderful" "down-home" Southern cooking "with no pretense", including all-day "greasy spoon" breakfast "complete with grits and biscuits"; the staff is "priceless", and while it may be a "dingy" "dive", it's "a dive with history."

Simpatico
▽ 19 | 16 | 18 | $27

23 N. Park Sq. NE (bet. Cherokee & Church Sts.), Marietta, 770-792-9086; www.willieraes.com

At this family-owned Marietta New American, which "shares a space" with sibling Willie Rae's, an "imaginative" menu keeps fans "coming back for more" (signature "egg rolls" are a "favorite" of many), and you can order from either kitchen; "consistently good" performance makes locals "glad" to have it "in the area."

Six Feet Under
20 | 14 | 18 | $18

415 Memorial Dr. SE (Oakland Ave.), 404-523-6664; www.sixfeetunderatlanta.com

This "cleverly named" seafood "shack" in Grant Park near Oakland Cemetery "serves up anything that swims", as well as one of the "best burgers in Atlanta" and a "top-notch beer selection"; an "eclectic", "competent" staff mans the "friendly bar" and downstairs dining area to the beat of a "rockin' jukebox" or on the rooftop deck overlooking the graveyard, which is "not to be missed on a pretty day."

Slope's BBQ
18 | 11 | 17 | $11

The Springs, 200 Johnson Ferry Rd. NE (Sandy Spring Circle), 404-252-3220
5865 Gateway Dr. (Hwy. 9), Alpharetta, 678-393-1913
34 E. Crossville Rd. (Crabapple Rd.), Roswell, 770-518-7000

Atlanta

F | **D** | **S** | **C**

(continued)

Slope's BBQ
10020 Hwy. 92 (Hwy. 5/Canton Hwy.), Woodstock, 770-516-6789
www.slopesbbq.com

"Nothin' says luvin' like something from the pit" of this "inexpensive" 'cue quartet that injects a little "personality in the chain-infested suburbs" with "flavorful" BBQ and "excellent" sides "prepared in true Southern style"; "counter service" is delivered with so much "country sarcasm" and "humor" that no one even notices the "bare-bones" decor.

Slovakia Restaurant
▽ 22 | 20 | 23 | $29

164 Roswell St. SE (Atlanta St.), Marietta, 770-792-4443;
www.slovakiarestaurant.com

For "a little bit of European class and hospitality" "in the suburbs", fans tout this "authentic" family-owned Eastern Euro spot in Marietta offering "healthy" portions of "surprisingly" "delicious" Slovakian eats, including "awesome" goulash, and "fantastic" desserts; owners "Stefan and Ivana are wonderful hosts" who provide "impeccable service" that makes "every diner feel like family."

Smokejack
19 | 17 | 18 | $21

29 S. Main St. (Old Milton Pkwy.), Alpharetta, 770-410-7611;
www.smokejackbbq.com

Owner "David Filipowicz has a winner" with this "upscale"-"casual" BBQ in a "great location" in historic Downtown Alpharetta where the "chef"-driven menu boasts "delicious" meats and "terrific" sides ("you have to try the fried pickles!"), served by a "friendly" staff in a "tasteful" renovated 1847 building; though foes fume over "exorbitant" prices, it's a "favorite" for the "horse and SUV set."

SoHo
22 | 19 | 21 | $35

Vinings Jubilee Shopping Ctr., 4300 Paces Ferry Rd. SE (Paces Mill Rd.), 770-801-0069; www.sohoatlanta.com

There's "no pretense to fine dining" at this "intimate" and "memorable" Vinings "hot spot", just an "interesting variety" of Eclectic dishes paired with an "amazing" wine list, and on Wednesday "flight nights", it's the "place to be"; oenophiles "learn a lot" from the "wine savvy" bartenders and appreciate the "energetic" vibe as well as the "good value" it offers.

Soleil
20 | 17 | 18 | $33

3081 Maple Dr. NE (E. Paces Ferry Rd.), 404-467-1790;
www.soleilbistro.com

The "wonderful" French fare is a "darn good value" at this bistro "tucked away" on a "quiet street behind the insanity of Buckhead", a "favorite" of many for Sunday brunch thanks to the "fabulous patio" fronting the "romantic" "old house"; "fantastic" service adds to the "charm", making this a "delightful place" for a "girlie lunch" or "pleasant light dinner."

vote at zagat.com

Atlanta

F | **D** | **S** | **C**

Son's Place ⊠⊅
▽ 19 | 8 | 14 | $12

100 Hurt St. NE (Dekalb Ave.), 404-581-0530

The "son of old Atlanta's favorite fryer" is cooking up batches of his own "soul food extraordinaire", including fried chicken "good enough to make you slap your mama", at this lunch-only meat and three in Inman Park; some find it "overpriced", while others say you "have to live in the city" to "appreciate" – and "find" – it.

SOTTO SOTTO ⊠
26 | 19 | 21 | $37

313 N. Highland Ave. NE (Elizabeth St.), 404-523-6678;
www.sottosottorestaurant.com

"Riccardo Ullio continues to set the bar" high for "elegant" Northern Italian cuisine with "dazzling performances in the kitchen" of his "super trattoria" that's the "highlight of Inman Park", where "heavenly" dishes are paired with a "well-chosen" wine list and the signature chocolate soup dessert is "divine"; the "courteous" service "seduces with small touches", "acoustical ceiling tiles" have "improved the din" in the "cozy" space and a "nifty little" patio offers a respite for "claustrophobics."

SOUPER JENNY ⊠⊅
24 | 14 | 20 | $11

Andrews Square Shopping Ctr., 56 E. Andrews Dr. NW (Roswell Rd.), 404-237-7687

"It's just soup, but it's just so-o good" gush groupies of this "'70s comfy-hip" Buckhead lunch spot that "doles out" "terrific fresh" bowls and other "outstanding", "healthy" fare in a recently expanded space; "free-spirited" Jenny is the "yang" to "NYC's Soup Nazi's yin" and her "hilarious, hyped-up" staff delivers "fast" service and the occasional song to those in the "lines out the door", and the "amazing" eats are "well worth" the "inconsistent hours"; N.B. now open Thursday nights.

SOUTH CITY KITCHEN
24 | 20 | 21 | $35

1144 Crescent Ave. NE (14th St.), 404-873-7358
1675 Cumberland Pkwy. (Atlanta Rd. SE), Smyrna, 770-435-0700
www.southcitykitchen.com

"Dixie meets Manhattan" at this "upscale" Midtown venue by the Fifth Group (Food Studio, La Tavola, Sala), a "long-term member of the can't-miss club" for fans of its "magnificent" "eclectic" Southern cuisine with a "new accent" brought to table by a "knowledgeable" staff; the renovated "old house" with a "trendy urban groove" can get "crowded" and "loud", but it's "worth enduring for the food"; N.B. a new location in Smyrna opened post-*Survey*.

South of France
17 | 15 | 17 | $32

Cheshire Square Shopping Ctr., 2345 Cheshire Bridge Rd. NE (Lavista Rd.), 404-325-6963

"Take a giant step back to 1979" at this Cheshire Bridge "sleeper" serving "warm and inviting" "butter-induced"

subscribe to zagat.com

Atlanta

F | D | S | C

French fare "that's so old-hat that it's almost new again" – and it "won't break the bank"; the setting is "quiet" and "romantic" with a "lovely" fireplace, and when singer Berne Poliakoff is there (Wednesdays–Saturdays) things get "surreal", but naysayers knock the "lackluster" food and beg "*plus ambiance s'il vous plaît.*"

Spice
20 | 22 | 19 | $41

793 Juniper St. NE (5th St.), 404-875-4242; www.spicerestaurant.com

"Impossibly hip", this "chic" Midtown New American is "what a trendy Intown" spot "should be" according to fans, with new chef Drew Van Leuvan's "well-thought-out" menu that "will tickle your tongue", served in a "modern" "stylish" space where "thirty- and fortysomethings" congregate; it can get "smoky" and "loud", however, and critics who find "too much attitude and not enough flavor" feel it's gotten "too cool for school."

Stoney River Legendary Steaks
24 | 22 | 22 | $39

5800 State Bridge Rd. (Medlock Bridge Rd.), Duluth, 770-476-0102
10524 Alpharetta Hwy. (E. Crossville Rd.), Roswell, 678-461-7900
www.stoneyriver.com

"Turn off the grill and head over" to this "serious" "mid-priced" steakhouse duo in Duluth and Roswell that "satisfies" the "carnivorous needs" of suburbanites with "flavorful" meats, "appetizing" sides and a "decent but compact wine selection", all served in a "tasteful" "cabin lodge setting"; "polite" waiters are "attentive" "without hovering", and the only "major downside is the wait for a table" but it's "worth it."

Strip
– | – | – | M

245 18th St. (17th St. NW), 404-385-2005; www.heretoserverestaurants.com

There's a bar on all three levels of Tom Catherall's new gargantuan surf 'n' turf in Atlantic Station, where Americanized sushi and steaks are served on bright cherry-red tables in an open, modern space or on the outdoor patio that offers refreshing views of the landscaped courtyard; as the evening progresses a club energy takes over, and there's even a pole for dancing if the mood strikes.

Sun Dial
19 | 24 | 20 | $43

Westin Peachtree Plaza, 210 Peachtree St., 71st fl. (Garnett St.), 404-589-7506; www.sundialrestaurant.com

"It's the "top of the world" – in Atlanta, anyway – at this New American on the 71st floor of the Westin Peachtree Plaza, where guests can take in the "stunning views" of the city from this "revolving" "rooftop" perch (but you may "need a drink" after that "glass elevator" ride up); "in-

vote at zagat.com

Atlanta F | D | S | C

spired" "seasonal" cuisine and "accommodating" service "top off" the experience; N.B. a post-*Survey* chef change is not reflected in the above Food score.

Sun in My Belly 24 | 22 | 16 | $15
2161 College Ave. NE (Murray Hill Ave.), 404-370-1088; www.suninmybelly.com

A "winner" "by the tracks" in a "gentrifying strip of Kirkwood", this BYO diner has fans cheering "hooray" for chef Alison Leuker's "phenomenal and fresh" breakfast choices "with a gourmet twist", "awesome Sunday brunch", "super" sandwiches and "giant portions" of "homestyle" dinner options; "hang out" on the "couch" or at "wooden tables" in the "relaxing" renovated hardware store, and while the service is "consistently flaky", it is "improving" according to insiders; P.S. "if you are anti-yuppie", "consider yourself forewarned."

Supper Club 23 | 22 | 23 | $37
The Shops of West Ponce, 308 W. Ponce de Leon Ave. (Ponce de Leon Pl.), Decatur, 404-370-1207; www.supperclubdecatur.com

"Don't take kids or a large party" to this "intimate" Decatur New American, the "perfect" "place for a romantic evening" amid drapery and candles in a "quiet" and "dark" setting, or seated "on pillows" in the private room; the menu "changes too often to pigeonhole" but "fresh ingredients" and "excellent presentation" result in "delicious" "offbeat" Euro-accented fare, and "wine pairings are second to none"; the service is "friendly" but "never over-attentive."

Surin of Thailand 21 | 14 | 17 | $22
810 N. Highland Ave. NE (Greenwood Ave.), 404-892-7789; www.surinofthailand.com

The "classic" "comfort" dishes at this "highly popular" Va-Highlands Thai (and sibling of Harry & Son's) are "reasonably priced" and "consistently" "drool-worthy", and it's a "great lunch quickie" (if you "can find a place to park"); "cool music" flows through the "dark, inviting" digs, which can get "crowded" and "noisy", and while the service is "friendly", the "long rows of 'pack-em-cheek-to-jowl' tables" "leave something to be desired."

Surin's Thai Bowl & Sushi Bar 18 | 10 | 15 | $15
The Peach, 2900 Peachtree Rd. NW (Sheridan Dr.), 404-841-2990

Surin's "straightforward" little sister at The Peach in Buckhead offers an "innovative format" of "make-your-own Thai bowls" that's just "authentic enough when you're in the mood" and makes for a "cheap, healthy meal" that's "quick and easy"; "tasty" sushi is available too, and a "friendly staff" attends to counter service, making this a "favorite" for either eat-in or takeout.

Atlanta   F | D | S | C

Sushi Avenue   22 | 16 | 21 | $21
131 Sycamore St. (Church St.), Decatur, 404-378-0228
The Shops of West Ponce, 308 W. Ponce de Leon Ave.
(Ponce de Leon Pl.), Decatur, 404-378-8448
Advocates of these Decatur raw-fin twins "would lay down in the street to keep these guys in town" since they "can't go wrong" with "amazingly fresh" sushi and "excellent" Japanese eats at "reasonable prices"; the "location on the square is hipper" but the "original" one has been "beautifully remodeled", and both boast "pleasant" staffs and an owner who's "an angel."

Sushi Huku   ▽ 28 | 20 | 23 | $35
Powers Ferry Landing, 6300 Powers Ferry Rd. NW
(Northside Dr.), 770-956-9559
"Feel like a tourist in Japan" at this Cobb County Japanese that's "the place to be" for "traditional" dishes, "serious sushi" and "great sashimi" that's "practically swimming"; an "exceptionally friendly staff" is "always willing to help" if you don't "know what to ask for" and the "intimate" space ensures that it might "take a while" to be seated "on a busy night."

Swallow at the Hollow   23 | 16 | 19 | $19
1072 Green St. (Woodstock St.), Roswell, 678-352-1975;
www.theswallowatthehollow.com
"How can you go wrong with a place that serves biscuits and honey as an appetizer" posit pros of this "laid-back" Roswell BBQ that pleases with "fantastic", "belt-loosening" 'cue served with "excellent sauces" and "homemade sides" ("gotta get the mac 'n' cheese!"); the "rustic" renovated barn is a "novel setting" for "Southern hospitality", "rednecks" and live country music on weekends; it's the "total package."

Swan Coach House ☒   17 | 22 | 20 | $21
3130 Slaton Dr. NW (W. Paces Ferry Rd.), 404-261-0636;
www.swancoachhouse.com
"Hats" are "optional, but certainly appropriate" at this "classic ladies' lunch spot" in Buckhead that's "one of the last true tearooms" around, serving "old-fashioned" Southern fare in the former coach house of the "historical" Swan House; the interior is "as charming as it gets" with "frilly" details, "bright" "floral wall covering" and the "best gift shop in town", so it's "always a treat" for "showers, birthdays" or even a "small wedding", but usually the "men stay home."

Table 1280   23 | 22 | 20 | $44
Woodruff Arts Ctr., 1280 Peachtree St. NE (bet. 15th & 16th Sts.),
404-897-1280; www.table1280.com
Part of the "ultraglam addition" to the Woodruff Arts Center in Midtown, this "highbrow" newcomer is where

vote at zagat.com   111

Atlanta

F | D | S | C

consulting chef Shaun Doty (ex MidCity Cuisine) has created an "artful", "cosmopolitan" New American menu with Italian and French influences "befitting" the "stylish", "modern" space, where even diners "feel like an exhibit"; while some wish the staff were "as talented as [arts center architect] Renzo Piano" when it comes to service, others predict it'll soon be one of the "tastiest spots to be spotted."

TAKA

26 | 14 | 21 | $38

375 Pharr Rd. NE (Grandview Ave.), 404-869-2802; www.taka-atlanta.com

"Insiders" are tickled by the "hilarious" e-mails they receive from chef Taka Moriuchi, an "absolute delight" who turns out "artistic" sushi and "sashimi that will make your head swim" at his Buckhead Japanese; even the "waiters are a joy" and "good about making recommendations" in the "small" venue that's "never crowded"; boosters say it's one of the "best in town – without the attitude."

TAMARIND

27 | 19 | 23 | $32

80 14th St. NW (bet. Spring & Williams Sts.), 404-873-4888; www.nanfinedining.com

"As genuine as the best in Bangkok", this "off-the-charts" Midtown Thai (and younger sibling of Nan) serves "perfect" "beautifully presented" cuisine that's "worth every penny", and an "impeccable staff" delivers "tip-top" service that "leaves an impression"; the "unassuming exterior" in a challenging location "right off the highway" masks an "upscale" yet "relaxed" setting where you can "see famous golfers" – "it's a favorite of past Masters champions."

TAQUERIA DEL SOL

24 | 14 | 15 | $13

1200B Howell Mill Rd. NW (Huff Rd.), 404-352-5812
359 W. Ponce de Leon Ave. (bet. Fairview Ave. & Ponce de Leon Pl.), Decatur, 404-377-7668
www.taqueriadelsol.com

The "lines snake into the parking lot" of these "new-school" Mexican-Southwestern twins in Decatur and Westside, but fans who are "hooked for life" swear it's "worth the wait" for the "addictive" fare at "rock-bottom prices" and "superb" margaritas made from a "dazzling array of tequilas"; expect "ultracasual" "minimalist" digs, and service that's usually "pleasant" but "can be a little prickly" "if you veer from the program" – i.e. "no sitting until you've ordered."

Taqueria Sundown

21 | 12 | 16 | $15

(fka Sundown Cafe)
2165 Cheshire Bridge Rd. NE (Lavista Rd.), 404-321-1118; www.sundowncafe.com

"Have a blast for $15 – if you splurge" at this "serve-yourself" Mexican in Cheshire Bridge that's "less crowded than sister Taqueria del Sol", but offers the "same menu", including "eclectic" tacos and "daily" specials that are a

Atlanta F | D | S | C

"hit every time", and "excellent margaritas"; it's an "easy place to grab a bite", but be forewarned – there are "long waits at lunchtime", the decor "needs some major work" and the service can be "rude."

Taurus 21 | 24 | 20 | $38
Brookwood Place Plaza, 1745 Peachtree St. NE (25th St.), 404-214-0641
There's "no bull" about "talented chef" Gary Mennie's (ex Canoe) "new take on the American chophouse" in South Buckhead that's proving to be a "strong newcomer" thanks to "amazing" New American cuisine, "excellent" meats, "small but unbelievable desserts" and a "diverse selection of wines", all brought to table by "energetic" servers; the "deliciously different" matador decor is "fresh and modern" but "still comfortable" and a "super bar" sports the "best skyline views" of Midtown and beyond.

Taverna Plaka 16 | 14 | 15 | $28
2196 Cheshire Bridge Rd. NE (Woodland Ave.), 404-636-2284; www.tavernaplakaatlanta.com
"It's perfectly all right to dance on the table" at this "tacky and wacky" Hellenic "dining experience" on Cheshire Bridge where it's "always a party" as "plates crash", "friendly" servers shout "*opa*" and "belly dancers shake their stuff"; "smush your own hummus" and "eat great Mediterranean fare" in the "festive" setting where "conversation is impossible", and while its appeal may be "Greek to" those who prefer "subtle dining", "it's a hoot" for the rest.

Tavern at Phipps 17 | 16 | 16 | $26
Phipps Plaza, 3500 Peachtree Rd. NE (Lenox Rd.), 404-814-9640; www.centraarchy.com
"Even if you're not one of the beautiful people" "you can enjoy watching their antics" at this "clubby" Buckhead American located in "one of the best malls around", where "waitresses in skimpy clothing" and "hot bartenders" "put on a show" in the "dark mahogany" setting that gets "noisy when busy, which is often"; fans rate the pub grub "way above average", but pickier patrons "go for the bar" scene and "eat elsewhere."

Ted's Montana Grill 18 | 17 | 17 | $22
133 Luckie St. NW (Spring St.), 404-521-9796
1874 Peachtree Rd. NE (Collier Rd.), 404-355-3897
Mill Creek, 1680 Mall of Georgia Blvd. (Buford Dr.), Buford, 678-546-3631
1360 Hwy. 85 N. (New Hope Rd.), Fayetteville, 770-460-9354
2500 Cobb Place Ln. NW (Cobb Place Blvd.), Kennesaw, 678-581-7890

(continued)

vote at zagat.com

Atlanta

(continued)
Ted's Montana Grill
The Avenues of West Cobb, 3625 Dallas Hwy. SW/Rte. 120 (Barrett Pkwy.), Marietta, 678-594-7242
Parkaire Landing Shopping Ctr., 640 Johnson Ferry Rd. (Lower Roswell Rd.), Marietta, 770-578-8337
The Forum, 5165 Peachtree Pkwy. NW/Hwy. 141 (Medlock Bridge Rd.), Norcross, 678-405-0305
The Avenue, 314 City Circle (Hwy. 54), Peachtree City, 678-829-0272
www.tedsmontanagrill.com
Fans of this "Old West"–inspired American chain "hope there's enough buffalo to go around" 'cause it "sure is good", as well as other items of "solid" "comfort food" made with "fresh ingredients"; the "handsome" "dark-wood" and "brass" setting "feels like a Gene Autry movie", and though "sloppy" service and "disappointing" eats leave cynics wishing they'd "leave the bison on the prairie", to others it goes "way beyond your normal burger joint."

10 Degrees South | 22 | 22 | 21 | $37 |
4183 Roswell Rd. NE (bet. Piedmont & Wieuca Rds.), 404-705-8870; www.10degreessouth.com
Surveyors "in the mood to try something different" head for this Buckhead South African for a "dining adventure" featuring "deliciously unique" fare and "warm" service; a "beautifully done expansion" "greatly improves the ambiance" (and Decor score) of the "sexy contemporary" space.

Terra Garden Grille | 21 | 17 | 17 | $20 |
Brookhaven Shopping Plaza, 3974 Peachtree Rd. NE (N. Druid Hills Rd.), 404-841-1032; www.terragrille.com
"Business" folks and "wealthy local" ladies are "happy" to have this "reliable" American in Brookhaven serving "tasty", "healthy dishes made with style" that are "better than you would expect at a strip mall"; the "relaxing" setting resembles an "upscale diner", where you "order at the counter", and while service can be "painfully slow", it's "always friendly."

Thai Chili | 23 | 16 | 19 | $21 |
Briarvista Shopping Ctr., 2169 Briarcliff Rd. NE (Lavista Rd.), 404-315-6750
Colony Sq., 1197 Peachtree St. NE (14th St.), 404-875-2275
www.thaichilicuisine.com
"One of Atlanta's oldest Thai" choices and "still one of the best", this "dependable" and "moderately priced" duo is touted for "traditional high-quality" fare that's "spicy if you like spicy", including "primo" pad Thai and some of the "best curry" in town; "Emory students and CDC staff" "get past the mall exterior" of the parent spot, while Midtowners can mingle on the "best patio in town", and service at both locations is "friendly and helpful."

Atlanta

F | D | S | C

Thomas Marketplace Rest.
▽ 21 | 11 | 21 | $14

State Farmers Mkt., 16 Forest Pkwy. (I-75, exit 237), Forest Park, 404-361-1367

"If you can't like" this "mecca of Southern home cooking" then you just "can't be pleased" declare devotees of this "family-run spot" "located in the State Farmers Market" in Forest Park, "one of the great meat and threes around" that "makes you feel at home" with "congenial" servers who deliver veggies "fresh" from the produce stands "right outside the front windows"; it's "excellent for breakfast", as well as a "fried food fix", with its signature "fried green tomatoes."

Thumbs Up ⊄
24 | 15 | 20 | $13

573 Edgewood Ave. NE (Bradley St.), 404-223-0690
1617 White Way (bet. East Point & Main Sts.), East Point, 404-768-3776

Even those who "live across the street" from this Inman Park diner "have to roll out of bed an hour early" to beat the "ridiculous" lines at what fans dub the "best homey breakfast joint in town" for its "wide range of choices" of "damn good Southern" fare; expect a "clean retro diner look" and "patient" servers who herd the masses; to "avoid the crowds", cognoscenti recommend the "East Point location", which "delivers the same delish menu" with "half the wait time."

TIERRA ⌧
25 | 18 | 25 | $34

1425B Piedmont Ave. NE (Westminster Dr.), 404-874-5951;
www.tierrarestaurant.com

Take a "superb" "culinary tour of South America" at this Midtown Pan-Latin where "knowledgeable and passionate owners" Ticha and Dan Krinsky "carefully" craft an "ever-changing seasonal menu" of "superb" dishes "with great integrity" that's matched with an "intriguing" wine list, while the signature tres leches cake is "to die for"; the "itty-bitty" space near the Botanical Gardens is unimposing from the outside, but the "pleasant bistro atmosphere" and "great" outdoor patio are "conducive to a comfortable evening."

Tin Drum Asia Café
18 | 12 | 14 | $11

4530 Old Perimeter Way (Ashford Dunwoody Rd.), 770-393-3006
Tech Sq., 88 Fifth St. (Veterans St.), 404-881-1368

Lunchers in-the-know "go 15 minutes before noon" to avoid the "lines out the door" of this "reliable" "quick service noodle house" in Midtown that offers "terrific", "simple and filling" Asian fusion fare with "a lot of flavor"; the "funky" modern space is "often" "packed" with the "business crowd", as well as "students" and "faculty" from Georgia Tech because the "price is right"; N.B. a Dunwoody branch opened post-*Survey*.

vote at zagat.com

Atlanta | F | D | S | C |

Toast | 20 | 19 | 20 | $25 |
The Biltmore, 817 W. Peachtree St. NW (6th St.), 404-815-9243; www.toastrestaurant.com
This "delightful cafe" "tucked into a quiet corner of Midtown" is a "bit hard to find", but "wows" those who do with "innovative" and "flavorful" New American fare, a "great brunch" and "good service"; the "industrial" setting has an "ultramodern feel" and the "quaint" patio "makes you forget you're in Atlanta"; insiders are "hopeful it will maintain its high standards" since the departure of original chef Drew Van Leuvan in 2005.

tomas ⊠ | ∇ 24 | 20 | 22 | $26 |
6025 Peachtree Pkwy. NW (Jay Bird Alley), Norcross, 770-447-0005
Surrounded by "suburban strip malls", this Norcross New American may not "look like much from the outside", but inside there are "so many things to love" – a menu that offers "something for every taste", "accommodating" service and "wood-and-leather" decor and an "open" feel that "makes it a pleasure" to dine; "for the quality", you might "normally expect to pay a stiff premium", but "not here."

Top Spice | 22 | 21 | 20 | $21 |
1529F Piedmont Ave. NE (Monroe Dr.), 404-685-9333; www.topspiceansleypark.com
Toco Hills Shopping Ctr., 3007 N. Druid Hills Rd. NE (Lavista Rd.), 404-728-0588; www.topspicetocohills.com
"Lots of college students, faculty, hospital staff" and others who "crave spicy food" "haunt" this Emory spot for its "great mix" of "high-end" Thai and Malaysian fare "so fresh" it "will shock you", served up in "just right portions"; "located in un-glamorous Toco Hills", it's "surprisingly" "elegant" inside "but not forbidding" and "having a bar is a big plus", as are the "courteous" and "attractive" servers, and "stellar" delivery; N.B. a newer Midtown location also offers "incredible taste for a decent price."

Touch of India | ∇ 15 | 10 | 16 | $18 |
Toco Hills Shopping Ctr., 3017 N. Druid Hills Rd. (Lavista Rd.), 404-728-8881
Pros who prefer their paratha be "predictable" pick this Emory Indian that's "been around forever", offering eats that are "pleasing to the palate" in a "fabulously Bollywood space"; but some find it "too expensive" for the "cafeteria" atmosphere, and feel there's "much better Indian food to be had" elsewhere.

Toulouse | 21 | 18 | 20 | $35 |
2293B Peachtree Rd. NE (Peachtree Memorial Dr.), 404-351-9533; www.toulouserestaurant.com
"Once you figure out how to get in", this South Buckhead New American with a "fine bistro" accent is a "great es-

Atlanta

cape right on Peachtree", offering "marvelous", "comforting" cuisine paired with "one of the best wine lists in town", all with an utter "lack of pretension"; oenophiles also appreciate the "superior tastings", and owner George Tice "makes you feel welcome" in the "wonderful", "romantic" loftlike space decorated with "great" paintings.

Trader Vic's   16 | 19 | 19 | $36
Hilton Atlanta, 255 Courtland St. NE (Baker St.), 404-221-6339; www.tradervicsatlanta.com

"Sometimes you just want kitsch that tastes good" and this "upscale chain" in the Downtown Hilton delivers with "extraordinary", albeit "pricey", "fruity cocktails with naked dolls in them" and "reliable" Pacific Rim fare in a "festive" setting with a "South Seas island theme"; but critics insist that original 'Trader' "Vic Bergeron himself would never approve" of the "mediocre eats or "snotty" service.

Trattoria La Strada   ▽ 19 | 11 | 17 | $25
2930 Johnson Ferry Rd. NE (Freeman Rd.), Marietta, 770-640-7008; www.lastradainc.com

There are "lots of favorites on the menu" of this "casual", "consistent" Marietta Italian where basic red-sauce fare is "prepared with imagination" and served by "attentive" waiters; critics carp it "doesn't look like much from the outside", "long waits" are common since "no reservations" are taken, it's "noisy" and there's "not enough parking."

Trattoria Monaco   ▽ 23 | 21 | 24 | $35
Plaza Shopping Ctr., 5530 Windward Pkwy. (GA 400), Alpharetta, 770-664-0056; www.monacorestaurants.com

Alpharettans applaud this "refreshing" "boutique" Italian in an "upscale strip mall" for finally "breaking the suburban mold" by putting "food and wine first" and "kids second" (though they are welcome) with their "outstanding" "seasonal" cuisine and "extensive" list of vino; the "proud" owner is praised for his "personal touch" and his staff delivers "first-class" service in the "elegant" yet "unpretentious" "white-tablecloth" space.

Twist   18 | 19 | 17 | $30
Phipps Plaza, 3500 Peachtree Rd. NE (Lenox Rd.), 404-869-1191; www.heretoserverestaurants.com

At Tom Catherall's (Shout, Prime, Strip, Goldfish) "high-energy" Eclectic venue "conveniently" located in Buckhead's Phipps Plaza, an "amazingly large variety" of small plates and "exceptional" sushi are "perfect for sharing", while "incredible cocktails" keep the "joint jumping"; the "diverse crowd" that "dresses to the nines" is "civilized at lunch" but turns "crazy" at night, when the "bar scene is a zoo", and "ear-shattering noise" drives many "outside when weather permits", while "confused", "inconsistent" eats and a "college vibe" drive others simply elsewhere.

vote at zagat.com

Atlanta

F | **D** | **S** | **C**

Twisted Taco ☻ — 13 | 11 | 14 | $16
66 12th St. NE (Crescent Ave.), 404-607-8771;
www.twistedtaco.com
The Midtown "business" crowd and anyone looking for a cowhide barstool and "plenty of drinks" head over to this Southwestern spot with the "best cheap eats in the neighborhood", albeit served up by a "grudging" staff; the two-story saloon-themed space with balconies front and back (and the occasional mechanical bull) is a "great lunch alternative", but realists point out it's nothing more than "a bar where you can get a taco."

TWO. URBAN LICKS ☻ — 20 | 25 | 18 | $37
820 Ralph McGill Blvd. NE (Freedom Pkwy.), 404-522-4622;
www.twourbanlicks.com
"Hipper than thou" and "louder than hell", Bob Amick's and Todd Rushing's (ONE. midtown kitchen and PieBar) "hot spot" near the Carter Center in Downtown "makes you feel cool just for showing up" in the "über-trendy" space, a reconstructed 19th-century forge; fans praise the "amazing" small plates, "excellent" "Creole"-inspired New American eats, "clever concoctions" of "infused" vodkas and "amazing barrel wine by the glass", but critics dismiss the fare as "mediocre and pricey" and warn the "indifferent" service could tax the "patience of Job."

Udipi Cafe — 21 | 7 | 15 | $14
1850 Lawrenceville Hwy. (Woodridge Dr.), Decatur, 404-325-1933
"No one misses the meat" at this "fantastic" vegetarian Indian in Decatur, an outpost of a national chain offering "excellent" fare and a "tasty" buffet at "unbelievably cheap" prices; sure, the "bland" decor "leaves a lot to be desired" but it's "always clean" and the staff is "very friendly"; N.B. it's BYO.

Umezono — ∇ 22 | 15 | 16 | $20
Windy Hill Plaza, 2086 Cobb Pkwy. SE (Windy Hill Rd.), Smyrna, 770-933-8808
The predictable "line forming at lunchtime" "is a clear sign" of the "quality" of this "real-deal" Japanese located in a no-frills Smyrna strip mall, where "fresh and delicious" sushi and "dependable" "appetizer-sized" dishes can be "cobbled together" for a "satisfying" experience; "reasonable prices" are an added attraction, so it's best to "avoid peak times" but if you can't the fare's "definitely worth the wait."

Uncle Julio's Casa Grande — 21 | 17 | 18 | $22
1860 Peachtree Rd. NW (Collier Rd.), 404-350-6767;
www.unclejulios.com
"Beware of the flying dough balls" from the "tortilla machine" that keeps kids "entertained" at this "upbeat" South Buckhead link in a Texas-based Tex-Mex chain offering "generous portions" of "fresh and delicious" eats

Atlanta F | D | S | C

and "great" margaritas; the staff "pays attention to detail" and handles "formidable crowds" "with aplomb."

Universal Joint ◐ 17 | 15 | 15 | $14
906 Oakview Rd. NE (E. Lake Dr.), Decatur, 404-373-6260; www.ujointbar.com

"Bring your dog and your shades" to this "favorite watering hole" (the "U-Joint" to regulars) in "charming" Oakhurst that's "always hopping with "low-key hipsters" who "bask in the sun" on their "great" outdoor patio; a "long beer list", "damn fine burgers" and other "classic" American pub grub, and "reasonable prices" add up to an "unbeatable combination" that excuses occasionally "slow" service.

Van Gogh's ⊠ 23 | 22 | 22 | $40
70 W. Crossville Rd. (Crabapple Rd.), Roswell, 770-993-1156; www.knowwheretogogh.com

"Paint your palate with a rainbow of tastes" at the Roswell "flagship" of the Sedgwick family's group (Aspen's, Vinny's, Pure Taqueria) that "has held up over the years" by offering "inventive" New American eats, including the "best crab cakes on the planet", as well as "friendly" service and a "lively scene" in their "gorgeous" "rabbit warren" of rooms; while some say it's "a little overpriced" and may be "losing its edge", for many it remains a popular "destination."

Varsity, The ∉ 17 | 12 | 17 | $9
61 North Ave. (Spring St.), 404-881-1706 ◐
11556 Rainwater Dr. (West Side Pkwy.), Alpharetta, 770-777-4004
2790 Town Center Dr. NW (Mall Blvd.), Kennesaw, 770-795-0802
6045 Dawson Blvd. (Jimmy Carter Blvd.), Norcross, 770-840-8519
www.thevarsity.com

Varsity Jr. ∉
1085 Lindbergh Dr. NE (Cheshire Bridge Rd.), 404-261-8843; www.varsityjr.com

"Fast food can't get any faster" than the American eats at this "iconic" Downtown drive-in where the "carhops are hoppin'" to bring you the "best chili dogs in the universe", "onion rings the size of hubcaps" and other eats, all "covered in good old American grease" ("can I have a side of Weight Watchers with that?"); its five branches might not "have the gritty feel of the original", but they're still part of the "Atlanta institution."

Vatica Indian Vegetarian Cuisine ▽ 24 | 8 | 25 | $12
Terrell Mill Junction Shopping Ctr., 1475 Terrell Mill Rd. SE (Powers Ferry Rd.), Marietta, 770-955-3740

"There is no menu" at this no-frills family-owned Indian in Marietta, so you can "just sit back and enjoy" the daily "home-cooked" offerings of "heavenly" vegetarian-only fare that "even carnivores love"; the "attentive" chef-owner and her "warm" and "funny" husband, the manager, make guests feel as if they're "eating in someone's house."

vote at zagat.com

Atlanta   F | D | S | C

VENI VIDI VICI   23 | 22 | 23 | $43
41 14th St. NE (bet. Peachtree & Spring Sts.), 404-875-8424;
www.buckheadrestaurants.com
A "transporting experience" awaits at this Midtown Italian from the Buckhead Life chain where "superb" "modern" cuisine, a "terrific" wine list and "outstanding" service make it a "fabulous" "place to celebrate something grand" (or run up your "expense account"), although "sometimes the din is deafening"; the "lovely smell of garlic" and the "wood-burning stove" "greets you at the door" of the "gorgeous" space "convenient to the Arts Center."

Vickery's   18 | 16 | 19 | $23
1106 Crescent Ave. NE (12th St.), 404-881-1106;
www.vickerys.com
"Like the Energizer Bunny", this "easygoing" Midtown venue "just keeps on going" with a "diverse" Southern-Eclectic menu of "comfort food" with "delicious" "twists"; "speedy service" and the "convenient" location make it a "dependable" lunch stop as well as a pre-"theater or symphony" option, the Sunday brunch is "amazing" and the patio is "perfect on a sunny day."

Villa Christina ⌀   19 | 21 | 20 | $40
4000 Summit Blvd. NE (Ashford Dunwoody Rd.), 404-303-0133;
www.villachristina.com
"Take a walk in the beautifully landscaped garden" and try your hand on the "putting green" at this Dunwoody Italian best known for its "great views" and "romantic" setting, but while some find the "pricey" menu "disappointing", many others laud the "predictable" yet "well-executed" fare; the "quiet atmosphere" "makes it great for business" or a "date", and "warm service" "makes it even more pleasurable"; N.B. Caffe Christina, the new take-out section, is located just inside the entrance.

Village Tavern   22 | 22 | 21 | $28
11555 Rainwater Dr. (Haynes Bridge Rd.), Alpharetta, 770-777-6490; www.villagetavern.com
"Consistency is everything" at this "upscale" New American that's one of the "top favorites in the Alpha-Roswell area" thanks to a "diverse" menu that "suits all tastes", a "beautifully appointed" dining room centered by a "magnificent" double-sided stone fireplace and "incredible" service; there's a "bustling bar scene" ("you can get a date and an ahi tuna salad all in under 60 minutes"), leading some to wonder "how can this be part of a chain?"

Vinings Inn ⌀   23 | 21 | 20 | $36
3011 Paces Mill Rd. SE (Paces Ferry Rd.), 770-438-2282;
www.viningsinn.com
"Step back in time" for some "creaky fun" at this "quaint" "old inn" dating back to 1853 that's one of Vinings' "fool-

Atlanta

proof options for a special occasion", thanks to "outstanding" cuisine that oozes "Southern charm", including some of the "best crab cakes in Atlanta", and "fabulous" service; the "cozy", "romantic" rooms with "crooked" floors have a "homey" feel and there's an "excellent" bar upstairs showcasing "great" live music.

Vinny's on Windward | 22 | 22 | 21 | $36 |
5355 Windward Pkwy. (off GA 400), Alpharetta, 770-772-4644; www.knowwheretogogh.com

"From the valet in front to the bartender in the back", this Alpharetta Italian (sibling of Aspens, Pure Taqueria and Van Gogh's) "has got it going" with "delicious" dishes, a "great wine list" and an "attentive" staff; the space is "beautiful", but the "open ceilings" and "terrible acoustics" add up to "high noise levels"; service can be "hurried" on the "weekends" and a few complain about "inconsistent" cooking, but pros argue "even their 'so-so' is better than what's available in the surrounding area."

Vinocity | 20 | 21 | 20 | $33 |
36 13th St. NE (W. Peachtree St.), 404-870-8886; www.vinocitywinebar.com

At this "fairly priced" Midtown wine bar and restaurant, "luscious" New American dishes and small plates "with a twist" "pair well with" the "head-spinning wine list", and the atmosphere is "cozy" in the "lovely" converted three-story house "hidden away" in a "super location"; "hospitable" service is one more reason so many aficionados "definitely recommend" it.

Violette ☒ | 21 | 21 | 20 | $27 |
2948 Clairmont Rd. NE (I-85), 404-633-3363; www.violetterestaurant.com

"The pickins' on this side of town are slim", so the "business" set and "budget-minded" *bec fins* appreciate this "approachable", "nicely packaged" Clairmont French bistro between I-75 and Buford Highway for its "fine" "country" fare that might just be "the best value in the South"; the "beautiful candlelit" space is "romantic" and "serene" even with the "wonderful" live entertainment nightly, and the staff "maintains high standards" of service.

Vortex Bar & Grill ● | 21 | 16 | 16 | $15 |
438 Moreland Ave. NE (Euclid Ave.), 404-688-1828
878 Peachtree St. NE (bet. 7th & 8th Sts.), 404-875-1667
www.thevortexbarandgrill.com

It's a "people watcher's paradise" at this hamburger pair in Little Five Points and Midtown that attracts an "eclectic" crowd with the "greatest burger in the history of man" along with "zillions of beer and liquor choices"; the decor is an "insane" mélange of "kitsch", and the "sassy" service is so "slow" some have "time to read *War and Peace*

Atlanta | F | D | S | C |

cover to cover" waiting for their orders; P.S. smokers are pleased "no rug rats are allowed."

Vreny's Biergarten ⊠ ▽ 20 | 16 | 18 | $23 |
4225 River Green Pkwy. (Peachtree Industrial Blvd.), Duluth, 770-623-9413; www.vrenysbiergarten.com

"*Trinkt, trinkt, trinkt,* just like you would in Munich" at this "touch of Bavaria" "in the back" of sibling Kurt's "50-year-old farmhouse" in Duluth, where "every hearty German treat one could imagine" can be washed down with one (or more) of their "hundreds of beers"; you can watch "German television" inside or sit on the patio that "feels like your back porch"; the only complaint heard is from Intown folks who "wish it were closer to the city."

Wahoo! A Decatur Grill 22 | 21 | 20 | $26 |
1042 W. College Ave. (E. Lake Dr.), Decatur, 404-373-3331; www.wahoogrilldecatur.com

Devotees "can't say enough about" this "discovery" in Decatur offering an "affordable" "fish-heavy" American menu and "easy breezy service with no pretension" in a "hard to find" spot where "parking's a chore"; local art adorns the "rough brick walls" of the "cozy", "inviting" space with a "glorious" garden patio, and while a few are "not impressed" by "lackluster" fare and "inconsistent" service, regulars report that "folks still line up out the door."

WATERSHED 25 | 19 | 21 | $30 |
406 W. Ponce de Leon Ave. (Commerce Dr.), Decatur, 404-378-4900; www.watershedrestaurant.com

"Superb hardly sums up" chef Scott Peacock's "whimsical, chic and nostalgic" "interpretations of Southern fare" at this "asset to Atlanta's dining scene" in Decatur, where cognoscenti caution "stay out of our way" on Tuesday nights, the only time the "best fried chicken in town" is served (topped off by the "best damn chocolate cake ever"); a "great staff" serves a "diverse clientele" in the "minimalist" (some say "cold") converted gas station space, and while wags dub the "pricey" affair "'Walletshed'", most agree it "never disappoints."

White House ⌀ 17 | 8 | 19 | $13 |
Peachtree Plaza, 3172 Peachtree Rd. NE (Mathieson Dr.), 404-237-7601

"If Buckhead really is a small town" this neighborhood "institution" "is Main Street" since it's "everything a small diner should be" with "terrific breakfasts" and Southern "comfort food" with a "Greek flair" and "colorful blue-haired matrons" providing "friendly" service; as a "power-player place" and "family fun farm" it's certainly "happenin'", but it's still "like eating in a time warp"– "not your daddy's, but your granddaddy's diner."

122 subscribe to zagat.com

Atlanta

| F | D | S | C |

Williamson Bros. Bar-B-Q | 20 | 13 | 16 | $14 |
*7040 Concourse Pkwy. (Hwy. 5), Douglasville,
770-949-5058*
*1425 Roswell Rd. NE (Powers Ferry Rd.), Marietta,
770-971-3201*
www.williamsonbros.com

A "mecca" of the smoke and spit, this family-owned BBQ trio serves up 'cue "just about any way you want" it, slathered with "your choice" of "tasty" sauce – purportedly "Newt had it flown to Washington when he was speaker"; the "good old-fashioned" fare is "worth the sacrifice of decor", and the "nice" folks running things offer a "conglomerate" of options, including "eat-in", "efficient" call-ahead takeout and retail sales.

Willie Rae's ⑤ | ∇ 20 | 15 | 19 | $21 |
*25 N. Park Sq. NE (bet. Cherokee & Church Sts.), Marietta,
770-792-9995; www.willieraes.com*

Simpatico's "cool" sibling in Downtown Marietta satisfies suburbanites with "creative", "consistent" Cajun and Southwestern eats, including the "best fish tacos east of the Mississippi" and "shrimp and grits" that are a "credit to the dish"; the "kid-friendly" "staff is always smiling" and "great local art makes things interesting" in the "cute" "joint" where fans "always feel at home."

Willy's Mexicana Grill | 20 | 11 | 16 | $10 |
*1100 Hammond Dr. NE (Peachtree Dunwoody Rd.),
770-512-0555*
*Peachtree Center Food Ct., 235 Peachtree St. NE (Memorial Dr.),
404-524-0821* ⑤
*Peachtree Sq., 2280 Peachtree Rd. NW (Peachtree Memorial Dr.),
404-351-4671*
1071 Piedmont Ave. NE (12th St.), 404-249-9054
*Roswell Wieuca Shopping Ctr., 4377 Roswell Rd. NE
(Wieuca Rd.), 404-252-2235*
832 Virginia Ave. (Doug Davis Dr.), 404-968-4756 ⑤
*1228 W. Paces Ferry Rd. NW (Northside Pkwy.),
404-816-2690*
*2074A N. Decatur Rd. (Clairmont Rd.), Decatur,
404-321-6060*
*Delk Spectrum Shopping Ctr., 2900 Delk Rd. SE
(Powers Ferry Rd.), Marietta, 770-690-0075*
www.willysmexicanagrill.com

"Lunchers with limited time to spare" and those who "don't want to cook" appreciate this "cheap and cheerful" Mexican chain deemed the "best of the bunch" thanks to "better, bigger" burritos made with "top-notch" fillings and "free salsa" at most locations; "lines move quickly" through the "nearly self service" drill in "unglamorous" but "clean" spaces, and the "primo location" of the Midtown outlet overlooking Piedmont Park makes it a "local favorite."

vote at zagat.com 123

Atlanta | F | D | S | C |

Wisteria | 24 | 20 | 22 | $37 |
471 N. Highland Ave. NE (bet. Colquitt Ave. & Freedom Pkwy.), 404-525-3363
"They provide relaxation at no extra charge" at this "hip but laid-back" "high-caliber hideaway" in Inman Park that's the "dining room away from home" for fans of chef Jason Hill's "fantastic" "Southern fare with a modern twist" that's paired with "varied and well-priced wines by the glass", and served by a "top-notch" staff; the "cozy" (but "loud") "urban" space in a century-old building has a "romantic" feel that makes it a "great first-date place", especially on a "weeknight" when it's relatively less "packed."

Wolfgang Puck Express | 17 | 13 | 15 | $17 |
Brookwood Village Shopping Plaza, 1745 Peachtree Rd. NE (25th St.), 404-815-1500; www.wolfgangpuck.com
South Buckheaders brag on their "little bit of Wolfgang at an affordable price" that "fits well in the neighborhood" since "there's a little something for everyone" from the "fast" "casual" Californian menu starring "great" "brick-oven pizzas" and "interesting" "short-order" fare that "beats burgers and chicken tenders by a mile"; while the decor may be "school cafeteria", the counter service is "quick", but puckrakers feel the food's "too express" and "barely good."

WOODFIRE GRILL | 24 | 21 | 22 | $41 |
1782 Cheshire Bridge Rd. NE (Piedmont Ave.), 404-347-9055; www.woodfiregrill.com
This Cheshire Bridge "altar to fresh food" is a "foodie's paradise" where chef Michael Tuohy's "outstanding" "homage to Californian cuisine", including a "tremendous cheese plate", and a "delectable wine list" that's "half price on Sundays" are served by an "attentive" staff in a "softly lit" space redolent with the "lovely smell of a wood fire"; while some smolder over "expensive" "small portions", most agree this "crowd-pleaser" is "burning up the competition" with "terrific" fare that's "worth every cent"; P.S. the new "casual" cafe is "quite a bargain."

YellowFin | ▽ 17 | 12 | 16 | $31 |
1170 Canton St. (Woodstock Rd.), Roswell, 678-277-9551; www.yellowfinblueroom.com
This New American with a seafood slant is proving to be a "great neighborhood bar and restaurant" for Roswell residents in search of a "nice dining experience" thanks to "wonderful" food and weekend live music; contemporary abstract art adorns the dining rooms, and a "nice patio" offers a respite on warm days.

Zab-E-Lee ⊠ | - | - | - | I |
4837 Old National Hwy. (Sullivan Rd.), College Park, 404-768-2705
Adventuresome souls sing the praises of this "excellent" Thai serving "tasty" fare "without the flash" in a "super-

124   subscribe to zagat.com

Atlanta | F | D | S | C |

sketchy" location near the airport; it's a "nice place even if the neighborhood is not", and a "good-value" "lunch spot" that's "worth" the trip according to those in-the-know.

Zapata ▽ | 24 | 13 | 23 | $18 |
5975 Peachtree Pkwy. (Jay Bird Alley), Norcross, 770-248-0052
"*Viva* Zapata" shout amigos of this "gourmet" Norcross Mexican serving "exquisite" soups and moles "like nothing you've had before" that'll "make you want to come back again and again"; live entertainment on Friday nights sets the "perfect mood" at this "hole-in-the-wall" that's "more than you would expect" from a spot "sharing space with a Starbucks and a mobile phone store", and it's a "great value for the $$$."

Zesto | 18 | 9 | 14 | $8 |
1181 E. Confederate Ave. SE (Moreland Ave.), 404-622-4254
377 Moreland Ave. NE (McLendon Ave.), 404-523-1973
544 Ponce de Leon Ave. NE (Monroe Dr.), 404-607-1118
151 Forest Pkwy. (Old Dixie Hwy.), Forest Park, 404-366-0564 ☾
www.zestoatlanta.com
"Hot damn", "you get good stuff" at this family-owned chain of "throwback burger joints" with "addictive" "fast-food-like" American fare "actually worth eating" since it's "prepared to order", including the "best shakes in town" and "tasty" Chubby Decker burger; the "retro decor and counter ladies seem to have traveled back to the '50s" at this "Atlanta mainstay for 50++ years" that's "still going strong."

Zocalo | 19 | 16 | 17 | $22 |
187 10th St. NE (Piedmont Ave.), 404-249-7576
123 E. Court Sq. (Church St.), Decatur, 404-270-9450
Purists praise this "*muy delicioso*" Midtown Mexican for its "authentic", "refined" south-of-the-border cuisine, including "mole to die for" and "sublime enchiladas", as well as "lethal" margaritas that'll "make you forget your name"; "parking is the pits", but the "open-air" patio and "earthy" decor "add even more character" to this "wonderfully relaxed" venue; N.B. a fast-food spin-off opened in Decatur post-*Survey*.

Zyka | 24 | 4 | 12 | $13 |
1677 Scott Blvd. (bet. Dekalb Industrial Way & N. Decatur Rd.), Decatur, 404-728-4444; www.zyka.com
"Montessori school cafeteria" decor in a converted "church rec room", "Styrofoam plates" and "plastic spoons" "can't deter" Decaturites from "nirvana" in the form of "seriously spicy" and "cheap" Indian fare that's "hands down the best in Atlanta"; service is "order-at-the-counter", the only beverage comes from a "water fountain" and the "weird location" is "hard to find", but "the trip is definitely worth it."

vote at zagat.com

Savannah

	F	D	S	C

Atlanta Bread Co.   16 | 12 | 14 | $11
5500 Abercorn St. (Janet Dr.), 912-691-1949;
www.atlantabread.com
See review in the Atlanta Directory.

Carrabba's Italian Grill   20 | 17 | 19 | $22
10408 Abercorn St. (Tibet Ave.), 912-961-7073;
www.carrabbas.com
See review in the Atlanta Directory.

ELIZABETH ON 37TH   27 | 26 | 27 | $52
105 E. 37th St. (Drayton St.), 912-236-5547;
www.elizabethon37th.com
A "fantastic romantic destination" near the Savannah historic district, this "magnificent" "fine-dining" doyenne is one of the "best tables in Georgia" "year after year" swear fans entranced by the "witty" "surprising tastes" of the "nouveau" Southern cuisine and "impeccable" service from an "excellent" staff; the "nostalgic" setting in a "fabulous" Greek Revival mansion (circa 1900) graced with "impressive artwork and antiques" is "superb", making it "a must" to be experienced "at least once in a lifetime."

45 South at the   20 | 22 | 19 | $39
Pirates' House Ⓢ
20 E. Broad St. (E. Bay St.), 912-233-1881;
www.thepirateshouse.com
For swashbuckling surveyors, this Savannah Continental is "worth the trip for the history lesson alone", housed in a building that dates back to 1753 with a pirate-themed interior that "can't be topped" according to fans; critics, however, keelhaul it as a "pricey" "tourist trap" that's "overrated in every way."

Garibaldi's   23 | 23 | 21 | $41
315 W. Congress St. (bet. Jefferson & Montgomery Sts.), 912-232-7118
It may be an "odd mix of sophistication and tourism" due to its historic Downtown location, but fans still find this Italian with a flair for seafood one of the "best of Savannah's fine-dining" choices, thanks to "wonderful" cuisine ("if the scored flounder was any better it would be illegal") and "unrivaled" service; the upstairs dining room, a former "ballroom", is "spectacular" and "different" from the moodier downstairs space, but no matter where they sit, regulars still consider it a "perennial favorite."

Savannah   F | D | S | C

Gottlieb's ⓈⒶ   26 | 21 | 25 | $53
1 W. Broughton St. (bet. Drayton & Whitaker Sts.), 912-234-7447; www.gottliebsfood.com
This team of three brothers from Savannah's "favorite food family" "has not forgotten their sweet tooth roots" at their Southern establishment that "started life as a bakery" and is now "one of the best" "upscale" spots in town, where "fabulous" Southern cuisine emphasizing local and organic produce and "famous" cakes from "family recipes" dating back to 1884 make it a "great experience"; servers are "there to please" and the "beautiful" space has a "comfortable feel."

Il Pasticcio   20 | 20 | 20 | $43
2 E. Broughton St. (Bull St.), 912-231-8888
A "favorite" of locals and tourists alike, this "upscale" Northern Italian in Downtown Savannah wins praise for "fresh and innovative" *alimento* and an "extensive wine list" offered up by a "knowledgeable" staff in a "beautifully decorated", "wide open" (read: "noisy") space; some critics, however, find it too "pricey" for service that's occasionally "poor to nonexistent."

Johnny Harris ⓈⒶ   17 | 18 | 16 | $21
1651 E. Victory Dr. (Wicklow St.), 912-354-7810; www.johnnyharris.com
"Dine like it's 1959" (actually 1936) at this "classic" Southern "family favorite" in Savannah, purportedly the city's "oldest restaurant", where "old timers still go and hold hands over BBQ" and "fine fried chicken", or have a "casual" "lobster dinner" "under the stars" in the main ballroom, but critics who crave "cutting-edge cuisine" come "for the nostalgia factor", "not the food."

Lady & Sons   22 | 17 | 19 | $24
102 W. Congress St. (Widdicker St.), 912-233-2600; www.ladyandsons.com
"Paula Dean may be a celebrity" on the Food Network, but "she is definitely not resting on her laurels" gush groupies of hers and her Savannah "temple of Southern delights" – "unapologetically fattening" "old-fashioned" "comfort" food "at its best"; don your "sweatpants" and "get there early", as the "lines form fast" despite "huge" "new digs", and while a few "local" cynics would leave the "overrated" eats "to the tour bus crowd", for others it's a "bargain" that's "worth" the "crazy waits."

Olde Pink House   24 | 24 | 22 | $42
23 Abercorn St. (Bay St.), 912-232-4286
Whether or not the "true old Savannah home" where it's housed is truly "haunted" as some say it is, this New American gives many "goose bumps" with "signature Southern desserts" and "excellent" cuisine, including the

vote at zagat.com

Savannah

"apricot-glazed flounder that'll make you wanna slap your mama"; choose between the "casual" "downstairs tavern" or "quieter", more "elegant" upstairs (the place opened in 1928 as a tearoom) and expect "attentive" service on either floor.

Sapphire Grill

26 | 24 | 24 | $44

110 W. Congress St. (Whitaker St.), 912-443-9962;
www.sapphiregrill.com

Those in-the-know attest "more should discover" this "real find" in Savannah that "can hold its own" against "comparable" big city spots with its "excellent", "fresh" Eclectic cuisine that creates "lasting memories" for fans and elicits many "compliments to the chef"; "cozy" dining areas in the multilevel space are "great places" for an "intimate dinner", and "excellent" service makes for a "relaxing experience" that's "almost worth a drive from Atlanta."

Other Outlying Areas

F	D	S	C

Bischero ▽ 20 | 21 | 19 | $26
237 Prince Ave. (Newton St.), Athens, 706-316-1006
Athenians find a "good alternative to the typical college town fare" at this "authentic" Italian praised for its "fresh pastas" and brick-oven pizzas that are among "the best in town", served in a "lovely" space featuring exposed-brick walls graced with large-scale paintings; some peripatetic participants even deem this entry "worth the drive from Atlanta."

Blue Willow Inn 18 | 19 | 19 | $22
294 N. Cherokee Rd. (Hightower Trail), Social Circle, 770-464-2131; www.bluewillowinn.com
"Even with gas prices the way they are", supporters insist this Social Circle Southerner is "worth the drive" for the "blue ribbon" buffet with a "gargantuan" selection of "homemade desserts" that makes it "hard not to eat too much"; housed in an "authentic" Greek Revival mansion, it's a "pleasant" "small-town" experience, but jaded cynics sniff this "touristy" "pig-out" palace is "proof there's no shortage of people who want to eat bad food in historic buildings."

CARGO PORTSIDE GRILL 25 | 18 | 24 | $31
1423 Newcastle St. (Gloucester St.), Brunswick, 912-267-7330; www.cargoportsidegrill.com
Aficionados deem this "friendly" Brunswick Eclectic an "essential stop" whenever they're in the area, and "worth a detour" when they're not, for "excellent" cuisine with an international flair, including "wonderful" "fresh" local seafood; "efficient" service and the "pleasant" space housed in a historic Downtown building also make it a "delight"; N.B. Alix Kenagy, the original chef-owner, recently sold it to her daughter Kate Buchanan, who has been cooking with her for years, a change that is not reflected in the above scores.

Crab Shack 18 | 20 | 18 | $24
40 Estill Hammock Rd. (Hwy. 80 E.), Tybee Island, 912-786-9857; www.thecrabshack.com
"Prepare to get messy" at this "Shangri-la of Low Country boil" (nothing fried here) on Tybee Island that "exceeds all expectations" with its "fresh" "Southern family" seafood; simply a "shack on a creek" with a "charming" outdoor deck, it "makes you want to become a beach bum", but crabby critics snap at the "inconsistent" eats "served on

vote at zagat.com

Other Outlying Areas   F D S C

plastic" to "tourists"; N.B. you can feed live captive alligators from the new Gator Deck.

Dillard House   17 | 14 | 17 | $22
768 Franklin St. (Hwy. 441), Dillard, 706-746-5348;
www.dillardhouse.com
You "won't leave hungry" from this "well-known" Southern all-you-can-eat located in a former farmhouse in Dillard serving "great country cooking" "family-style"; Atlantans "love the drive" and "doggy bags" make it a "great value", and while some dismiss it as "overrated" and "overpriced", many others feel it's "worth" the trip; just be sure to wear "loose-fitting clothing" and "comfy shoes for standing in line."

D. Morgan's ☒   - | - | - | E
28 W. Main St. (Erwin St.), Cartersville, 770-383-3535;
www.dmorgans.com
Those in-the-know "head north" to this "surprising find" in Cartersville, where "culinary pioneer" Derek Morgan is fulfilling a "lifelong dream" by offering a "fine-dining experience" featuring "excellent" New American cuisine and "fantastic" service; it's housed in a 125-year-old building that still boasts the original hardwood pine floors and exposed-brick walls, and there's also a "charming" wine cellar lounge.

Doc Chey's Asian Kitchen   17 | 13 | 16 | $13
Michaels Bldg., 320 E. Clayton St. (Jackson St.), Athens, 706-546-0015; www.doccheys.com
See review in the Atlanta Directory.

East West Bistro   23 | 17 | 21 | $27
351 E. Broad St. (Jackson St.), Athens, 706-546-9378;
www.eastwestbistro.com
"Far better than you'd expect in Athens", this "can't-miss classic" draws "locals", "Dawgs fans" and those in search of a "date spot" with a Med/Asian–accented New American menu that "pleases the taste buds", though a few feel it "tries to be too creative" at times; it's "always busy", especially on "football weekends", so you'll "get to know those waiting with you", and a "great bar" scene adds to the "lively" experience.

FIVE & TEN   28 | 21 | 24 | $39
1653 S. Lumpkin St. (Milledge Ave.), Athens, 706-546-7300;
www.fiveandten.com
A "true find" in Athens, Hugh Acheson's "high-end" New American is "worth the drive from Atlanta even on a 'school' night" for his "exquisite" cuisine that makes "clever use" of "local and seasonal ingredients", "rivaling" big-city counterparts at "lower prices"; the wine list is "outstanding" and the service "charming", but the "neat old house" is rather "small", so reservations are advis-

Other Outlying Areas   F | D | S | C

able, or else beat the crowds and go for the early-bird prix fixe, a "great value" at $20.

George's of Tybee   ▽ 22 | 18 | 23 | $50
1105 Hwy. 80 (Byers St.), Tybee Island, 912-786-9730
Those who have made the "beautiful drive" "across the marsh" to Tybee Island just outside of Savannah report the "outstanding" New American cuisine from a "young talented chef" at this "first class haven" is some of the "best food in Southeast Georgia"; though it's "a little pricey" and the ambiance is "so-so", most agree it's "well worth" the trip.

Georgia's - The New   ▽ 25 | 26 | 27 | $59
Taste of the South
The Ritz-Carlton Lodge, Reynolds Plantation,
1 Lake Oconee Trail (Hwy. 44), Greensboro, 706-467-7135;
www.ritzcarlton.com
This "classy" "signature restaurant" at the Ritz-Carlton Lodge of the Reynolds Plantation on Lake Oconee offers a "nice change" to the property's other "casual dining options" with "excellent" Southern cuisine delivered by "respectful" servers; the "pleasant" "lodge-style" dining room with a huge two-sided stone fireplace "looks and feels like something out of the Old South."

Le Clos   18 | 22 | 21 | $47
Château Élan Winery & Resort, 100 Rue Charlemagne
(Hwy. 211), Braselton, 678-425-0900;
www.chateauelan.com
At this "small", "pricey" New French on the grounds of the Château Élan winery in "rural" Braselton, "pretty good" fare from a five-course tasting menu is paired with the house's wines, and served in a formal setting (jackets are required); but disgruntled critics cry "give me a break" from "outrageous" tabs for "average" service and "mediocre" food.

Linger Longer Bar and Grill   ▽ 24 | 24 | 25 | $56
The Ritz-Carlton Lodge, Reynolds Plantation,
1 Lake Oconee Trail (Hwy. 44), Greensboro, 706-467-0600;
www.ritzcarlton.com
For "steak like it ought to be", but "an hour and a half away from where you would expect it", peripatetic pros praise this American chophouse overlooking the Oconee golf course at the Ritz-Carlton Lodge Reynolds Plantation, where "excellent" surf 'n' turf is served in a "lovely" "relaxing" Craftsman-style space; "impeccable" service is also par for the course.

Varsity, The ⇗   17 | 12 | 17 | $9
1000 W. Broad St. (Milledge Ave.), Athens, 706-548-6325;
www.thevarsity.com
See review in the Atlanta Directory.

Other Outlying Areas   F | D | S | C

Whistle Stop Cafe   ▽ 16 | 19 | 17 | $20
443 McCrackin St. (Juliette Rd.), Juliette, 478-992-8886;
www.thewhistlestopcafe.com
It's more than "lights, camera, action" at this "small town" spot "way off the beaten path" in Juliette, famous for being the "movie set" of *Fried Green Tomatoes,* now that "Southern cooking including the fixin's" takes center stage these days; you'd "better come hungry" to the renovated 1922 general store "at the end of a tiny street"; N.B. wine, beer and dinner have been added to the script.

Williamson Bros. Bar-B-Q   20 | 13 | 16 | $14
1600 Marietta Hwy. (Hwy. 575, exit 16A), Canton, 770-345-9067;
www.williamsonbros.com
See review in the Atlanta Directory.

Indexes

CUISINES
LOCATIONS
SPECIAL FEATURES

All restaurants are in the greater Atlanta Metropolitan area unless otherwise noted (S=Savannah; O=Other Outlying Areas).

CUISINES

American (New)
Anthony's
Aqua Blue
Aria
Bacchanalia
Bazzaar
B.E.D.
BluePointe
Buckhead Diner
Canoe
Cherry
City Grill
Clubhouse
Corner Cafe
dick and harry's
dish
D. Morgan's/O
East West Bistro/O
Eclipse di Luna/Sol
Einstein's
Feast
Feed Store
Fickle Pickle
Five & Ten/O
Five Seasons Brew.
Food 101
Food Studio
George's of Tybee/O
Globe
Grace 17.20
Haven
Hi Life Kitchen
Java Jive
Lobby at Twelve
MidCity Cuisine
Misto
Mitra
Olde Pink House/S
ONE. midtown
Park 75
PieBar
Pleasant Peasant
Quinones/Bacchanalia
Rainwater
Rathbun's
Real Chow Baby
Repast
Rest. Eugene
River Room
R. Thomas Deluxe
Rustic Gourmet
Sage on Sycamore
Simpatico
Spice
Sun Dial
Supper Club
Table 1280
Taurus
Toast
tomas
Toulouse
TWO. urban licks
Van Gogh's
Village Tavern
Vinocity
YellowFin

American (Traditional)
American Roadhse.
Atkins Park
Belly General
Blue Ribbon Grill
Brake Pad
Brickery G&B
Brookwood Grill
Cheesecake Factory
Chicago's Steak
Dailey's
Downwind
ESPN Zone
Feed Store
Garrison's Broiler
George's
Gold Star Cafe
Gordon Biersch
Greenwoods
High Cotton
Houston Mill
Houston's
Joey D's
Linger Longer B&G/O
Majestic
Manuel's Tavern
Marlow's Tavern
Mick's
Murphy's
Norcross Station
Paul's
Righteous Room
Roasters
Sun in My Belly
Tavern at Phipps

Cuisines

Ted's Montana
Terra Garden
Varsity
Varsity/O
Wahoo!
Zesto

Argentinean
Pampas Steak

Asian
BluePointe
Malaya
Real Chow Baby
Savu
Sia's
Trader Vic's

Asian Fusion
Roy's
Tin Drum Asia Café

Bakeries
Alon's
Bread Garden
Corner Cafe
Joli Kobe Bakery
La Madeleine/Bakery
Pao de Mel

Bangladeshi
Panahar

Barbecue
Barbecue Kitchen
Bobby & June's
Daddy D'z
Dreamland BBQ
Dusty's BBQ
Fat Matt's Rib
Harold's BBQ
Hometown BBQ
Johnny Harris/S
Old South BBQ
One Star Ranch
Pig-N-Chik
P.R.'s BBQ
Rib Ranch
Rolling Bones BBQ
Slope's BBQ
Smokejack
Swallow/Hollow
Williamson Bros. BBQ
Williamson Bros. BBQ/O

Brazilian
Boi Na Braza
Fire of Brazil
Fogo de Chão
Pao de Mel
Sal Grosso

Cajun
Atkins Park
Gumbeaux's
Hal's on Old Ivy
Huey's
McKinnon's
Pappadeaux Seafood
Redfish
Willie Rae's

Californian
Raging Burrito
Wolfgang Puck Exp.
Woodfire Grill

Caribbean
Bridgetown Grill

Chinese
(* dim sum specialist)
Bamboo Garden
Canton Cooks
Canton House*
China Cooks
China Delight*
Chin Chin
Chopstix
City Garden
Fortune Cookie
Grand China
Happy Valley*
Hong Kong Harbour*
House of Chan
Hsu's Gourmet
Lee's Golden Buddha
Little Szechuan
Mu Lan
Orient at Vinings
P.F. Chang's
Pung Mie

Coffee Shops/Diners
Cafe Intermezzo
Crescent Moon
Majestic
OK Cafe
Original Pancake

vote at zagat.com

Cuisines

Ria's Bluebird
Silver Grill
Silver Skillet
Sun in My Belly
Thumbs Up

Contemporary Louisiana
Emeril's

Continental
Après Diem
Carbo's Cafe
Ecco
45 S./Pirates' Hse./S
Joli Kobe Bakery
Nikolai's Roof
Pano's & Paul's
Petite Auberge
Ritz/Buckhead Café

Creole
Hal's on Old Ivy
Huey's
McKinnon's
Pappadeaux Seafood
Redfish

Cuban
Coco Loco
Fuego Spanish
Havana Sandwich
Las Palmeras
Salsa

Delis
Atlanta Bread
Atlanta Bread/S
Fabiano's Deli
Goldberg's Bagel
Jason's Deli
Muss & Turner's
New Yorker
Oak Grove
111 MLK
Pangaea
Provisions to Go
Rising Roll Sandwich

Dessert
Alon's
Aria
Atlanta Bread
Cafe Intermezzo
Cheesecake Factory

Dailey's
Gottlieb's/S
Jake's
La Madeleine/Bakery
Olde Pink House/S
Paolo's Gelato

Eastern European
Slovakia

Eclectic
Café Tu Tu Tango
Cargo Portside Grill/O
East Andrews Cafe
Eats
Eatzi's
Loaf & Kettle
Muss & Turner's
Roman Lily Cafe
Sapphire Grill/S
Shout
SoHo
Twist
Vickery's

European
Babette's Cafe
Bazzaar
Kurt's
Seeger's

Fondue
Dante's Down/Hatch
Melting Pot

French
Au Rendez Vous
Floataway Cafe
Joël
La Madeleine/Bakery
Les Fleurs De Lis
Nikolai's Roof
South of France

French (Bistro)
Anis Bistro
Cafe Alsace
Le Giverny
Pastis
Seasons de Provence
Soleil
Toulouse
Violette

Cuisines

French (Brasserie)
Au Pied de Cochon

French (New)
Atmosphere
B.E.D.
Epicurean
Le Clos/O
Ritz/Buckhead Din. Rm.

German
Vreny's Biergarten

Greek
Athens Pizza
Avra Greek Tavern
Downwind
Kyma
Taverna Plaka

Hamburgers
Johnny Rockets
Moe's & Joe's
Universal Joint
Vortex B&G
Zesto

Hawaiian
Roy's

Health Food
Flying Biscuit
Terra Garden

Hot Dogs
Varsity
Varsity/O
Zesto

Ice Cream Parlors
Jake's
Paolo's Gelato

Indian
Andy's Indian
Bollywood Masala
Bombay Grill
Haveli Indian
Himalayas Indian
Madras Saravana
Minerva Indian
Palace
Raja Indian
Santoor Indian
Touch of India

Udipi Cafe
Vatica Indian
Zyka

Irish
Fadó Irish Pub
Meehan's Pub

Italian
(N=Northern; S=Southern)
Alfredo's
Ali-Oli
Antica Posta (N)
Azio/Little Azio
Bambinelli's (S)
Baraonda (S)
Benedetti's
Bischero/O
Brio Tuscan Grille (N)
Brooklyn Cafe (N)
Buca di Beppo
Cafe Prego
Carrabba's Italian
Carrabba's Italian/S
Ciao Bella
di Paolo (N)
Dominick's
Eats (S)
Enoteca Carbonari
Figo Pasta
Floataway Cafe
Fratelli di Napoli (S)
Fritti
Garibaldi's/S
Il Localino
Il Pasticcio/S (N)
Ippolito's
La Grotta (N)
La Tavola
Lombardi's
Maggiano's
Misto
Nino's
Oscar's Villa Capri
Osteria 832
Pasta da Pulcinella (N)
Pasta Vino (N)
Portofino
Pricci
Roasted Garlic
Salvatore (S)
Sotto Sotto (N)
Tratt. La Strada
Tratt. Monaco
Veni Vidi Vici

vote at zagat.com 137

Cuisines

Villa Christina
Vinny's/Windward

Japanese
(* sushi specialist)
Atlantic Seafood Co.*
Benihana*
City Garden*
Edo
Genki*
Haru Ichiban*
Hashiguchi*
Imari*
Kobe Steaks
Lee's Golden Buddha
MF Sushibar*
Nagoya*
Nakato*
Nickiemoto's*
Ru San's*
Sushi Ave.*
Sushi Huku*
Taka*
Umezono*

Korean
(* barbecue specialist)
88 Tofu House
Hae Woon Dae BBQ*

Lebanese
Byblos
Cedars
Mezza Lebanese
Nicola's

Malaysian
Penang
Top Spice

Mediterranean
Ali-Oli
Ambra
Basil's
Café Lily
Carpe Diem
Cedars
Eno
Gilbert's Med.
Grape
Krog Bar
Lobby at Twelve
Milan Med.
Mosaic

Ritz/Buckhead Din. Rm.
Roasted Garlic
Shipfeifer

Mexican
Bajarito's
Chipotle
El Azteca
El Taco Veloz
Jalisco
Mexico City
Nuevo Laredo
Pappasito's Cantina
Pure Taqueria
Raging Burrito
Rio Grande Cantina
Rosa Mexicano
Sala – Sabor
Taqueria del Sol
Taqueria Sundown
Willy's Mexicana
Zapata
Zocalo

Moroccan
Imperial Fez

Noodle Shops
Doc Chey's Asian
Doc Chey's Asian/O
Genki
Noodle
Tin Drum Asia Café

Pacific Rim
Trader Vic's

Pan-Asian
Aqua Blue
Eurasia Bistro
Nickiemoto's
Noodle
Pacific Rim Bistro
Red & Green
Silk

Pan-Latin
La Fonda Latina
Loca Luna
Pura Vida
Tierra

Persian/Iranian
Persepolis

Cuisines

Peruvian
Machu Picchu

Pizza
Athens Pizza
Baraonda
Bischero/O
Cameli's Pizza
Everybody's Pizza
Fellini's Pizza
Fritti
Grant Central Pizza
Il Forno
Johnny's NY Pizza
Mellow Mushroom
Osteria 832
Oz Pizza
Pasta Vino
Ray's NY Pizza
Savage Pizza
Shorty's
Wolfgang Puck Exp.

Pub Food
Brick Store Pub
Fadó Irish Pub
Gordon Biersch
Manuel's Tavern
Marlow's Tavern
Meehan's Pub
Moe's & Joe's
Universal Joint

Sandwiches
Alon's
Atlanta Bread
Atlanta Bread/S
Blue Eyed Daisy
Bread Garden
Fabiano's Deli
Fickle Pickle
Goldberg's Bagel
Havana Sandwich
Jake's
Jason's Deli
Loaf & Kettle
New Yorker
111 MLK
Pangaea
Rising Roll Sandwich

Seafood
Atlanta Fish
Atlantic Seafood Co.
Blackstone
Cabernet
Chequers Seafood
Chops/Lobster Bar
Crab Shack/O
Dantanna's
dick and harry's
Fishmonger
Fontaine Oyster Hse.
Garibaldi's/S
Goldfish
McCormick/Schmick
Oceanaire
Pappadeaux Seafood
Prime
Ray's in the City
Ray's on the River
Red Snapper
Six Feet Under
Strip
Wahoo!
YellowFin

Small Plates
(See also Spanish tapas specialist)
Bazzaar (American/European)
Café Tu Tu Tango (Eclectic)
Cherry (New American)
East Andrews Cafe (Eclectic)
Ecco (Continental)
Enoteca Carbonari (Italian)
Feast (American)
Grape (Mediterranean)
Krog Bar (Mediterranean)
Mezza Lebanese (Lebanese)
Milan Med. (Mediterranean)
Mix (Asian/Mediterranean)
Noche (Southwestern)
Pura Vida (Pan-Latin)
Shout (Eclectic)
Silk (Pan-Asian)
Twist (Eclectic)
Vinocity (New American)

Soul Food
Busy Bee Cafe
Fat Matt's Chicken
Fat Matt's Rib
Horseradish Grill
Justin's
P.R.'s BBQ
Son's Place

Soup
Souper Jenny

vote at zagat.com

Cuisines

South African
10 Degrees S.

Southern
Agnes & Muriel's
Barbecue Kitchen
Blue Eyed Daisy
Blue Ridge Grill
Blue Willow Inn/O
Bobby & June's
Colonnade
Dillard House/O
Elizabeth on 37th/S
Fat Matt's Chicken
Fat Matt's Rib
Flying Biscuit
Food 101
Georgia's New Taste/O
Gottlieb's/S
Greenwoods
Horseradish Grill
Johnny Harris/S
Justin's
Lady & Sons/S
Mary Mac's
Matthew's Cafeteria
OK Cafe
Pittypat's Porch
P.R.'s BBQ
Real Food
Rest. Eugene
Ritz/Atlanta Grill
Silver Grill
Silver Skillet
Son's Place
South City Kitchen
Swan Coach Hse.
Thomas Mktpl.
Thumbs Up
Vickery's
Vinings Inn
Watershed
Whistle Stop Cafe/O
White House
Wisteria

Southwestern
Agave
Ambra
Asada
Georgia Grille
Moe's SW Grill
Nava
Noche
Sia's
Twisted Taco
Willie Rae's

Spanish
(* tapas specialist)
Eclipse di Luna/Sol*
Fuego Spanish*
Loca Luna*

Steakhouses
Aspens/Steak
Benihana
Blackstone
Bone's
Brookwood Grill
Cabernet
Capital Grille
Chicago's Steak
Chops/Lobster Bar
Cowtippers
Dantanna's
Fire of Brazil
Fleming's/Steak
Fogo de Chão
Garrison's Broiler
Hal's on Old Ivy
Highland Tap
Kobe Steaks
Linger Longer B&G/O
LongHorn Steak
McKendrick's Steak
Morton's Steak
New York Prime
Outback Steak
Palm
Pampas Steak
Prime
Ray's Killer Creek
Ruth's Chris
Sal Grosso
Stoney River Steak
Strip
Taurus

Tex-Mex
Caramba Cafe
Jalisco
La Paz
Pappasito's Cantina
Uncle Julio's

Thai
Annie's Thai
Bangkok Thai
Harry & Sons

Cuisines

Jitlada
King & I
Little Bangkok
Mali
Nan Thai
Northlake Thai
Pad Thai
Penang
Phuket Thai
Rice Thai
Sawadee Thai
Surin of Thailand
Surin's Thai
Tamarind
Thai Chili
Top Spice
Zab-E-Lee

Vegetarian
Cafe Sunflower
Flying Biscuit
Madras Saravana
Rainbow
R. Thomas Deluxe
Udipi Cafe
Vatica Indian

Vietnamese
Com Dunwoody/Vietnam
Nam
Pho Hoa
Pho 79

LOCATIONS

ATLANTA

Acworth/Cobb/Kennesaw/Marietta/Smyrna
Aspens/Steak
Atkins Park
Atlanta Bread
Azio/Little Azio
Blackstone
Carrabba's Italian
Chicago's Steak
Chin Chin
Doc Chey's Asian
El Taco Veloz
Hashiguchi
Haveli Indian
House of Chan
Houston's
Ippolito's
Johnny Rockets
Johnny's NY Pizza
La Madeleine/Bakery
LongHorn Steak
Mellow Mushroom
Melting Pot
Moe's SW Grill
Muss & Turner's
Old South BBQ
Outback Steak
Pao de Mel
Pappadeaux Seafood
Pappasito's Cantina
Ray's on the River
Rib Ranch
Roasters
Ru San's
Sal Grosso
Seasons de Provence
Simpatico
Slovakia
South City Kitchen
Sushi Huku
Ted's Montana
Tratt. La Strada
Umezono
Varsity
Vatica Indian
Williamson Bros. BBQ
Willie Rae's
Willy's Mexicana

Airport/Southside/College Park
Barbecue Kitchen
Brake Pad
Daddy D'z
Feed Store
Harold's BBQ
Zab-E-Lee
Zesto

Alpharetta/Cumming/Roswell/Stockbridge
Andy's Indian
Aqua Blue
Atlanta Bread
Atlantic Seafood Co.
Benihana
Brookwood Grill
Buca di Beppo
Byblos
Cabernet
Cheesecake Factory
Chicago's Steak
Chin Chin
Chipotle
dick and harry's
di Paolo
Dreamland BBQ
El Azteca
Fickle Pickle
Fire of Brazil
Fishmonger
Fratelli di Napoli
Greenwoods
Il Forno
Ippolito's
Jason's Deli
Johnny's NY Pizza
Marlow's Tavern
Meehan's Pub
Mellow Mushroom
Melting Pot
Minerva Indian
Moe's SW Grill
Nagoya
One Star Ranch
Outback Steak
Pampas Steak
Pappadeaux Seafood

Locations

Pasta Vino
Pastis
P.F. Chang's
P.R.'s BBQ
Pure Taqueria
Rainwater
Ray's Killer Creek
Ray's NY Pizza
Real Food
Red & Green
Rice Thai
Rising Roll Sandwich
Roasted Garlic
Roasters
Salvatore
Santoor Indian
Slope's BBQ
Smokejack
Stoney River Steak
Swallow/Hollow
Tratt. Monaco
Van Gogh's
Varsity
Village Tavern
Vinny's/Windward
YellowFin

Atlantic Station/Westside

Ambra
Bacchanalia
Figo Pasta
Food Studio
Lobby at Twelve
Misto
Nuevo Laredo
Pangaea
Provisions to Go
Quinones/Bacchanalia
Real Chow Baby
Rosa Mexicano
Strip
Taqueria del Sol

Brookhaven

Bajarito's
Chin Chin
Haven
Meehan's Pub
Mix
Terra Garden

Buckhead

Ali-Oli
Anis Bistro
Annie's Thai
Anthony's
Antica Posta
Aria
Atlanta Bread
Atlanta Fish
Au Pied de Cochon
Basil's
BluePointe
Blue Ridge Grill
Boi Na Braza
Bone's
Bridgetown Grill
Brio Tuscan Grille
Buckhead Diner
Cafe Prego
Café Tu Tu Tango
Capital Grille
Carbo's Cafe
Cedars
Cheesecake Factory
Chipotle
Chops/Lobster Bar
Chopstix
Ciao Bella
Clubhouse
Coco Loco
Corner Cafe
Dantanna's
Dante's Down/Hatch
East Andrews Cafe
Eatzi's
Eclipse di Luna/Sol
El Azteca
Emeril's
ESPN Zone
Fadó Irish Pub
Fellini's Pizza
Fogo de Chão
Genki
Goldberg's Bagel
Grand China
Grape
Hal's on Old Ivy
Hashiguchi
Horseradish Grill
Houston's
Jason's Deli
Joël
Johnny Rockets
Kyma
La Fonda Latina
La Grotta
La Madeleine/Bakery
Lee's Golden Buddha
LongHorn Steak

vote at zagat.com

Locations

Maggiano's
McKinnon's
Milan Med.
Moe's SW Grill
Morton's Steak
Mosaic
Nava
New Yorker
New York Prime
OK Cafe
One Star Ranch
Outback Steak
Palm
Pano's & Paul's
Pasta Vino
Portofino
Pricci
Prime
Raja Indian
Ray's NY Pizza
Rio Grande Cantina
Ritz/Buckhead Café
Ritz/Buckhead Din. Rm.
Roasters
Roy's
Ru San's
Ruth's Chris
Seeger's
Soleil
Souper Jenny
Surin's Thai
Swan Coach Hse.
Taka
Tavern at Phipps
10 Degrees S.
Twist
White House
Willy's Mexicana

Buford Hwy./Chamblee/Doraville

Athens Pizza
Bombay Grill
Canton House
China Delight
88 Tofu House
El Taco Veloz
Hae Woon Dae BBQ
Happy Valley
Havana Sandwich
Himalayas Indian
Little Szechuan
Machu Picchu
Panahar
Penang
Pho Hoa
Pho 79
Phuket Thai
Pig-N-Chik
Pung Mie

Cabbagetown/Candler Park/Inman Park/Grant Park

Agave
Asada
Fellini's Pizza
Flying Biscuit
Fritti
Grant Central Pizza
Il Localino
Johnny's NY Pizza
Krog Bar
La Fonda Latina
Rathbun's
Redfish
Ria's Bluebird
Roman Lily Cafe
Six Feet Under
Son's Place
Sotto Sotto
Thumbs Up
Wisteria

Cheshire Bridge

Alfredo's
Colonnade
Hong Kong Harbour
Jitlada
Johnny's NY Pizza
Little Bangkok
Nakato
Nino's
Original Pancake
Red Snapper
South of France
Taqueria Sundown
Taverna Plaka
Varsity
Woodfire Grill

Clairmont

Violette

Decatur/DeKalb/Emory

Athens Pizza
Atlanta Bread

Locations

Bamboo Garden
Benedetti's
Bollywood Masala
Brick Store Pub
Cafe Alsace
Café Lily
Carpe Diem
Chipotle
Crescent Moon
Doc Chey's Asian
Downwind
Dusty's BBQ
Edo
Epicurean
Eurasia Bistro
Everybody's Pizza
Feast
Fellini's Pizza
Figo Pasta
Floataway Cafe
Fortune Cookie
Houston Mill
Jake's
Johnny's NY Pizza
Le Giverny
LongHorn Steak
Madras Saravana
Mellow Mushroom
Mexico City
Mezza Lebanese
Mick's
Moe's SW Grill
Nicola's
Noodle
Oak Grove
Outback Steak
Oz Pizza
Petite Auberge
Raging Burrito
Rainbow
Rustic Gourmet
Sage on Sycamore
Shorty's
Supper Club
Sushi Ave.
Taqueria del Sol
Thai Chili
Top Spice
Touch of India
Udipi Cafe
Universal Joint
Wahoo!
Watershed
Willy's Mexicana

Zocalo
Zyka

Douglasville
Gumbeaux's
Johnny Rockets
Outback Steak
Williamson Bros. BBQ

Downtown/Underground
Azio/Little Azio
B.E.D.
Benihana
Busy Bee Cafe
City Grill
Dailey's
Haveli Indian
Hsu's Gourmet
Johnny Rockets
Les Fleurs De Lis
Loaf & Kettle
Lombardi's
McCormick/Schmick
Mick's
Morton's Steak
Nikolai's Roof
Noodle
111 MLK
Pacific Rim Bistro
Pittypat's Porch
Ray's in the City
Ritz/Atlanta Grill
Rolling Bones BBQ
Ruth's Chris
Sun Dial
Ted's Montana
Trader Vic's
TWO. urban licks
Varsity
Willy's Mexicana

Duluth/Gwinnett/Norcross
Athens Pizza
Atlanta Bread
Bamboo Garden
Carrabba's Italian
Chin Chin
Chipotle
Dominick's
Dreamland BBQ
El Taco Veloz
Garrison's Broiler
Grace 17.20
Grape

vote at zagat.com

Locations

Haru Ichiban
Hi Life Kitchen
Hometown BBQ
Ippolito's
Jason's Deli
Johnny Rockets
Kurt's
La Madeleine/Bakery
LongHorn Steak
Melting Pot
Norcross Station
Original Pancake
Outback Steak
Palace
Pappadeaux Seafood
P.F. Chang's
Rising Roll Sandwich
Sia's
Stoney River Steak
Ted's Montana
tomas
Varsity
Vreny's Biergarten
Zapata

Dunwoody/Sandy Springs

Atlanta Bread
Au Rendez Vous
Brickery G&B
Bridgetown Grill
Brio Tuscan Grille
Brooklyn Cafe
Cafe Intermezzo
Cafe Sunflower
Canton Cooks
Cheesecake Factory
Chequers Seafood
Chicago's Steak
China Cooks
Chin Chin
Com Dunwoody/Vietnam
Doc Chey's Asian
Eatzi's
El Taco Veloz
Fire of Brazil
Fishmonger
Five Seasons Brew.
Fleming's/Steak
Food 101
Garrison's Broiler
Goldberg's Bagel
Goldfish
Grape

High Cotton
Houston's
Il Forno
Ippolito's
Jason's Deli
Joey D's
Joli Kobe Bakery
Kobe Steaks
La Grotta
La Madeleine/Bakery
LongHorn Steak
Maggiano's
McCormick/Schmick
McKendrick's Steak
Meehan's Pub
Mellow Mushroom
Moe's SW Grill
Oscar's Villa Capri
Persepolis
P.F. Chang's
Pig-N-Chik
Ray's NY Pizza
Roasters
Ruth's Chris
Savu
Sawadee Thai
Slope's BBQ
Tin Drum Asia Café
Villa Christina
Willy's Mexicana

East Atlanta

Azio/Little Azio
Grant Central Pizza
Salsa

East Point

LongHorn Steak
Oz Pizza
Thumbs Up

Fairburn

Oz Pizza

Fayetteville

Ted's Montana

Forest Park

Thomas Mktpl.
Zesto

Hapeville

Rising Roll Sandwich

Locations

Intown/Midtown
Agnes & Muriel's
Après Diem
Avra Greek Tavern
Azio/Little Azio
Bangkok Thai
Baraonda
Bazzaar
Bobby & June's
Bread Garden
Cameli's Pizza
Cherry
Chin Chin
Cowtippers
Eats
Ecco
Einstein's
Eno
Enoteca Carbonari
Fabiano's Deli
Flying Biscuit
Fuego Spanish
Gilbert's Med.
Globe
Gold Star Cafe
Gordon Biersch
King & I
Las Palmeras
Loca Luna
Mary Mac's
Mellow Mushroom
MF Sushibar
Mick's
MidCity Cuisine
Mitra
Moe's SW Grill
Mu Lan
Nan Thai
Nickiemoto's
Noodle
Oceanaire
ONE. midtown
Park 75
Pasta da Pulcinella
PieBar
Pleasant Peasant
Repast
Rising Roll Sandwich
Ru San's
Shout
Silk
Silver Grill
Silver Skillet
South City Kitchen
Spice
Table 1280
Tamarind
Ted's Montana
Thai Chili
Tierra
Tin Drum Asia Café
Toast
Top Spice
Twisted Taco
Veni Vidi Vici
Vickery's
Vinocity
Vortex B&G
Willy's Mexicana
Zocalo

Jonesboro
Harold's BBQ

Kirkwood
Sun in My Belly

Little Five Points
Savage Pizza
Vortex B&G
Zesto

Morningside/Poncey-Highlands/Virginia Highlands
Alon's
American Roadhse.
Atkins Park
Atmosphere
Babette's Cafe
Belly General
Caramba Cafe
dish
Doc Chey's Asian
Eclipse di Luna/Sol
El Azteca
Everybody's Pizza
Fat Matt's Chicken
Fat Matt's Rib
Fellini's Pizza
Fontaine Oyster Hse.
Food 101
George's
Harry & Sons
Highland Tap
Java Jive
La Fonda Latina

vote at zagat.com

Locations

La Tavola
Majestic
Mali
Manuel's Tavern
Moe's & Joe's
Murphy's
Nam
Noche
Osteria 832
Pad Thai
Paolo's Gelato
Pura Vida
Righteous Room
Sala – Sabor
Surin of Thailand
Willy's Mexicana
Zesto

Morrow
Carrabba's Italian

Newnan/Palmetto/Peachtree City
Blue Eyed Daisy
Carrabba's Italian
Chin Chin
Original Pancake
Outback Steak
Ted's Montana

Peachtree Hills/South Buckhead
Benihana
Cafe Intermezzo
Cafe Sunflower
City Garden
El Azteca
Fellini's Pizza
Figo Pasta
Fratelli di Napoli
Georgia Grille
Houston's
Huey's
Imari
Imperial Fez

Atlanta Bread
Carrabba's Italian
Elizabeth on 37th
45 S./Pirates' Hse.
Garibaldi's
Gottlieb's

Jalisco
Justin's
Malaya
Mick's
Moe's SW Grill
Paul's
Rest. Eugene
R. Thomas Deluxe
Salsa
Shipfeifer
Taurus
Toulouse
Uncle Julio's
Willy's Mexicana
Wolfgang Puck Exp.

Snellville/Stone Mountain/Tucker
Bambinelli's
Blue Ribbon Grill
Crescent Moon
Jason's Deli
Matthew's Cafeteria
Northlake Thai
Original Pancake
Outback Steak

Vinings
Canoe
Garrison's Broiler
Grape
La Madeleine/Bakery
La Paz
Marlow's Tavern
Meehan's Pub
Mellow Mushroom
Orient at Vinings
River Room
SoHo
Vinings Inn

Woodstock
Chin Chin
Slope's BBQ

SAVANNAH

Il Pasticcio
Johnny Harris
Lady & Sons
Olde Pink House
Sapphire Grill

Locations

OTHER OUTLYING AREAS

Athens
Bischero
Doc Chey's Asian
East West Bistro
Five & Ten
Varsity

Braselton
Le Clos

Brunswick
Cargo Portside Grill

Canton
Williamson Bros. BBQ

Cartersville
D. Morgan's

Dillard
Dillard House

Greensboro
Georgia's New Taste
Linger Longer B&G

Juliette
Whistle Stop Cafe

Social Circle
Blue Willow Inn

Tybee Island
Crab Shack
George's of Tybee

Special Features

SPECIAL FEATURES

(Indexes list the best in each category. Multi-location restaurants' features may vary by branch.)

Breakfast
(See also Hotel Dining)
American Roadhse.
Atlanta Bread
Atlanta Bread/S
Barbecue Kitchen
Belly General
Bobby & June's
Corner Cafe
Crescent Moon
Flying Biscuit
Goldberg's Bagel
Gold Star Cafe
Huey's
Jason's Deli
Java Jive
La Madeleine/Bakery
Majestic
Matthew's Cafeteria
New Yorker
Oak Grove
OK Cafe
Original Pancake
Pangaea
Ria's Bluebird
R. Thomas Deluxe
Silver Skillet
Son's Place
Thomas Mktpl.
Thumbs Up
White House
Willy's Mexicana

Brunch
Agnes & Muriel's
American Roadhse.
Après Diem
Atkins Park
Atmosphere
Babette's Cafe
Basil's
Blue Ridge Grill
Bollywood Masala
Brake Pad
Brio Tuscan Grille
Buckhead Diner
Cafe Alsace
Cafe Intermezzo
Café Lily
Canoe
Carpe Diem
Cheesecake Factory
Chequers Seafood
Corner Cafe
Einstein's
Fadó Irish Pub
Five & Ten/O
Flying Biscuit
Food 101
Gilbert's Med.
Himalayas Indian
Horseradish Grill
Java Jive
La Tavola
Les Fleurs De Lis
Manuel's Tavern
Mick's
Murphy's
OK Cafe
Pangaea
Park 75
Pastis
Pleasant Peasant
Ray's on the River
Real Food
Ritz/Atlanta Grill
Ritz/Buckhead Café
River Room
Roman Lily Cafe
R. Thomas Deluxe
Sage on Sycamore
Soleil
South City Kitchen
Spice
Toast
Vickery's
Village Tavern
Wahoo!
Watershed
Zocalo

Buffet Served
(Check availability)
Andy's Indian
B.E.D.
Blue Willow Inn/O
Bollywood Masala
Bombay Grill

Special Features

Byblos
Cedars
Chequers Seafood
Georgia's New Taste/O
Gilbert's Med.
Haveli Indian
Himalayas Indian
Lady & Sons/S
Madras Saravana
Panahar
Pappadeaux Seafood
Persepolis
Ray's on the River
Ritz/Atlanta Grill
Ritz/Buckhead Café
Santoor Indian
Touch of India
Udipi Cafe
Wahoo!

Business Dining
Anthony's
Antica Posta
Aria
Atlanta Fish
Bacchanalia
Blue Ridge Grill
Boi Na Braza
Bone's
Buckhead Diner
Cabernet
Cafe Intermezzo
Canoe
Capital Grille
Carbo's Cafe
Chops/Lobster Bar
City Grill
Dailey's
dick and harry's
Elizabeth on 37th/S
Emeril's
Eno
Fire of Brazil
Fleming's/Steak
Fogo de Chão
Food Studio
45 S./Pirates' Hse./S
Georgia Grille
Horseradish Grill
Il Pasticcio/S
Joël
Joey D's
Kyma
La Grotta
Lobby at Twelve
Maggiano's
McKendrick's Steak
MidCity Cuisine
Morton's Steak
Nan Thai
Nava
New York Prime
Nikolai's Roof
Oceanaire
Palm
Pano's & Paul's
Paul's
Pittypat's Porch
Pricci
Prime
Quinones/Bacchanalia
Real Food
Rest. Eugene
Ritz/Atlanta Grill
Ritz/Buckhead Din. Rm.
Rosa Mexicano
Roy's
Ruth's Chris
Seeger's
Sia's
South City Kitchen
Table 1280
Tamarind
Taurus
Trader Vic's
Van Gogh's
Veni Vidi Vici
Villa Christina
Vinings Inn
Vinny's/Windward

BYO
Alon's
Blue Willow Inn/O
Dillard House/O
Figo Pasta
Loaf & Kettle
Nicola's
Panahar
Sun in My Belly
Udipi Cafe
Vatica Indian
Zab-E-Lee

Celebrity Chefs
Aria, *Gerry Klaskala*
Atlanta Fish, *Robert Holley*
Babette's Cafe, *Marla Adams*
Bacchanalia, *Anne Quatrano, Clifford Harrison*

Special Features

Five & Ten/O, *Hugh Acheson, Chuck Ramsey*
Floataway Cafe, *Anne Quatrano*
Georgia Grille, *Karen Hilliard*
Joël, *Joël Antunes*
Krog Bar, *Kevin Rathbun*
La Grotta, *Antonio Abizanda*
Lobby at Twelve, *Nick Oltarsh*
MF Sushibar, *Chris Kinjo*
Nan Thai, *Nan Niyomkul*
ONE. midtown, *Richard Blais*
Park 75, *Robert Gerstenecker*
Paul's, *Paul Albrecht*
Provisions to Go, *Anne Quatrano, Clifford Harrison*
Quinones/Bacchanalia, *Anne Quatrano, Clifford Harrison*
Rathbun's, *Kevin Rathbun*
Ritz/Buckhead Din. Rm., *Bruno Menard*
Roy's, *Roy Yamaguchi*
Seeger's, *Guenter Seeger*
Shout, *Ian Winslade*
Sotto Sotto, *Riccardo Ullio*
Taurus, *Gary Mennie*
Twist, *Peter Kaiser*
TWO. urban licks, *Scott Serpas*
Veni Vidi Vici, *Jamie Adams*
Watershed, *Scott Peacock*
Woodfire Grill, *Michael Tuohy*

Child-Friendly

(Alternatives to the usual fast-food places; * children's menu available)

American Roadhse.*
Asada*
Athens Pizza*
Atkins Park*
Atlanta Bread*
Atlanta Bread/S*
Atlanta Fish*
Atlantic Seafood Co.*
Babette's Cafe*
Bajarito's*
Bambinelli's*
Baraonda
Barbecue Kitchen*
Basil's
Blue Ribbon Grill*
Bobby & June's
Brake Pad
Brickery G&B*
Bridgetown Grill*
Brio Tuscan Grille*
Brookwood Grill*
Buckhead Diner
Byblos*
Cafe Sunflower*
Cameli's Pizza
Caramba Cafe*
Carrabba's Italian*
Carrabba's Italian/S*
Cheesecake Factory
Chequers Seafood*
Chin Chin*
City Garden
Clubhouse*
Coco Loco*
Colonnade
Corner Cafe*
Crescent Moon*
Dailey's*
Doc Chey's Asian*
Dominick's*
Eats
Einstein's*
El Azteca*
El Taco Veloz*
ESPN Zone*
Eurasia Bistro
Everybody's Pizza
Fat Matt's Chicken
Fellini's Pizza
Fickle Pickle*
Flying Biscuit*
Food 101*
Fortune Cookie
Fratelli di Napoli*
Fuego Spanish
Garrison's Broiler*
Georgia's New Taste/O*
Goldberg's Bagel*
Gold Star Cafe
Grand China*
Grant Central Pizza
Haven
High Cotton*
Horseradish Grill*
Houston's*
Imari
Ippolito's*
Jake's*
Jalisco*
Jason's Deli*
Java Jive
Johnny Harris/S*
Johnny Rockets*
Johnny's NY Pizza*

152 subscribe to zagat.com

Special Features

Lady & Sons/S
La Madeleine/Bakery*
La Paz*
Lee's Golden Buddha*
Linger Longer B&G/O*
LongHorn Steak*
Madras Saravana*
Maggiano's*
Marlow's Tavern*
Mary Mac's*
McCormick/Schmick*
Meehan's Pub*
Mellow Mushroom
Melting Pot
Mexico City*
Mick's*
MidCity Cuisine*
Moe's SW Grill*
Murphy's*
Muss & Turner's*
Nicola's
Nino's
Norcross Station*
Nuevo Laredo*
OK Cafe
Old South BBQ*
Original Pancake*
Outback Steak*
Pangaea
Pappadeaux Seafood*
Pasta Vino*
Prime*
P.R.'s BBQ*
Raging Burrito*
Rainwater*
Ray's in the City*
Ray's on the River*
Real Chow Baby*
Real Food*
Ria's Bluebird
Rising Roll Sandwich*
Ritz/Buckhead Café*
Roasted Garlic*
Roasters*
Roman Lily Cafe
R. Thomas Deluxe*
Sage on Sycamore*
Sala – Sabor*
Salsa*
Savu
Shipfeifer
Silver Grill
Silver Skillet
Six Feet Under*
Smokejack*
Soleil
Son's Place*
Souper Jenny
Stoney River Steak*
Sun in My Belly*
Swallow/Hollow
Tavern at Phipps*
Ted's Montana*
Terra Garden*
Thomas Mktpl.
Thumbs Up
Tratt. La Strada*
Uncle Julio's*
Varsity*
Village Tavern*
Vinny's/Windward*
Vreny's Biergarten*
Watershed*
Whistle Stop Cafe/O*
White House*
Willie Rae's
Willy's Mexicana*
Wisteria*
Zapata*
Zesto*
Zocalo*

Delivery/Takeout
(D=delivery, T=takeout)
Agave (T)
Agnes & Muriel's (T)
Alfredo's (T)
Ali-Oli (T)
Anis Bistro (T)
Antica Posta (T)
Aqua Blue (T)
Asada (T)
Aspens/Steak (T)
Atkins Park (T)
Atlanta Fish (T)
Atlantic Seafood Co. (T)
Atmosphere (T)
Au Rendez Vous (T)
Babette's Cafe (T)
Bambinelli's (T)
Basil's (T)
Bazzaar (T)
Belly General (D,T)
Blackstone (T)
BluePointe (T)
Blue Ridge Grill (T)
Bollywood Masala (T)
Brio Tuscan Grille (T)

Special Features

Brookwood Grill (T)
Buckhead Diner (T)
Byblos (T)
Cabernet (T)
Cafe Alsace (T)
Cafe Intermezzo (T)
Café Lily (T)
Cafe Sunflower (T)
Café Tu Tu Tango (T)
Canoe (T)
Cheesecake Factory (T)
Chequers Seafood (T)
Cherry (T)
Chicago's Steak (T)
Chops/Lobster Bar (T)
Chopstix (T)
Ciao Bella (T)
City Grill (T)
Coco Loco (T)
Colonnade (T)
Cowtippers (T)
Crab Shack/O (T)
Crescent Moon (T)
dick and harry's (T)
di Paolo (T)
dish (T)
D. Morgan's/O (T)
Eclipse di Luna/Sol (T)
Eno (T)
Eurasia Bistro (T)
Feed Store (T)
Fishmonger (T)
Five & Ten/O (T)
Five Seasons Brew. (T)
Flying Biscuit (T)
Fontaine Oyster Hse. (T)
Food 101 (T)
Garrison's Broiler (T)
Georgia Grille (T)
Grace 17.20 (T)
Greenwoods (T)
Hal's on Old Ivy (T)
Haven (T)
High Cotton (T)
Highland Tap (T)
Hi Life Kitchen (T)
Horseradish Grill (T)
Houston's (T)
Imari (T)
Imperial Fez (T)
Ippolito's (T)
Jalisco (T)
Java Jive (T)
Joey D's (T)
Kurt's (T)
Kyma (T)
Lady & Sons/S (D,T)
La Grotta (D,T)
La Tavola (T)
Le Giverny (T)
Les Fleurs De Lis (T)
Loaf & Kettle (T)
Loca Luna (T)
Lombardi's (T)
LongHorn Steak (T)
Marlow's Tavern (T)
Mary Mac's (T)
McCormick/Schmick (T)
McKinnon's (T)
Meehan's Pub (T)
MidCity Cuisine (T)
Milan Med. (T)
Misto (T)
Mitra (T)
Murphy's (T)
Muss & Turner's (T)
Nava (T)
Nickiemoto's (T)
Nicola's (T)
Nino's (T)
Noche (T)
Norcross Station (T)
111 MLK (T)
Original Pancake (T)
Oscar's Villa Capri (T)
Osteria 832 (T)
Outback Steak (T)
Pacific Rim Bistro (T)
Palm (T)
Pampas Steak (T)
Panahar (T)
Pappadeaux Seafood (T)
Pappasito's Cantina (T)
Pastis (T)
Persepolis (T)
Petite Auberge (T)
P.F. Chang's (T)
Pleasant Peasant (T)
Portofino (T)
Pricci (T)
Prime (T)
Pura Vida (T)
Rainwater (T)
Rathbun's (T)
Ray's in the City (T)
Ray's on the River (T)
Real Food (T)
Red Snapper (T)

Rest. Eugene (T)
Ria's Bluebird (T)
River Room (T)
Roasted Garlic (T)
Roman Lily Cafe (T)
Roy's (T)
R. Thomas Deluxe (T)
Rustic Gourmet (T)
Ruth's Chris (T)
Sage on Sycamore (T)
Sala – Sabor (T)
Salvatore (T)
Sapphire Grill/S (T)
Savu (T)
Shipfeifer (T)
Shout (T)
Silk (T)
Silver Grill (T)
Silver Skillet (T)
Simpatico (T)
Six Feet Under (T)
Slovakia (T)
Smokejack (T)
Son's Place (T)
South City Kitchen (T)
South of France (T)
Sun in My Belly (D,T)
Swallow/Hollow (T)
Swan Coach Hse. (T)
Taverna Plaka (T)
Tavern at Phipps (T)
Ted's Montana (T)
10 Degrees S. (T)
Terra Garden (T)
Thumbs Up (T)
Tierra (T)
Tin Drum Asia Café (T)
Toast (T)
tomas (T)
Tratt. La Strada (T)
Twist (T)
TWO. urban licks (T)
Universal Joint (T)
Veni Vidi Vici (T)
Vickery's (T)
Villa Christina (T)
Village Tavern (T)
Vinings Inn (T)
Vinny's/Windward (T)
Violette (T)
Vreny's Biergarten (T)
Wahoo! (T)
Watershed (T)
Whistle Stop Cafe/O (T)
White House (T)

Willie Rae's (T)
Zocalo (T)
Zyka (T)

Dining Alone
(Other than hotels and places with counter service)
Alon's
Ambra
Andy's Indian
Anis Bistro
Blue Eyed Daisy
Blue Ribbon Grill
Busy Bee Cafe
Chipotle
Com Dunwoody/Vietnam
Corner Cafe
Eats
Everybody's Pizza
Feast
Figo Pasta
Flying Biscuit
Houston's
Imari
Jake's
Jason's Deli
Java Jive
La Madeleine/Bakery
Les Fleurs De Lis
Loaf & Kettle
MF Sushibar
Murphy's
Nicola's
Nino's
Noodle
111 MLK
Pangaea
Paul's
R. Thomas Deluxe
Rustic Gourmet
Salsa
Shorty's
Soleil
Son's Place
Sun in My Belly
Surin's Thai
Tamarind
Taqueria del Sol
Taqueria Sundown
10 Degrees S.
Terra Garden
Thai Chili
Tierra
Tin Drum Asia Café
Uncle Julio's

Special Features

Entertainment
(Call for days and times of performances)
Aqua Blue (jazz)
Atkins Park (guitar)
Atmosphere (jazz)
Au Pied de Cochon (jazz trio)
Bazzaar (DJ)
Blackstone (varies)
Brookwood Grill (piano)
Byblos (belly dancing)
Café Tu Tu Tango (varies)
Carbo's Cafe (piano)
Carpe Diem (DJ)
Chicago's Steak (varies)
Chopstix (piano)
Coco Loco (guitar/vocals)
Dailey's (jazz/piano)
Dante's Down/Hatch (jazz)
East Andrews Cafe (varies)
Fadó Irish Pub (Irish bands)
Fat Matt's Rib (blues)
Five Seasons Brew. (jazz)
Fuego Spanish (flamenco)
Goldfish (piano)
Grape (varies)
Hal's on Old Ivy (piano/vocals)
Imperial Fez (belly dancing)
Lady & Sons/S (singing waiters)
Loca Luna (Latin/salsa)
Manuel's Tavern (improv)
Marlow's Tavern (varies)
McKinnon's (open mike/piano)
Mexico City (guitar)
Nickiemoto's (drag shows)
Pampas Steak (tango)
Park 75 (piano)
Pastis (jazz)
Pura Vida (tango)
Ray's on the River (jazz)
Ritz/Atlanta Grill (jazz)
Ritz/Buckhead Café (jazz trio)
River Room (guitar/jazz)
Sala – Sabor (Latin band)
Smokejack (blues)
South of France (guitar/vocals)
Swallow/Hollow (country)
Tavern at Phipps (varies)
Twisted Taco (varies)
TWO. urban licks (blues)
Vinings Inn (varies)
Vinny's/Windward (jazz trio)
Violette (varies)

Family-Style
Colonnade
Com Dunwoody/Vietnam
Dillard House/O
Dreamland BBQ
Dusty's BBQ
Everybody's Pizza
Fratelli di Napoli
Greenwoods
Il Localino
Maggiano's
Melting Pot
Nicola's
Old South BBQ
Orient at Vinings
P.F. Chang's

Fireplaces
Agave
Ali-Oli
Blackstone
Blue Ridge Grill
Blue Willow Inn/O
Cabernet
Carbo's Cafe
Ciao Bella
Colonnade
Elizabeth on 37th/S
Fadó Irish Pub
Fishmonger
Fogo de Chão
Food Studio
45 S./Pirates' Hse./S
Garrison's Broiler
Georgia's New Taste/O
Grape
Greenwoods
Harold's BBQ
Highland Tap
Horseradish Grill
Houston Mill
Houston's
Justin's
Kurt's
La Madeleine/Bakery
Le Giverny
Linger Longer B&G/O
Moe's SW Grill
Olde Pink House/S
Pastis
Persepolis
Portofino
Rainwater
Real Food
Redfish

Special Features

Ruth's Chris
Savu
South City Kitchen
South of France
Stoney River Steak
10 Degrees S.
Van Gogh's
Village Tavern
Vinings Inn
Violette

Gracious Hosts
Aqua Blue, *John Metz*
Babette's Cafe, *Marla Adams*
Byblos, *Nelly Perez*
Café Lily, *Angelo/Anthony Pitillo*
Chopstix, *Philip Chan*
di Paolo, *Susan Thill*
Fishmonger, *Nik Panatotolous*
Imperial Fez, *Rafih/Rita Benjelloun*
La Grotta, *Sergio Favalli*
McKendrick's Steak, *Doug McKendrick*
Murphy's, *Tom Murphy*
Ritz/Buckhead Din. Rm., *Claude Guillaume*
Salsa, *Alexander Palacios*
Sia's, *Sia Moshk*
Tierra, *Ticha & Dan Krinsky*
Van Gogh's, *Chris/Michele Sedgwick*

Historic Places
(Year opened; * building)
1771 Olde Pink House/S*
1790 Greenwoods*
1797 Anthony's*
1800 Swan Coach Hse.*
1847 Smokejack*
1853 Vinings Inn*
1855 Pastis*
1880 D. Morgan's/O*
1890 Pleasant Peasant*
1890 Rathbun's*
1890 Vinocity*
1898 Lady & Sons/S
1900 Elizabeth on 37th/S*
1900 Manuel's Tavern*
1900 Mu Lan*
1900 Sage on Sycamore*
1900 Wisteria*
1902 Food Studio*
1912 City Grill*
1913 Les Fleurs De Lis*
1913 Loaf & Kettle*
1917 Blue Willow Inn/O*
1917 Dillard House/O*
1920 Seeger's*
1920 South City Kitchen*
1920 Spice*
1922 Atkins Park
1922 Soleil*
1922 Whistle Stop Cafe/O*
1924 Johnny Harris/S
1924 Toast*
1927 Colonnade
1928 Varsity
1929 Majestic*
1940 Asada*
1945 Mary Mac's*
1945 Silver Grill
1947 Busy Bee Cafe*
1947 Harold's BBQ
1947 Moe's & Joe's*
1948 White House
1949 Zesto
1955 Matthew's Cafeteria
1956 Silver Skillet

Hotel Dining
Château Élan Winery & Resort
  Le Clos/O
Crowne Plaza Buckhead
  Milan Med.
Crowne Plaza Ravinia Hotel
  La Grotta
Embassy Suites Hotel
  Ruth's Chris
Emory Inn
  Le Giverny
Four Seasons Atlanta
  Park 75
Glenn Hotel
  B.E.D.
Hilton Atlanta
  Nikolai's Roof
  Trader Vic's
InterContinental Buckhead
  Au Pied de Cochon
Ritz-Carlton Atlanta
  Ritz/Atlanta Grill
Ritz-Carlton Buckhead
  Ritz/Buckhead Café
  Ritz/Buckhead Din. Rm.
Ritz-Carlton Lodge
  Georgia's New Taste/O
  Linger Longer B&G/O
Twelve Hotel
  Lobby at Twelve

Special Features

Westin Buckhead
  Palm
Westin Peachtree Plaza
  Sun Dial
W Hotel
  Savu

Jacket Required
Le Clos/O
Ritz/Buckhead Din. Rm.
Seeger's

Late Dining
(Weekday closing hour)
Après Diem (12 AM)
Atkins Park (varies)
Au Pied de Cochon (24 hrs.)
Brake Pad (12 AM)
Brick Store Pub (12 AM)
Buckhead Diner (12 AM)
Cafe Intermezzo (varies)
Café Tu Tu Tango (varies)
Canton Cooks (2:30 AM)
Canton House (12 AM)
China Cooks (2 AM)
Dantanna's (3 AM)
88 Tofu House (24 hrs.)
El Taco Veloz (varies)
Fadó Irish Pub (1:30 AM)
Fellini's Pizza (2 AM)
Fontaine Oyster Hse. (12 AM)
Fuego Spanish (12 AM)
Gordon Biersch (12 AM)
Hae Woon Dae BBQ (6 AM)
Happy Valley (12 AM)
Hashiguchi (varies)
Hong Kong Harbour (1 AM)
Krog Bar (12 AM)
Loca Luna (12 AM)
Majestic (24 hrs.)
Manuel's Tavern (1 AM)
Marlow's Tavern (varies)
Meehan's Pub (varies)
Moe's & Joe's (12 AM)
ONE. midtown (12 AM)
PieBar (12 AM)
Ray's NY Pizza (varies)
Righteous Room (1 AM)
R. Thomas Deluxe (24 hrs.)
Twisted Taco (2:30 AM)
TWO. urban licks (12 AM)
Universal Joint (12 AM)
Vortex B&G (varies)
Zesto (12 AM)

Meet for a Drink
Après Diem
Aqua Blue
Aria
Atkins Park
Atlanta Fish
Atmosphere
Au Pied de Cochon
Avra Greek Tavern
Basil's
Bazzaar
BluePointe
Blue Ridge Grill
Bone's
Brio Tuscan Grille
Buckhead Diner
Cabernet
Cafe Intermezzo
Café Tu Tu Tango
Capital Grille
Carbo's Cafe
Carpe Diem
Cherry
Chops/Lobster Bar
City Grill
Dailey's
Dantanna's
Dante's Down/Hatch
dick and harry's
East Andrews Cafe
East West Bistro/O
Eclipse di Luna/Sol
Einstein's
Emeril's
Eno
Feast
Five Seasons Brew.
Fleming's/Steak
Fontaine Oyster Hse.
Food 101
Food Studio
Genki
George's
Goldfish
Gordon Biersch
Grape
Hal's on Old Ivy
Highland Tap
Hi Life Kitchen
Horseradish Grill
Joël
Justin's
Krog Bar
Le Giverny

subscribe to zagat.com

Special Features

Lobby at Twelve
Manuel's Tavern
McCormick/Schmick
Meehan's Pub
MidCity Cuisine
Milan Med.
Mix
Moe's & Joe's
Nava
Oceanaire
ONE. midtown
Paul's
PieBar
Portofino
Pricci
Prime
Pure Taqueria
Ray's Killer Creek
Real Food
Righteous Room
Rosa Mexicano
Roy's
R. Thomas Deluxe
Sala – Sabor
Sapphire Grill/S
Savu
Shout
Smokejack
SoHo
Soleil
South City Kitchen
Spice
Strip
Table 1280
Taqueria Sundown
Taurus
Tavern at Phipps
Tratt. La Strada
Twist
Twisted Taco
TWO. urban licks
Van Gogh's
Veni Vidi Vici
Vickery's
Villa Christina
Village Tavern
Vinny's/Windward
Vinocity
Vortex B&G
Zocalo

Microbreweries
Five Seasons Brew.
Gordon Biersch

Natural/Organic
(These restaurants often or always use organic, local ingredients)
Aria
Bacchanalia
Belly General
Blue Eyed Daisy
Blue Ridge Grill
Canoe
Carpe Diem
Elizabeth on 37th/S
Five & Ten/O
Floataway Cafe
Food Studio
Globe
Gottlieb's/S
Joël
MidCity Cuisine
ONE. midtown
Park 75
Provisions to Go
Quinones/Bacchanalia
Rainbow
Rathbun's
Rest. Eugene
R. Thomas Deluxe
Rustic Gourmet
Seeger's
Sia's
Smokejack
South City Kitchen
Supper Club
Table 1280
Thomas Mktpl.
Tierra
Toast
Tratt. Monaco
Van Gogh's
Watershed
Wisteria
Woodfire Grill

Noteworthy Newcomers
Avra Greek Tavern
B.E.D.
Blue Eyed Daisy
Com Dunwoody/Vietnam
Ecco
Enoteca Carbonari
Feast
Fleming's/Steak
Food 101
Globe
Krog Bar

vote at zagat.com

Special Features

Lobby at Twelve
Mix
Paul's
PieBar
Pure Taqueria
Quinones/Bacchanalia
Red & Green
Redfish
Repast
Rosa Mexicano
Seasons de Provence
Shorty's
Strip
Table 1280
Taurus

Offbeat
Agave
Agnes & Muriel's
Après Diem
Au Rendez Vous
Avra Greek Tavern
Benihana
Blue Eyed Daisy
Brake Pad
Bridgetown Grill
Buca di Beppo
Cafe Sunflower
Café Tu Tu Tango
Carpe Diem
Com Dunwoody/Vietnam
Dante's Down/Hatch
Doc Chey's Asian Eats
Eclipse di Luna/Sol
Einstein's
Fat Matt's Chicken
Fat Matt's Rib
Feast
Fellini's Pizza
Figo Pasta
Floataway Cafe
Flying Biscuit
Food Studio
Fritti
Hae Woon Dae BBQ
Imperial Fez
Java Jive
Krog Bar
La Fonda Latina
Loaf & Kettle
Loca Luna
Majestic
Mellow Mushroom
MF Sushibar
Misto
Nicola's
Noodle
OK Cafe
Osteria 832
Pangaea
Paolo's Gelato
Pasta da Pulcinella
PieBar
Pittypat's Porch
Pure Taqueria
Raging Burrito
Righteous Room
Roman Lily Cafe
R. Thomas Deluxe
Ru San's
Rustic Gourmet
Sapphire Grill/S
Shorty's
Six Feet Under
SoHo
Souper Jenny
Sun in My Belly
Supper Club
Taqueria del Sol
Taverna Plaka
10 Degrees S.
Tierra
Universal Joint
Varsity/O
Vortex B&G
Zocalo

Outdoor Dining
(G=garden; P=patio; S=sidewalk; T=terrace; W=waterside)

Agave (P)
Anis Bistro (P)
Après Diem (P)
Aqua Blue (P)
Aria (P)
Asada (P)
Atmosphere (P)
Au Pied de Cochon (P)
Babette's Cafe (P)
Bambinelli's (P)
Baraonda (P)
Basil's (P)
Blue Ribbon Grill (P)
Bollywood Masala (P)
Brake Pad (P)
Brick Store Pub (S)
Bridgetown Grill (P)
Brio Tuscan Grille (P,T)

160   subscribe to zagat.com

Special Features

Brooklyn Cafe (P,S)
Brookwood Grill (P)
Byblos (P)
Cafe Intermezzo (P,S,T)
Café Lily (P)
Cafe Prego (P)
Café Tu Tu Tango (S)
Canoe (P,W)
Carbo's Cafe (P,S)
Carpe Diem (P)
Carrabba's Italian/S (P)
Cedars (P)
Cheesecake Factory (P)
Chequers Seafood (P)
Cherry (P)
Chipotle (P)
Ciao Bella (P)
Cowtippers (P)
Crab Shack/O (T,W)
Dantanna's (P)
dick and harry's (P)
dish (P)
Doc Chey's Asian (P)
Downwind (T)
Eclipse di Luna/Sol (P)
Einstein's (P)
El Azteca (P)
Emeril's (P)
Eno (S)
Everybody's Pizza (P)
Fadó Irish Pub (P)
Fat Matt's Rib (P)
Fickle Pickle (G,P)
Fishmonger (P)
Five Seasons Brew. (P)
Floataway Cafe (P)
Flying Biscuit (P)
Fontaine Oyster Hse. (P)
Food 101 (P)
Food Studio (P)
Fritti (P)
Fuego Spanish (P)
Genki (P)
George's (P)
Georgia's New Taste/O (P,W)
Globe (P)
Goldfish (P)
Gordon Biersch (P)
Grace 17.20 (P)
Grape (P)
Hal's on Old Ivy (P)
Haven (P)
High Cotton (P)
Hi Life Kitchen (P)
Horseradish Grill (P)
Houston Mill (T)
Houston's (P)
Huey's (P)
Jitlada (P)
Joël (P)
Joey D's (P)
Justin's (P,S)
Krog Bar (P)
La Fonda Latina (P)
La Tavola (P)
Linger Longer B&G/O (T)
Loca Luna (P)
Mali (P)
Marlow's Tavern (P)
McCormick/Schmick (P,T,W)
Meehan's Pub (P)
Mellow Mushroom (P)
MidCity Cuisine (P)
Milan Med. (P)
Misto (P)
Mitra (P)
Moe's & Joe's (P)
Mosaic (G,P)
Mu Lan (P)
Murphy's (P)
Muss & Turner's (P)
Nava (P)
Nickiemoto's (P)
Nicola's (P)
Nino's (P)
Noche (P)
Noodle (P)
Norcross Station (P)
111 MLK (S)
Osteria 832 (P)
Oz Pizza (S)
Pacific Rim Bistro (P)
Pampas Steak (P)
Pangaea (P)
Paolo's Gelato (P)
Pappadeaux Seafood (P)
Pappasito's Cantina (P)
Pasta da Pulcinella (P)
Pasta Vino (P)
Pastis (T)
P.F. Chang's (P)
PieBar (P)
Portofino (P)
Rainwater (P)
Rathbun's (P)
Ray's on the River (P,W)
Real Chow Baby (P)
Real Food (P)
Ritz/Atlanta Grill (T)
Ritz/Buckhead Café (P)

vote at zagat.com

Special Features

River Room (G,P,S)
Roasted Garlic (P)
Rolling Bones BBQ (P)
Roman Lily Cafe (P)
Roy's (P)
R. Thomas Deluxe (P)
Rustic Gourmet (P)
Ruth's Chris (P)
Sage on Sycamore (S)
Sala – Sabor (P)
Savage Pizza (P)
Savu (P)
Shipfeifer (P)
Shout (T)
Silk (P)
Six Feet Under (P)
Smokejack (P)
SoHo (G,P)
Soleil (P)
Sotto Sotto (P)
Souper Jenny (P)
South City Kitchen (P)
Sun in My Belly (P)
Table 1280 (P)
Taka (P)
Taqueria del Sol (P,T)
Taverna Plaka (P)
Tavern at Phipps (P)
Thai Chili (P)
Tierra (T)
Toast (G,P)
tomas (P)
Tratt. Monaco (P)
Twist (P)
Twisted Taco (P,T)
TWO. urban licks (P)
Uncle Julio's (P)
Universal Joint (P)
Veni Vidi Vici (P)
Vickery's (P)
Villa Christina (G)
Village Tavern (P)
Vinings Inn (P)
Vinny's/Windward (P)
Vinocity (T)
Violette (P)
Vortex B&G (P)
Vreny's Biergarten (T)
Wahoo! (P)
Woodfire Grill (T)
Zocalo (P)

People-Watching
Aria
Atlanta Fish

Atmosphere
Au Pied de Cochon
Barbecue Kitchen
B.E.D.
BluePointe
Buckhead Diner
Cafe Intermezzo
Café Tu Tu Tango
Canoe
Cherry
Colonnade
Cowtippers
dick and harry's
East West Bistro/O
Eats
Eclipse di Luna/Sol
Einstein's
Emeril's
Feast
Fellini's Pizza
Flying Biscuit
Fogo de Chão
Food 101
Food Studio
Goldfish
Hal's on Old Ivy
Highland Tap
Horseradish Grill
Il Pasticcio/S
Java Jive
Joël
Krog Bar
Kyma
La Fonda Latina
Lobby at Twelve
Maggiano's
Majestic
MF Sushibar
Mix
Nan Thai
Nava
New York Prime
Noche
Oceanaire
OK Cafe
ONE. midtown
Palm
Paul's
PieBar
Pricci
Prime
Rathbun's
Real Food
Rolling Bones BBQ
Rosa Mexicano

Special Features

R. Thomas Deluxe
Sala – Sabor
Sapphire Grill/S
Seeger's
Shout
SoHo
South City Kitchen
Spice
Strip
Table 1280
Tamarind
Taurus
Tavern at Phipps
Thomas Mktpl.
Twist
TWO. urban licks
Van Gogh's
Veni Vidi Vici
Vortex B&G
White House
Woodfire Grill

Power Scenes
Atlanta Fish
Au Pied de Cochon
BluePointe
Bone's
Buckhead Diner
Capital Grille
Chops/Lobster Bar
Chopstix
City Grill
Elizabeth on 37th/S
Fleming's/Steak
Joël
Joey D's
Kyma
La Grotta
Lobby at Twelve
Manuel's Tavern
Morton's Steak
Nan Thai
Nava
Oceanaire
ONE. midtown
Palm
Pano's & Paul's
Paul's
Pricci
Prime
Quinones/Bacchanalia
Rest. Eugene
Ritz/Buckhead Din. Rm.
Ruth's Chris

Seeger's
South City Kitchen
Spice
Table 1280
Twist
Veni Vidi Vici

Private Rooms
(Restaurants charge less at off times; call for capacity)
Agave
Ali-Oli
Antica Posta
Aqua Blue
Aria
Atlanta Fish
Au Pied de Cochon
Bazzaar
BluePointe
Blue Ridge Grill
Boi Na Braza
Bollywood Masala
Bone's
Brio Tuscan Grille
Canoe
Capital Grille
Cherry
Chops/Lobster Bar
Chopstix
City Grill
dick and harry's
Ecco
Emeril's
Eno
Feed Store
Fleming's/Steak
Floataway Cafe
Fogo de Chão
Food 101
Food Studio
Fritti
Goldfish
Grace 17.20
Haru Ichiban
Hashiguchi
Hi Life Kitchen
Horseradish Grill
Il Localino
Imari
Ippolito's
Joël
Justin's
Kobe Steaks
Kurt's

vote at zagat.com

Special Features

La Grotta
Le Giverny
Maggiano's
Manuel's Tavern
McCormick/Schmick
McKendrick's Steak
McKinnon's
Melting Pot
MidCity Cuisine
Mitra
Morton's Steak
Mosaic
Nan Thai
New York Prime
Nikolai's Roof
Nino's
Oceanaire
Palm
Pampas Steak
Portofino
Pricci
Prime
Rainwater
Ray's in the City
Ray's on the River
Real Food
Rest. Eugene
Ritz/Buckhead Din. Rm.
River Room
Roy's
Ruth's Chris
Sage on Sycamore
Sal Grosso
Seeger's
Shout
Sia's
Silk
Slovakia
Soleil
Spice
Stoney River Steak
Supper Club
Swan Coach Hse.
Tierra
tomas
Toulouse
Tratt. Monaco
Twist
TWO. urban licks
Van Gogh's
Veni Vidi Vici
Villa Christina
Vinings Inn
Violette
Woodfire Grill

Prix Fixe Menus
(Call for prices and times)

Au Rendez Vous
Bacchanalia
Boi Na Braza
Cedars
Chequers Seafood
Dillard House/O
Fire of Brazil
Fogo de Chão
Imperial Fez
Johnny Harris/S
Little Szechuan
Madras Saravana
MidCity Cuisine
Nicola's
Pano's & Paul's
Park 75
Quinones/Bacchanalia
Real Chow Baby
Ritz/Atlanta Grill
Ritz/Buckhead Din. Rm.
Roy's
Rustic Gourmet
Sal Grosso
Salsa
South of France

Quick Bites

Alon's
Andy's Indian
Bajarito's
Baraonda
Barbecue Kitchen
Blue Eyed Daisy
Bread Garden
Cafe Intermezzo
China Cooks
Chipotle
Chopstix
Coco Loco
Com Dunwoody/Vietnam
Corner Cafe
Eatzi's
Eclipse di Luna/Sol
88 Tofu House
El Taco Veloz
Everybody's Pizza
Fabiano's Deli
Fellini's Pizza
Figo Pasta
Goldberg's Bagel
Jason's Deli
Johnny Rockets
Lobby at Twelve

Special Features

Majestic
Matthew's Cafeteria
Moe's SW Grill
New Yorker
Nino's
Noodle
Nuevo Laredo
Oak Grove
OK Cafe
111 MLK
Orient at Vinings
PieBar
Provisions to Go
Pure Taqueria
Raging Burrito
Ray's NY Pizza
Rolling Bones BBQ
Ru San's
Shorty's
Souper Jenny
Surin of Thailand
Surin's Thai
Taqueria del Sol
Taqueria Sundown
10 Degrees S.
Tin Drum Asia Café
Varsity
Varsity/O
Willy's Mexicana
Wolfgang Puck Exp.

Quiet Conversation
Alfredo's
Ali-Oli
Anis Bistro
Anthony's
Antica Posta
Atmosphere
Babette's Cafe
Bacchanalia
Basil's
B.E.D.
Benihana
Blackstone
Blue Eyed Daisy
Blue Ridge Grill
Bone's
Cafe Alsace
Cafe Intermezzo
Carbo's Cafe
Chopstix
Ciao Bella
City Grill
di Paolo

Eclipse di Luna/Sol
Edo
Elizabeth on 37th/S
Epicurean
Eurasia Bistro
Fishmonger
Fleming's/Steak
Food Studio
Georgia Grille
Georgia's New Taste/O
Harry & Sons
Haru Ichiban
Imari
La Grotta
Le Giverny
McCormick/Schmick
McKendrick's Steak
McKinnon's
Melting Pot
Mosaic
Mu Lan
Nakato
Nam
Nikolai's Roof
Nino's
Palm
Pano's & Paul's
Park 75
Petite Auberge
Portofino
Prime
Quinones/Bacchanalia
Redfish
Red Snapper
Rest. Eugene
Rice Thai
Ritz/Buckhead Din. Rm.
Rustic Gourmet
Sapphire Grill/S
Seasons de Provence
Seeger's
Sia's
Silk
Soleil
South City Kitchen
South of France
Supper Club
Tamarind
10 Degrees S.
Tierra
Top Spice
Toulouse
Tratt. La Strada
Villa Christina

vote at zagat.com

Special Features

Vinings Inn
Violette
Wisteria

Raw Bars
Aqua Blue
Atlanta Fish
Au Pied de Cochon
Benihana
Chops/Lobster Bar
dick and harry's
Edo
Fontaine Oyster Hse.
Garrison's Broiler
Goldfish
Gumbeaux's
McCormick/Schmick
Oceanaire
Ray's in the City
Ray's on the River
Six Feet Under
Strip
Twist

Reserve Ahead
Anthony's
Aria
Bacchanalia
Café Lily
Cafe Prego
Canoe
45 S./Pirates' Hse./S
Georgia's New Taste/O
Le Clos/O
Nikolai's Roof
Nino's
Quinones/Bacchanalia
Rest. Eugene
Ritz/Buckhead Din. Rm.
Seeger's
Sotto Sotto
South City Kitchen
Spice
Sun Dial
Taurus
10 Degrees S.
Veni Vidi Vici

Romantic Places
Alfredo's
Ali-Oli
Anis Bistro
Antica Posta
Après Diem
Aria
Atmosphere
Babette's Cafe
Bacchanalia
Basil's
Bazzaar
B.E.D.
Blue Ridge Grill
Cabernet
Cafe Intermezzo
Carbo's Cafe
Cargo Portside Grill/O
Ciao Bella
City Grill
Dante's Down/Hatch
dick and harry's
di Paolo
dish
Eclipse di Luna/Sol
Edo
Elizabeth on 37th/S
Eno
Epicurean
Feast
Five & Ten/O
Fleming's/Steak
Food 101
Food Studio
Georgia Grille
Georgia's New Taste/O
Haven
Imperial Fez
Joël
Kyma
La Grotta
Le Giverny
McCormick/Schmick
McKendrick's Steak
Mosaic
Mu Lan
Nikolai's Roof
Pano's & Paul's
Park 75
Paul's
Pleasant Peasant
Portofino
Quinones/Bacchanalia
Rainwater
Rest. Eugene
Rice Thai
Ritz/Atlanta Grill
Ritz/Buckhead Din. Rm.
Rustic Gourmet
Sage on Sycamore
Sapphire Grill/S
Seasons de Provence

Special Features

Seeger's
Sia's
Soleil
Sotto Sotto
South City Kitchen
South of France
Supper Club
Tamarind
Top Spice
Toulouse
Van Gogh's
Villa Christina
Vinings Inn
Vinocity
Violette
Wisteria
Woodfire Grill

Senior Appeal
Alfredo's
Ali-Oli
Atlanta Fish
Au Pied de Cochon
Au Rendez Vous
Babette's Cafe
Bacchanalia
Blackstone
Blue Ribbon Grill
Blue Willow Inn/O
Bobby & June's
Brickery G&B
Brio Tuscan Grille
Cabernet
Carbo's Cafe
Colonnade
Dillard House/O
di Paolo
Fleming's/Steak
Food 101
Georgia Grille
Greenwoods
Hal's on Old Ivy
La Grotta
LongHorn Steak
Mary Mac's
McKinnon's
Morton's Steak
Nikolai's Roof
OK Cafe
Olde Pink House/S
Original Pancake
Pano's & Paul's
Paul's
Petite Auberge
Pittypat's Porch

Pleasant Peasant
Portofino
P.R.'s BBQ
Ray's on the River
Red Snapper
Silver Grill
Silver Skillet
Son's Place
South City Kitchen
Swan Coach Hse.
Thomas Mktpl.
Tratt. La Strada
Village Tavern
Vinings Inn
Violette

Singles Scenes
Agave
Après Diem
Athens Pizza
Atkins Park
Azio/Little Azio
B.E.D.
BluePointe
Bridgetown Grill
Café Tu Tu Tango
Capital Grille
Cherry
Doc Chey's Asian
East West Bistro/O
Eats
Einstein's
Everybody's Pizza
Fat Matt's Rib
Fellini's Pizza
Fleming's/Steak
Flying Biscuit
Fritti
Genki
Grape
Hal's on Old Ivy
Haven
Highland Tap
La Fonda Latina
Lobby at Twelve
LongHorn Steak
Majestic
Mellow Mushroom
Misto
Mix
Murphy's
Nickiemoto's
Noodle
ONE. midtown
Pangaea

vote at zagat.com 167

Special Features

PieBar
Pricci
Pure Taqueria
Repast
Rosa Mexicano
R. Thomas Deluxe
Ru San's
Savage Pizza
Savu
Spice
Strip
Surin of Thailand
Tavern at Phipps
Twist
Twisted Taco
TWO. urban licks
Vickery's

Sleepers
(Good to excellent food, but little known)
Bangkok Thai
Barbecue Kitchen
Bread Garden
Busy Bee Cafe
Cargo Portside Grill/O
China Cooks
China Delight
George's of Tybee/O
Georgia's New Taste/O
Gottlieb's/S
Gumbeaux's
Hae Woon Dae BBQ
Haru Ichiban
Himalayas Indian
House of Chan
Imari
Kurt's
Les Fleurs De Lis
Linger Longer B&G/O
Loaf & Kettle
Northlake Thai
Old South BBQ
Pho Hoa
Provisions to Go
Rustic Gourmet
Sapphire Grill/S
Seasons de Provence
Shorty's
Slovakia
Sushi Huku
tomas
Tratt. Monaco
Umezono

Vatica Indian
Zapata

Special Occasions
Anthony's
Aria
Au Pied de Cochon
Bacchanalia
B.E.D.
BluePointe
Canoe
Cargo Portside Grill/O
Chops/Lobster Bar
di Paolo
D. Morgan's/O
Elizabeth on 37th/S
Emeril's
Eno
Fleming's/Steak
Food Studio
Georgia's New Taste/O
Horseradish Grill
Imperial Fez
Joël
Kurt's
La Grotta
Linger Longer B&G/O
Morton's Steak
Nan Thai
New York Prime
Nikolai's Roof
Oceanaire
Olde Pink House/S
Pano's & Paul's
Park 75
Prime
Quinones/Bacchanalia
Rest. Eugene
Ritz/Atlanta Grill
Ritz/Buckhead Din. Rm.
Sapphire Grill/S
Seeger's
Sia's
Sotto Sotto
Table 1280
Van Gogh's
Villa Christina

Teen Appeal
Athens Pizza
Benihana
Bollywood Masala
Brickery G&B
Buca di Beppo
Cheesecake Factory

Special Features

Chipotle
Dante's Down/Hatch
Downwind
Einstein's
ESPN Zone
Everybody's Pizza
Fellini's Pizza
Ippolito's
Jake's
Johnny Rockets
La Paz
LongHorn Steak
Mellow Mushroom
Mexico City
Noodle
Outback Steak
Pappadeaux Seafood
Pasta Vino
Varsity
Varsity/O
Zesto

Theme Restaurants

Avra Greek Tavern
Benihana
Bollywood Masala
Buca di Beppo
Café Tu Tu Tango
Cheesecake Factory
Dante's Down/Hatch
ESPN Zone
Fadó Irish Pub
Fire of Brazil
Fogo de Chão
Johnny Rockets
Kobe Steaks
Melting Pot
Pampas Steak
Sal Grosso
Taverna Plaka
Ted's Montana
Uncle Julio's
Varsity

Transporting Experiences

Alfredo's
Bacchanalia
BluePointe
Bollywood Masala
Byblos
Com Dunwoody/Vietnam
Elizabeth on 37th/S
Fadó Irish Pub
Hae Woon Dae BBQ
Hashiguchi
Imperial Fez
Joël
MF Sushibar
Nan Thai
Pittypat's Porch
Quinones/Bacchanalia
Supper Club

Trendy

Anis Bistro
Aria
Au Pied de Cochon
Bacchanalia
B.E.D.
BluePointe
Buckhead Diner
Canoe
Capital Grille
Cargo Portside Grill/O
Cherry
Chops/Lobster Bar
dick and harry's
dish
East West Bistro/O
Ecco
Eclipse di Luna/Sol
Einstein's
Emeril's
Eno
Five & Ten/O
Floataway Cafe
Flying Biscuit
Fogo de Chão
Food 101
Food Studio
Fratelli di Napoli
Fritti
Highland Tap
Hi Life Kitchen
Horseradish Grill
Il Pasticcio/S
Joël
Krog Bar
Kyma
La Tavola
Lobby at Twelve
Maggiano's
MF Sushibar
MidCity Cuisine
Nam
Nan Thai
Nava
Noche
ONE. midtown
Palm

vote at zagat.com

Special Features

PieBar
Pricci
Prime
Pure Taqueria
Rathbun's
Ray's Killer Creek
Real Food
Repast
Rosa Mexicano
Roy's
Ru San's
Sala – Sabor
Sapphire Grill/S
Seeger's
Shout
Sia's
SoHo
Sotto Sotto
South City Kitchen
Spice
Stoney River Steak
Strip
Surin of Thailand
Table 1280
Taqueria del Sol
Taurus
Toast
Twist
TWO. urban licks
Veni Vidi Vici
Village Tavern
Vinocity
Woodfire Grill

Views
Agave
Canoe
Capital Grille
Cherry
Dillard House/O
Downwind
Horseradish Grill
Linger Longer B&G/O
Nikolai's Roof
ONE. midtown
Pappadeaux Seafood
Ray's on the River
River Room
Roman Lily Cafe
Ruth's Chris
Six Feet Under
Sun Dial
Taurus
TWO. urban licks

Villa Christina
Vinocity

Visitors on Expense Account
Au Pied de Cochon
Bacchanalia
BluePointe
Blue Ridge Grill
Boi Na Braza
Bone's
Canoe
Carbo's Cafe
Chops/Lobster Bar
Chopstix
City Grill
dick and harry's
Elizabeth on 37th/S
Emeril's
Fleming's/Steak
Fogo de Chão
Food Studio
45 S./Pirates' Hse./S
Kyma
La Grotta
McKendrick's Steak
Morton's Steak
Nava
Nikolai's Roof
Oceanaire
Palm
Pano's & Paul's
Park 75
Pricci
Prime
Quinones/Bacchanalia
Ritz/Atlanta Grill
Ritz/Buckhead Din. Rm.
Ruth's Chris
South City Kitchen
Spice
Sun Dial
Table 1280
Tratt. La Strada
Van Gogh's
Veni Vidi Vici
Villa Christina

Wine Bars
Eno
Enoteca Carbonari
Epicurean
Fuego Spanish
Grape
Krog Bar

Special Features

Murphy's
Pura Vida
SoHo
Supper Club
Terra Garden
Vinocity

Winning Wine Lists
Antica Posta
Aria
Atlanta Fish
Bacchanalia
Blue Ridge Grill
Bone's
Buckhead Diner
Canoe
Carbo's Cafe
Cargo Portside Grill/O
Chops/Lobster Bar
City Grill
dick and harry's
dish
Elizabeth on 37th/S
Emeril's
Eno
Epicurean
Fleming's/Steak
Floataway Cafe
Food 101
Food Studio
Grace 17.20
Grape
Horseradish Grill
Il Pasticcio/S
Joël
Kyma
La Grotta
Lobby at Twelve
McKendrick's Steak
MidCity Cuisine
Morton's Steak
Murphy's
Nava
Nikolai's Roof
ONE. midtown
Pano's & Paul's
Park 75
Portofino
Pricci
Prime
Quinones/Bacchanalia

Rathbun's
Ritz/Atlanta Grill
Ritz/Buckhead Din. Rm.
Rustic Gourmet
Ruth's Chris
Seeger's
Sia's
SoHo
South City Kitchen
Table 1280
Toulouse
Tratt. La Strada
TWO. urban licks
Van Gogh's
Veni Vidi Vici
Villa Christina
Vinings Inn
Vinocity
Woodfire Grill

Worth a Trip
Acworth
   Seasons de Provence
Athens
   East West Bistro/O
   Five & Ten/O
Braselton
   Le Clos/O
Brunswick
   Cargo Portside Grill/O
Cartersville
   D. Morgan's/O
Dillard
   Dillard House/O
Greensboro
   Georgia's New Taste/O
   Linger Longer B&G/O
Norcross
   Grace 17.20
Palmetto
   Blue Eyed Daisy
Savannah
   Elizabeth on 37th/S
   45 S./Pirates' Hse./S
   Il Pasticcio/S
   Olde Pink House/S
Social Circle
   Blue Willow Inn/O
Tybee Island
   George's of Tybee/O

vote at zagat.com

Wine Vintage Chart

This chart is designed to help you select wine to go with your meal. It is based on the same 0 to 30 scale used throughout this *Survey*. The ratings (prepared by our friend **Howard Stravitz**, a law professor at the University of South Carolina) reflect both the quality of the vintage and the wine's readiness for present consumption. Thus, if a wine is not fully mature or is over the hill, its rating has been reduced. We do not include 1987, 1991–1993 vintages because they are not especially recommended for most areas. A dash indicates that a wine is either past its peak or too young to rate.

	'85	'86	'88	'89	'90	'94	'95	'96	'97	'98	'99	'00	'01	'02	'03	'04
WHITES																
French:																
Alsace	24	–	22	27	27	26	25	25	24	26	23	26	27	25	22	–
Burgundy	26	25	–	24	22	–	28	29	24	23	26	25	24	27	23	24
Loire Valley	–	–	–	–	–	20	23	22	–	24	25	26	27	25	23	
Champagne	28	25	24	26	29	–	26	27	24	23	24	24	22	26	–	–
Sauternes	21	28	29	25	27	–	21	23	25	23	24	24	28	25	26	–
German	–	–	25	26	27	25	24	27	26	25	25	23	29	27	25	25
California (Napa, Sonoma, Mendocino):																
Chardonnay	–	–	–	–	–	–	–	–	–	–	24	25	28	27	26	–
Sauvignon Blanc/Sémillon	–	–	–	–	–	–	–	–	–	–	–	–	27	28	26	–
REDS																
French:																
Bordeaux	24	25	24	26	29	22	26	25	23	25	24	28	26	23	25	23
Burgundy	23	–	21	24	26	–	26	28	25	22	27	22	25	27	24	–
Rhône	–	–	26	29	29	24	25	22	24	28	27	27	26	–	25	–
Beaujolais	–	–	–	–	–	–	–	–	–	–	–	24	–	25	28	25
California (Napa, Sonoma, Mendocino):																
Cab./Merlot	27	26	–	–	28	29	27	25	28	23	26	22	27	25	24	–
Pinot Noir	–	–	–	–	–	–	–	–	24	24	25	24	27	28	26	–
Zinfandel	–	–	–	–	–	–	–	–	–	–	–	–	26	26	28	
Italian:																
Tuscany	–	–	–	–	25	22	25	20	29	24	28	24	26	24	–	–
Piedmont	–	–	24	26	28	–	23	26	27	25	25	28	26	18	–	–
Spanish:																
Rioja	–	–	–	–	–	26	26	24	25	22	25	25	27	20	–	–
Ribera del Duero/Priorat	–	–	–	–	26	26	27	25	24	26	26	27	20	–	–	

On the go.
In the know.

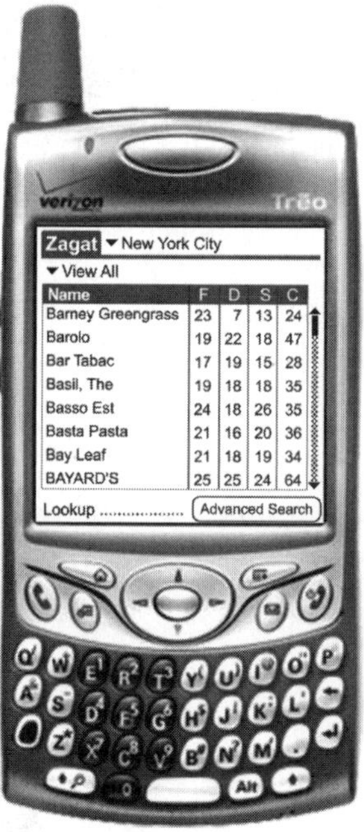

ZAGAT TO GO[SM]

For Palm OS, Windows Mobile, BlackBerry and mobile phones

- Unlimited access to Restaurant, Nightlife and Lifestyle guides in over 65 U.S. and international cities.

- Search and browse by ratings, cuisines, neighborhoods and Top Lists.

- Access to the latest guide content and software updates as they are released.

Available at mobile.zagat.com